BREAKING OPEN
THE WORD OF GOD
Resources for Using the Lectionary
for Catechesis in the RCIA
Cycle C

Edited by
Karen Hinman Powell
Joseph P. Sinwell

PAULIST PRESS
New York / Mahwah

Library of Congress Cataloging-in-Publication Data

Breaking open the word of God : resources for using the lectionary
    for catechesis in the RCIA cycle C / edited by Karen Hinman
    Powell, Joseph P. Sinwell.
      p.   cm.
    Bibliography: p.
    ISBN 0-8091-2973-6 (pbk.) : $12.95
    1. Bible—Study. 2. Catholic Church. Ordo initiationis
Christianae adultorum. 3. Lectionaries. 4. Christian education of
adults. I. Powell, Karen Hinman, 1953–   . II. Sinwell, Joseph P.
BS592.B76 1988
268′.434—dc19   88-3534
                                                CIP

Published by Paulist Press
997 Macarthur Boulevard
Mahwah, New Jersey 07430

Printed and bound in the
United States of America

CONTENTS

Introduction to Cycle C

Breaking Open the Word of God: Resources for Using the Lectionary for Catechesis in RCIA for Cycle C is the third volume in a three-part series which demonstrates how the lectionary can be a source of catechesis in implementing the Rite of Christian Initiation of Adults. The other volumes which focus on the lectionary Cycles A and B have received an enthusiastic response from catechumenal leaders. This volume focuses on the readings in Cycle C and emphasizes using the lectionary in catechesis throughout the entire year.

The use of the lectionary can incorporate catechesis with the vibrant faith of a celebrating Christian community. Articles in this book focus on the use of the lectionary, ministries in the catechumenate, major and minor liturgies and conversion. It contains outlines of catechetical sessions on themes found in the Sunday and Holy Day readings of Cycle C. A Scripture commentary precedes each liturgical season.

Experienced ministers in the adult catechumenate have authored the session outlines which utilize a variety of models. Catechumenate teams can use these sessions as resources for adapting the lectionary to local needs. Flexibility and adaptability are key ingredients to an effective and creative use of the lectionary in catechesis.

The use of the outlines presumes:

1. That the parish offers on-going catechesis for catechumens throughout the liturgical year. This book is a resource for the catechumenate period of the RCIA only. Hence during Lent the Scrutinies (which are for the elect) are omitted.

2. That the parish has extended the period of catechesis with adult catechumens for one to three years.

3. That the parish celebrates the rite of dismissal for catechumens in a Eucharistic liturgy.

4. That the parish catechumenate teams promote the principles of adult religious education in the catechumenate.

5. That catechumens and team members have available their own copy of the Sacred Scriptures during catechetical sessions.

Although this volume is primarily intended for use in parish catechumenates, a variety of pastoral ministers could easily adapt it for personal reflections, Scripture sharing, post-RENEW processes and other adult religious education activities.

Again, we wish to acknowledge the cooperation and creativity of those whose efforts have contributed to this book: Mr. Robert Hamma of Paulist Press for his support and Mrs. Marie White and Ms. Michele Kelly for their diligent assistance.

This resource can be another pastoral tool for all adults who are discovering and sharing the word of God with one another. Using the lectionary in catechesis can help each adult to continue to respond to the challenge of living God's word in community.

INTRODUCTORY ARTICLES

The Power of the Word: A Lectionary-Based Catechesis

By Maureen Kelly

A few years ago, I sat with a new group of catechumens and candidates and listened as a former catechumen now more than a neophyte related a part of her story. She had called the week before and asked if she could come to the catechumenal session to enlist some of the present catechumens and candidates in a hunger project which she and her husband were spearheading in the city. As Connie spoke, I heard her refer to the Gospel reading of the feeding of the multitudes which she and her husband had reflected on months before. She related how the reading had caused them to ask the question: "How do we feed the hungry?" She went on to say that the hunger project was a direct result of asking that question. One could not help but be moved by the witness Connie was giving of the power of the word to both shape and sustain conversion.

The bottom line in any catechumenal process is conversion of the whole person to the mind and attitude of Jesus and the Church. The key to this conversion is the breaking open of the word week after week with catechumens and candidates—breaking open the word in such a way that those doing it discover both the nourishment and confrontation of the spirit of the Gospel in their human experience.

The Lectionary and the Goals of the Catechumenate

It is often difficult for catechists, priests and directors of catechumenates to "buy into" using the lectionary as the prime source book for catechesis. There are fears that everything won't be covered or that we will be creating a post-Reformation Church where we neglect the handing on of doctrine, as well as the practical anxiety of how do we do this.

The first two fears are fears I had when I first heard about using the lectionary as the basic "text" for catechesis. It was not until I experienced a dismissal and breaking open the word at a Beginnings and Beyond Institute that I became motivated enough to try it. My experience of it, and of what happens formationally to all participants including sponsors and catechists, was such that I became convinced of its central importance. Not only were my fears unfounded but I also came to see that there was an innate power and force in the method which was the dynamic of a much deeper conversion for the groups involved.

Paragraph 19 of the R.C.I.A. states that the formation of catechumens is achieved through four elements: catechesis, community, liturgy and apostolic works.

Catechesis. The use of the lectionary brings these four areas together with integrity. One comes to know in some fullness both the person and the message of the Lord when one is invited into that word each week. As for the fear that everything will not be covered, the method of always asking "What questions do these readings raise for you about the Church or the Catholic way of life?" tends to be an authentic way of getting at the questions that are really in the hearts of catechumens and inquirers. Basic principles of good adult education are respected and catechetical questions and issues are raised out of the experiences that are real starting points for catechetical sessions. The rhythm of the Church year also opens up a variety of doctrinal questions.

Community. Using methods of shared reflection and prayer with the Scriptures tends to help people get to the realization of the community as a living body struggling with living the Christian way of life in the marketplace. The experience of community that flows from wrestling with the Scriptures is qualitatively different than one which concentrates only on the breaking open of traditions.

Liturgy. Ideally the breaking of the word and the catechetical session begin in the context of the gathering of the assembly at the Sunday Eucharist. Catechumens celebrate the liturgy of the word with the faithful and are dismissed after the homily to break open the word and be nourished by it. Dismissal is not a negative experience. Catechumens find that their hunger for the Eucharist deepens as they are nourished by the presence of Jesus in the word. The dismissal also causes the faithful to ask some hard questions about themselves and what being a Catholic means for them today.

Apostolic Works. An important area of conversion and catechumenal formation assists catechumens and candidates to live and spread the Gospel in all areas of their lives. Many catechumenates across the country provide projects and experiences for catechumens in this area. A catechesis that is based on the word and the often asked question "What do I feel myself being called to change in my life?" provides a strong on-going impetus with apostolic work for the catechumen and the initiated, as was seen in Connie's experience.

In answer to the above-mentioned fears that all of Catholic doctrine will not be covered if one uses the lectionary, one readily sees that many doctrinal questions and issues rise from the use of the lectionary in a well balanced manner. Not only that, but the use of the lectionary in this manner over a year's time gives the initiated the skills they need to continue to live in the on-going process of conversion.

The Structure of the Session

The practical question is: "How does one do this breaking open of the word? How do we structure it?" This volume will give you many different approaches and ideas for each Sunday. A typical Sunday agenda might look like this:

9:30   Gather with the assembly for liturgy of the word
          Dismissal after the homily

10:00   Coffee/rolls as catechumens and catechists gather

10:10   Time for prayer, meditation or discussion with catechumens

10:30   Sponsors and spouses join the catechumens at the end of the Eucharist
          Catechetical session as presented in this volume

12:00   Closing prayer and dismissal

I would like to elaborate a bit on the various elements of this schedule. The gathering of the assembly and the dismissal of candidates happens every Sunday as long as there are catechumens. The dismissal should take place after the homily. It is a good idea to make the dismissal a solemn moment by calling the catechist forward and presenting the lectionary to him or her with these or similar words: "N., this community sends you forth to break open the word with our candidates. Go in peace."

After the catechumens and candidates are settled in the gathering place, the catechist reads one of the day's Scriptures. Following the rereading of the text one of several activities may be done: a guided meditation (whereby catechumens are invited to place themselves in the text or in a similar situation); a journal exercise recalling a life event similar to the readings; a time of spontaneous prayer or prayer based on the psalm response; quiet meditation; reflection and/or discussion of some point of the homily.

As you will notice the time for this segment is short. It is not always necessary to use the reading that your catechetical session is based on. Sometimes this segment of time can be given over to reflection on the question "What struck you in today's homily" or on reviewing decisions that catechumens and candidates may have made in the previous week's discussion.

When sponsors and spouses arrive there are as many options for catechetical sessions as there are persons and Scriptures. This book is filled with sample sessions and methods, so I need not deliberate more about this here.

The closing prayer and dismissal can be as simple or as complicated as you would like. Again samples are provided in this book. Some parishes ask a sponsor/candidate team to prepare the closing prayer for each week based on that week's readings. Creativity leaves open all sorts of possibilities here.

In general the structure of Sunday morning is simple. The process is simple when the lectionary is used as the basis. The sessions in this book are good guidelines for creating a process which will work best for your people.

Preparing for the Session

Preparation for the Sunday morning session is essential for effective use of time and materials. There are many ways a team member may prepare to be the facilitator for Sunday morning. The method presented here has been developed by Karen Hinman Powell and is most effective for team members. There are seven steps to this method. *All seven* are essential!

First, find the readings for the given Sunday in the lectionary. Read all three readings slowly and thoughtfully at least three times, preferably one time aloud. Underline thought patterns, significant words and phrases in all the readings. Jot down connections you notice between the readings. The purpose of this step is to become familiar with the texts for the given Sunday.

Second, work with the Gospel. Read the Gospel slowly and deliberately one more time. Visualize the Gospel. Where is this text taking place? At what time of day or night? What season of the year? Ask yourself: Do time and place make any difference in the reading? Name all the characters. With whom do you identify? Of these characters, who is the principal person in the Gospel? What is his or her problem? Find a passage from the text which articulates the problem of the principal person from his or her other perspective. Finding the problem in the text of the Gospel is essential. What is Jesus' response? How does Jesus deal with the problem? Again find the answer in the text. How do the other characters respond to the situation? Situate the text by visualizing it, sensing it (feeling, seeing, smelling, hearing that passage). Place yourself in the text.

Third, once you have done the work of visualizing the text (and only then), read commentaries about the passage. Some helpful resources are *Unfinished Images* available through Wm. H. Sadlier Company and *Share the Word* from the Paulist Evangelization Center. Commentaries assist in stretching beyond our own images, understandings, and interpretations of this passage. Note any connections between the commentaries, your reflections, and readings. How do commentaries enlighten, challenge, and affirm your understanding of this passage?

Fourth, set all readings, visualizations, commentaries aside and go before God to pray with this Gospel. Questions you may sit with are: What meaning do these readings offer for my life? for the life of the catechumens? for the Church? for the world? Where do you find yourself in the Gospel (e.g., are you the man born blind, the family, his neighbors, the Pharisees, Jesus)? What similarities and/or differences do you find in your world and the world of the principal character? Does this passage recall for you a concrete example or situation in your life? If so describe that time in detail. In what ways do the readings call you to growth? to new awareness? How do you meet this challenge? What is the hard word that the Gospel calls you to hear? How do you or will you respond? These are just some ways of being with the Gospel. There are many ways to pray with the word. Methods of praying with the Scripture are left to your creativity.

Fifth, after reading texts, visualizing, attending to commentaries, and praying with the Gospel, talk with the pastor/presider for the liturgy at which the catechumens will be present. Ask him to share with you briefly the focus of his homily. The catechumenal session builds upon the word and upon how that word is broken open by the homilist. Therefore, it is helpful to speak with the presider in the planning stages.

Sixth, with all of the data gathered, list the questions about the Catholic Christian tradition which could emerge. For example from the Feast of the Baptism of Our Lord questions about baptism could emerge. Readings on the call of the disciples could lead to questions about the origin of the Catholic Church and/or what it means that Peter is the rock of the Church. On Sundays when a letter is read (e.g., from the bishop, about reconciliation, peace pastoral, economic pastoral), questions could emerge about these issues. The issues raised about our tradition emerge as candidates live this tradition with us on each and every Sunday of the year. These issues and concerns emerge from our living and being together.

Seventh and last, realizing the wealth of information in word, in experiences, in homily, the team member sets aside preparation materials and designs a process to be used with catechumens on Sunday morn-

ing. The team member decides how to use the Gospel, what other texts of the day will be used, what symbols can be used effectively from the Scriptures for prayer or reflection, what context needs to be addressed, and what catechetical issues may emerge based on his or her experience with the catechumens.

Ministries for the Catechumenate Period

By Karen Hinman Powell

A variety of ministries are necessary for the implementation of the Rite of Christian Initiation of Adults (RCIA). These ministries are described throughout the RCIA; however there is a special section entitled "Ministries and Offices" in paragraphs 9 to 13 which specifically highlights the various ministries. In these paragraphs the ministry of the faithful, sponsor, godparent, bishop, priest, deacon, and catechist are described consecutively. The descriptions in this section are by no means complete and the entire ritual book needs to be read and studied in order to fully comprehend the ministries here described. These descriptions, however, capture only those areas which need to be highlighted or which may not be fully described in the Rite.

A description of all the ministries necessary for this process would be quite lengthy, too lengthy for the chapter of this book. The Rite of Christian Initiation of Adults defines the initiation process as one to be implemented and initiated "in stages." Four periods are described throughout the process: precatechumenate, catechumenate, purification and enlightenment, and mystagogia. The purpose of this article is to highlight the ministries needed for the period of the catechumenate—the period when we "break open the word" with our catechumens. The ministries have been limited in this article to include: the faithful, sponsor, pastor/priest and catechist. Each ministry needed for this period has specific responsibilities. Each ministry requires different skills and gifts. In this article these skills and responsibilities will be described.

Ministry of the Faithful—The People of God

Paragraph #9 of the Rite states that during the catechumenate "the faithful participate in celebrations belonging to the period of the catechumenate. The faithful take an active part in responses, prayers, singing, acclamations." The ministry of the assembly during the catechumenate period is primarily a liturgical ministry where the call to witness through our celebration is an essential skill. The faithful are called to "participate" in celebrations of the rites. But what rites? These rites include the Rite of Acceptance into the Order of Catechumens, Minor Exorcisms, Blessings, Presentations of the Creed and Lord's Prayer (if these are celebrated during the catechumenate period, which the Rite suggests they may be), and in weekly Sunday celebrations of the word (after which catechumens are dismissed in a friendly way). There is a real variety of liturgies in which to participate.

What does it mean to participate? The Rite states in paragraph #9 that the faithful are to "take an active part in responses, prayers, singing, and acclamations." The ministry of the assembly is *not* passive! To participate is first of all to be present, to attend the liturgies, to motivate our parishioners to want to be present (instead of dreading the fact that "Mass will be longer today"). Second, to participate is to be involved—to sing, to pray, to respond, to acclaim. To participate is not to be a spectator! This directive has something to say about the quality of our liturgy. This directive is a challenge to be creative in enabling the ministry of the faithful to be carried out. To do this we must change our focus in planning from what happens in the sanctuary and in the catechumens to begin to focus on what is happening in the assembly and asking the question of how we enable the faithful to fully participate. Enabling this assembly means knowing the assembly and determining the steps necessary to encourage, educate, and support the people of God to carry out this role.

It is important to note that the Rite does not indicate that all members of the people of God know each candidate or catechumen personally. Nor does it say that the parish attends the catechumenal sessions. The ministry of the assembly is one of witness, of prayer, of song, and of celebration of the word. In and through the celebration of the community the catechumens and candidates are drawn closer to God. The ministry of the faithful is a ministry of who we are more than of what we do.

. . . . PAUSE TO REFLECT . . . .

How is the ministry of the assembly fulfilled in your parish during the period of the catechumenate? What are your parish strengths? What are the areas you need to work on? Describe your participation in the rites as a people of God. Name one concrete step you will take this month to better enable this ministry in your parish.

Ministry of Sponsor

The ministry of the sponsor is a ministry appointed by the parish to be carried out during the catechumenate period. The sponsor is appointed "to journey with the catechumen during the catechumenate period." Sponsors are persons who "know and assist the candidates and who stand as witnesses to the candidates' moral character, faith, and intentions." (#10)

The ministry of the sponsor is primarily one of peer ministry—adult to adult. To fully understand the ministry of the sponsor one could look to Alcoholics Anonymous or any twelve step program (Overeaters Anonymous, Gamblers Anonymous, Al-Anon, Adult Children of Alcoholics, etc.) for a model of what a sponsor is to be. These twelve step programs see the role of sponsor as vital to recovery of the individual. The sponsor/sponsoree relationship is mutually beneficial. In AA there are various methods of relating to a sponsor. Some sponsoring relationships are friendships. Some have highly structured relationships where daily or occasional phone calls to one another are important. Other relationships are easy-going and flexible. The role of the sponsor is to help the sponsoree to work the steps, to listen to the sponsoree, to share experience, faith, and hope with the sponsoree, to pray together, to attend meetings together, to read materials and discuss them, to offer time and encouragement, and to place the person in God's hands. Is this not a good analogy for the ministry of sponsor for the catechumenate?

The role of the sponsor is to listen, to listen, and to listen some more. The sponsor is the witness to how God works in our lives. Someone once said that to become a Catholic the spirit is "caught not taught." It is through the sponsor that this spirit can be caught. The sponsor walks with the candidate throughout the catechumenate period, that is from the Rite of Acceptance into the Order of Catechumens to the Rite of Election. At that time the godparent steps in. About ninety percent of the time the sponsor is chosen by the candidate to be the godparent. The sponsor is a co-journeyer with the catechumen. They are not persons with all the answers, but "partners on the way."

What skills does a sponsor need for this important ministry? First and foremost skills of listening are necessary. Skills in sharing faith are also essential. These can be taught in sponsor formation sessions. Lastly sponsors need confidence in the faith they have been given in order to share this faith and live it with others. Affirmation and support of sponsors is key.

. . . . PAUSE TO REFLECT . . . .

How are your sponsors selected? What part do they play in the catechumenate period? What expectations do you have of them? How can you better enable your sponsors to carry out their ministry?

Ministry of the Priest/Pastor

The ministry of the priest/pastor during the catechumenate period is an important element. "What am I to do?" and "How do we involve the pastor?" are questions often asked by pastors and by team members. The questions are especially focused during the catechumenate period because catechumens are dismissed after the homily and the priest/pastor stays to complete the celebration of the Eucharist. Most priests wonder: How do I get involved?

The ministry of the priest is key. First he is to preside at the rites. To preside means to know the rite, to know the essential elements and flow of the rite, to be able to name the central symbol and/or the central action of each of the rituals and to then allow the ritual to happen. This means that priests cannot come into the sanctuary fifteen minutes before Mass and look at what has been prepared. To preside means to study and to know the rites. This takes time and preparation.

Second, the priest is to preach—to break open the word of God. Catechumens and candidates are dismissed after the homily to reflect on "what they have heard" and on "what they did not hear." The liturgy of the word, which includes the homily, is the stepping stone for the catechesis of the catechumenate period. A good homily can really challenge, affirm, and call to conversion the catechumens and candidates present. The catechumenate, after all, is a call to conversion of the whole person. This homily is a key to the catechetical formation process.

Third, during the catechumenate period the priest is the link to the rest of the parish for what is happening in the catechumenate. He approves sponsors. He may be a spiritual director. It is important, also, that during this time the priest/pastor come to know the candidates and catechumens. Each parish situation is different. Each priest is different. The pastor and catechumenate team members and leaders need to sit down together and reflect on how to work together. Cooperation (not competition) is important here!

. . . . PAUSE TO REFLECT . . . .

How well do you as pastor or presider know the rites? How much time do you spend in preparation? How are you involved in the catechumenate process? How would you like to be involved? How well do you enable your catechumenate team members to carry out this process? How are your homilies received? Do you break open the word of the day? How well do you do this? What skills would you like to enhance to better preside? to better proclaim the word? What resources are available to you to do so?

Ministry of Catechist

The ministry of catechist in the RCIA is an "important office for the progress of the catechumens and the growth of the community." (#16) Catechists are to have an active part in the rites (the Rite of Acceptance into the Catechumenate) and may perform minor exorcisms and blessings. In addition catechists teach/form catechumens: "filled with the spirit of the Gospel, adapted to the liturgical signs and cycle of the church year, suitable to the needs of catechumens, and enriched by local traditions." (#16) The catechist has quite a job!

How is this ministry specified during the catechumenate period? What does this mean? What skills are required? First of all catechesis is taken from the Greek which means "to echo or resound the word." A catechist is therefore one who resounds the word of God, whose life is to echo this word. Paragraph #75 of the Rite states the content of the catechesis of the catechumenate, indicating that this period is one of "pastoral formation and guidance and training in the Christian life." There are four specific areas of catechesis which are discussed: (1) catechesis accommodated to the liturgical year which leads to "appropriate" acquaintance with dogma, (2) formation in a community way of life which includes formation in prayer, witness, discernment, and conversion, (3) formation in liturgy which purifies and strengthens, and (4) formation in the apostolic works of the Christian life. Holistic catechesis, catechesis of the heart, mind, relationships, service, and spirit, is called for. The catechist has the responsibility to see to it that all four areas are carried out and balanced in the formation process of the candidate since no one area is given greater emphasis than any other area in the Rite. All four components are given equal attention.

The catechist is a person of faith. The catechist is not a Bible expert, is not a doctrine expert, a spirituality expert, or a theology expert. Rather, the catechist is informed in these areas and knows how to make connections between faith and life, between doctrine and life, between theology and life, so that the faith life, the formation and the growth of the catechumens is assured. The catechist is not someone who knows "all the answers" but is a resource, someone who knows how to live the questions.

What are essential skills of a catechist? First and foremost catechists must be able to share faith. To share faith they must have faith and be able to articulate it.

Second, in order to enable catechumens to grow in faith, catechists need to have good communication skills. Skills in attending, information and opinion seeking, and clarification are important. In working with a group, skills in redirecting a group, handling talkative and silent members, are essential. Active listening skills are important to good communication skills.

Third, catechists must be informed or be willing to be informed on Church teaching, Scripture, moral issues, etc., as these issues arise within the catechumenate. This does not mean that catechists have to be experts in these areas. In many places the best team members are not the experts! This point means that catechists need to know what resources—books, people, workshops—are available to assist them in the holistic formation process of the catechumens.

Fourth, team members need to look at the formation process holistically—to become a Catholic is not only "to know" all the doctrine of the Church. Catechists need to understand the process as a conversion process whereby formation of the whole person is essential. (See paragraph #75 once more). This means that catechists must confront the conflict—internal to their own hearts and external in other Catholics—which says "they don't know enough" on the one hand and on the other hand which says "they are in a formation process which is providing catechumens tools and skills to live their lives as Catholic Christians each and every day for the rest of their lives." This conflict is not an easy one in which to stand. Nor is this conflict going to disappear. To face the conflict catechists need to be convinced themselves of this fact. They also need to raise the consciousness of the whole parish and the catechumens to the fact that there are four components. Once again the four elements of catechesis found in paragraph #75 are: doctrine accommodated to the liturgical year, formation in liturgy, formation in the Christian life, and formation in apostolic works. Catechists need to honestly challenge and invite parish teams and catechumens to grow equally in all four areas.

Fifth, catechists during the catechumenate period need to know how to break open the word of God— how to use the liturgy of the word in order to ensure the holistic formation of the catechumen in doctrine accommodated to the liturgical year, in liturgy, in Christian life, in apostolic works. Breaking open the word of God demands prayer and understanding of the Sunday Scriptures, listening to the catechumens' issues and concerns, and knowing the teachings of the Church, such that all three of these elements are brought together into a dynamic process. Catechists need to grow in the ability to create sessions in touch with these three elements. This book is a great resource in this regard—a stepping stone in how to create Sunday morning catechetical sessions. Breaking open the word also means having the skill to lead these sessions—a skill which grows with experience and time. Novice catechists need supervision in this area of planning and leading, of breaking open the word, and other catechetical sessions.

Sixth, during the catechumenate the catechist is to celebrate minor exorcisms and blessings. Catechists need skill in understanding the nature of exorcisms and blessings, skill in preparing for and presiding at these liturgies. Catechists need to understand the importance of these rites for the whole process that they may be integrated more fully into the dynamics of the catechumenate period.

Lastly, catechists need to be people of prayer. Ultimately this is God's work in which we share. Catechists need to do what they have to do. They need to take the steps to make the process work. Then they must "Let go and let God" do the rest.

. . . . PAUSE TO REFLECT . . . .

How are catechists selected for the catechumenate period? How are they formed? What do catechists do during the catechumenate period in your parish? Is the catechesis for the catechumenate period in your parish accommodated to the liturgical year? Do catechists give equal importance and emphasis to doctrine accommodated to the liturgical year, formation in liturgy, formation in the Christian life, formation in apostolic works? How often do your catechists celebrate minor exorcisms and blessings? What is one area of the catechumenate period in which your catechists need assistance? How will you help them?

Conclusion

This article is not meant to be an exhaustive list of the ministries of the RCIA nor of the ministries for the catechumenate period. There are obviously other important ministries left out—catechumenate director, deacon, spiritual director, hospitality, etc. All of these ministries are important for the catechumenate period; however, the ministries described in this chapter are the essential ministries for the catechumenate period. The others I have just mentioned vary from parish to parish, from situation to situation. The ministries described here are some of those listed in the chapter on ministries and offices in the Rite.

The Rites of the Catechumenate: An Invitation to Discipleship

By Richard N. Fragomeni

It has been written that the primary language of religious consciousness is the language of symbol, poetry and the complexus of ritual that affectively triggers a transformation of desire in the human subject.[1] It has also been written that the foundational Christian conversion is the conversion of affectivity which ignites the imagination and invites the human subject into realms of commitment to further conversion, generating an energy that can make a difference in human affairs.[2] It has again been written that the Rite of Christian Initiation of Adults is a ritual text that has as its aim the formation of Christian disciples through the catechetical testimony and support of an apostolic community and the vibrant celebration of the various prescribed rites of passage.[3]

This article is written to describe a certain group of these initiatory rites, central to the period of the catechumenate: the celebrations of the word of God, the minor exorcisms, the blessings of the catechumens, and the anointing of the catechumens. This essay will briefly examine each of these four rites as they are presented in the most recent edition of the RCIA.[4] The examination of these texts is grounded in what has been written above: that by a robust entry into the world of the symbolic through the rites of the RCIA, catechumens and the community of the faithful are invited into a vowed commitment of apostolic testimony by language and ritual that touch the heart and open up the possibility for conversion and the reorientation of desire.

I. The Celebrations of the Word of God

The catechumenate period begins with the celebration of the Rite of Acceptance into the Order of Catechumens.[5] This celebration initiates the inquirers into the household of Christ and brings them into communion with the faithful at the table of the word of God. The word catechumen means "the one who is formed by the resounding word." Thus, those who are seeking to be baptized are called into a formative journey, being nurtured by the Scripture readings that resound in the Christian assemblies. The revised text notes the importance of these celebrations (Pars. 81–84) and enumerates three occasions when the word is to be celebrated with the catechumens: 1) at celebrations held specifically for the catechumens themselves; 2) at the Sunday assembly when catechumens gather with the community for the liturgy of the word; 3) at celebrations that are held in conjunction with the catechetical sessions during the time of the catechumenate.

A model for a celebration of the word (occasions 1 and 3, above) is offered in paragraphs 85–89. It consists of 1) a gathering song, 2) a selection of readings from the Scriptures which are to be chosen for their relevance to the formation of the catechumens, 3) a brief homily, and 4) the concluding rites, which may include a minor exorcism, a blessing or an anointing with oil. This model, following the fundamental structure of the liturgy of the word in the Sunday assembly, is open to a variety of adaptations and ministries. For instance, the homily may be offered by a catechist who has the gift of preaching; the readings may be proclaimed in a style that allows for a variety of voices to participate; the celebration may include the possibility of shared vocal prayer and the focused use of silent time.

The ritual text invites parish leadership to ground the catechetical formation of catechumens in the celebrations of the word, both within and without of the Sunday assembly. The RCIA sees the main purpose of these celebrations for the catechumens as fourfold:

1. to implant in their hearts the teachings they are receiving: for example, the morality characteristic of the New Testament, the forgiveness of injuries and insults, a sense of sin and repentance, the duties Christians must carry out in the world;

2. to give them instruction and experience in the different aspects and ways of prayer;

3. to explain to them the signs, celebrations, and seasons of the liturgy;

4. to prepare them gradually to enter the worship assembly of the entire community. (Par. 82)

Liturgy planners and catechists are well advised to read paragraph 13 of the Directory for Masses with Children[6] when reading the second and third purposes cited above. In a paragraph describing the formation of children and their preparation for full participation in the liturgical life of the Church, the Directory warns the reader: "Such celebrations, however, should avoid having too didactic a character." The celebrations of the word instruct and explain in a holistic manner. These celebrations are to speak the language of the heart in images and metaphors, not in a didactic and wooden way as in the mere dissemination of concepts. It is the downfall of conversion to make it simply a matter of giving information from jug to mug.

From the RCIA text we can make two observations about the significance of the celebrations of the word for the formation of catechumens. First, the formation of Christians fundamentally takes place within the experience of the primary language of religious consciousness. The conversion of the heart is radical and it is achieved by God's word that resounds in the genre of narrative, parables, wisdom sayings, prophetic images, covenant codes, laments and hymns of praise, proclaimed in the community and received in the Spirit. Second, the celebrations of the word invite the catechumens to surrender to God and into the world that God has created in Christ through the Spirit. To this end, the catechumens are formed by the word in prayer and are invited by the experience of the word to become the members of the living word of God that regenerates history and reverses the order of domination and oppression. Growing strong in the hearing of the word, the catechumens prepare for the mission of the Church and the struggle with the powers of evil. From St. Paul they are exhorted:

> So stand your ground, with truth a belt round
> your waist, and uprightness a breastplate,
> wearing for shoes on your feet the eagerness
> to spread the gospel of peace and always car-
> rying the shield of faith so that you can use it
> to quench the burning arrows of the Evil One.
> And then you must take salvation as your hel-
> met and the sword of the Spirit, that is, the
> word of God (Eph 6:14–17, *The New Jerusa-*
> *lem Bible*).

II. The Minor Exorcisms

Knowing the struggle and the energy needed to be a disciple of the living word, the RCIA encourages the catechumens on their journey with three other rites and prayers during this stage of their formation. The first of these are the minor exorcisms. Par. 90 of the text tells us that these prayers, "directly addressed to God" (although sample prayers F, G, H and I are addressed to Christ), are to assist the catechumens and draw their attention to the need for God's assistance on the way.

The minor exorcisms may take place during a celebration of the word, or at the beginning or end of a catechetical session. When there is a spiritual need, these exorcisms may take place privately for an individual catechumen. The text gives a clear indication that those who can preside over a celebration of a minor exorcism are presbyters, deacons and qualified catechists appointed by the bishop.

The ritual is simple. The catechumens kneel or bow. The presider with outstretched hands says one of the sample prayers given in the text. With this, the ritual concludes. What immediately comes to mind is the necessity of situating this ritual within the context of the proclamation of the word and a more comprehensive form of prayer, which might include specific mentioning of matters in the life of the catechumens needing God's assistance and healing. Without such a scriptural and prayerful context, the exorcism might be misunderstood as a form of magical remedy, casually associated with the utterance of certain prescribed formulae.

Eleven prayers of exorcism are given. They seem to have been written in a twofold pattern or model, traditionally familiar to the Roman rite. First, God or Christ is addressed. The address includes the mentioning of some memory of what God or Christ has accomplished. For example, prayer H, addressed to Christ begins:

> Lord Jesus Christ,
> sent by the Father and anointed by the Spirit,
> when you read in the synagogue at Nazareth
> you fulfilled the words of the prophet Isaiah
> that proclaimed liberty to captives
> and announced a season of forgiveness.

Second, these prayers make petition for the catechumens that they be rescued from evil and become strong in the service of God. Some prayers are more elaborate than others in the images evoked for the liberation of the catechumens from the powers of darkness. All of them, nevertheless, follow this twofold pattern.

When celebrating these minor exorcisms during the period of the catechumenate, the presider may discover that none of the exorcism prayers meets the need of language and image that is necessary for the meaningful celebration of the rite of exorcism. Using the given texts as samples of what can be prayed, and maintaining the traditional twofold division of such prayers, an intelligent, creative and pastoral adaptation can certainly be made, and in some cases, no doubt, will have to be made. When making these adaptations, the poetic use of the images and references about God and Christ, proclaimed in the readings preceding the minor exorcisms, could be incorporated and woven into the texture of the prayer. This connection would bring to the prayer a deepening of the meaning of the Scriptures and a linkage of the scriptural texts with the life of the catechumens. This same sort of adaptation could be employed with the prayers of blessing for the catechumens which we shall now examine.

III. The Blessings of the Catechumens

Par. 95 of the revised rite gives the purpose of blessing catechumens:

> The blessings of the catechumens are a sign of God's love and of the Church's tender care. They are bestowed on the catechumens so that, even though they do not as yet have the grace of the sacraments, they may still receive from the church courage, joy and peace as they proceed along the difficult journey they have begun.

Like the minor exorcisms that we examined above, the blessing of catechumens usually takes place at the end of a celebration of the word, at the conclusion of a catechetical session, or, when there is a special need, in private.

The ritual is simple: the presider, who can be a presbyter, deacon, or qualified catechist, stretches out his or her hands over the heads of the catechumens and says one of the nine prayers in the ritual book. A parish catechumenal team could suggest that the entire assembly extend hands in solidarity with the catechumens so as to enrich the gesture of blessing to include all the faithful in the action. If it can be conveniently done, the rubrics invite the catechumens forward to the presider "who lays hands on them individually." The catechumens then leave. It is to be noted that the imposition of hands, the primary sacramental gesture of touch, while included in these blessings, is missing from the minor exorcisms. One wonders about the reason for such an omission.

The blessing prayers offered in the text are addressed to God through Christ. They are of diverse form, while all invoking the blessing and sanctification of God upon the catechumens who are preparing for baptism and the rebirth in the Holy Spirit. As mentioned above, an adaptation of these blessing prayers and the creation of new ones from the context of the scriptural passages proclaimed and the needs of the catechumens may well be necessary in certain pastoral situations.

The blessings of the catechumens and the minor exorcisms seem to form a complementary set of encouragement and support rituals. Very similar in shape and intent, these rituals are envisioned to be celebrated regularly during the period of the catechumenate in conjunction with the catechesis and growth that are characteristic of this part of the journey in faith.

IV. The Anointing of the Catechumens

The last of the rites which we will examine in this article falls under the general heading: "Optional Rites During the Catechumenate." There are two rites that come under this heading: the anointing of the catechumens and the presentations of the Lord's Prayer and the Creed. The presentations will not be handled here. The presentations of the Lord's Prayer and the Creed are made optional during the period of the catechumenate. The RCIA places them in the Lenten season, ordinarily to be celebrated between the scrutinies.

The anointing of the catechumens, through the use of the oil of catechumens, "may be celebrated wherever this seems beneficial or desirable" (Par. 98). The ritual states that the usual minister for the anointing is either a presbyter or a deacon. It seems that the use of oil for any sacramental action in the Roman tradition is reserved for the ministry of the ordained. This will cause some confusion, no doubt, in areas where the laity are the main ministers of initiation. The inconsistency in this directive is made clear when we examine the rite itself.

The rite takes place after the homily in a celebration of the word. While provisions are made for the anointing to take place privately, the context of the proclamation of scripture in the assembly grounds the meaning of the anointing more clearly. The ritual is in two parts:

(1) The oil of the catechumens is usually blessed by the bishop of the diocese at the annual Mass of Chrism. If this blessed oil is used, the presider prays a prayer of exorcism over the catechumens. These exorcism prayers are found in Par. 94 of the ritual text, or created by the presider to suit the occasion, as explained above. It will be noted that a catechist may celebrate an exorcism. Here is the inconsistency. When an anointing with oil concludes the exorcism prayer, the ministers cited are only the presbyter and the deacon. When the exorcism prayer is done alone, however, the catechist is included as a possible minister.

If the oil to be used has not been blessed by the bishop, a priest celebrant is to bless the oil with a brief blessing prayer that is given in the ritual text.

(2) When the exorcism prayer or blessing has been completed, the presider faces the catechumens and says:

> We anoint you with the oil of salvation
> in the name of Christ our Savior.
> May he strengthen you with his power,
> who lives and reigns for ever and ever.

The catechumens respond "Amen," and the presider anoints each of them with the oil of catechumens in silence. The ritual suggests that a blessing of the catechumens may follow the anointing. This suggestion seems redundant and a mere duplication of the anointing itself. The anointing with oil can be done several times during the catechumenate period, bringing strength to the catechumens on their journey of conversion.

We have examined the four rites of the catechumenate. It is now the task of the local parish ministers to adapt these rites intelligently and pastorally (Par. 35) so that these rites can indeed become symbolic discourse and invitation to Christian discipleship. What we have done in this essay, to use a metaphor familiar in liturgical circles, is to describe the "dry bones" of these rites. By intelligent and pastoral adaptation, communities will make these dry bones breathe and give life to those who journey with us on the road of reconciliation and awakened faith. These rites anticipate with eagerness the communion that the assembly of the baptized will share with the catechumens at the table of bread and wine: a communion with the cosmos, with Christ and with the future that God is creating.

Notes

1. David N. Power, O.M.I., *Unsearchable Riches: The Symbolic Nature of the Liturgy* (New York: Pueblo Publishing Company, 1984).

2. Walter Conn, "Passionate Commitment: The Dynamics of Affective Conversion," *Cross Currents* 34 (Fall 1984):329–336.

3. Mark Searle, "Faith and Sacraments in the Conversion Process," in *Conversion and the Catechumenate*, edited by Robert Duggan (New York: Paulist Press, 1984), pp. 64–84.

4. This article is employing the recent White Book edition of the RCIA that has been published by the International Commission on English in the Liturgy, Washington, D.C., 1986.

5. Cf. my commentary on the rite: "Acceptance into the Order of Catechumens," in *Catechumenate: A Journal of Christian Initiation*, Vol. 9, No. 3, January 1987, pp. 2–11.

6. S.C.D.W., *Pueros Baptizatos*, 1, November 1973, found in translation in Austin Flannery, O.P., general editor, *Vatican Council II: The Conciliar and Post-Conciliar Documents* (New York: Costello Publishing Company, 1984), pp. 254–270.

Conversion: Heart of the R.C.I.A.

By Ron Oakham, O.Carm.

The Second Vatican Council set into motion change and changes in the Church. Quite often we have implemented the changes (new and/or renewed ways of doing things), but have not internalized the change (the basic assumptions) from which the changes emanate. This is true about the implementation of the Rite of Christian Initiation of Adults. In many parishes ritual changes have been instituted, but the understanding of what initiation is about has remained fixed in a pre-Vatican II mentality.

In this article, I want to explore one of the basic assumptions upon which the R.C.I.A. is built. I'll begin by sharing with you a couple of contemporary stories and ancient rites.

Journeys and Rites

Paul lived alone in an apartment across the street from the church. On Sundays he would watch our congregation gather before and after Mass on the church steps. From his window he could see a number of happy people; he could hear the chatter and the laughter. He could also see the hurting people and how they were being cared for by their friends. The scene only made Paul feel the pain of his loneliness and isolation all the more. To escape this pain, he would retreat into the darkness of his apartment, take some of his drugs, and wander away into some fantasy world in his mind.

One Sunday Paul took a very different and dramatic step. Instead of withdrawing to his "drug counter," he put on his jacket and walked across the street into the midst of these unknown yet familiar people.

Bill, an active parishioner, noticed Paul coming toward the church steps looking a little uneasy in unfamiliar surroundings. Excusing himself from his group of friends, Bill went over and introduced himself to Paul. After talking briefly, Bill invited Paul to sit with him and his family for the Mass. With that simple gesture of hospitality a long and hard journey for Paul was begun.

In the course of the next three years Paul experienced a lot of pain and much growth. Through the assistance of Bill, he was able to acknowledge that he had a drug problem which he could not control. Eventually, Paul checked into a drug rehabilitation center and suc-

cessfully overcame his addictions. Throughout this time members of the community, organized by Bill, visited Paul and prayed for him. When he returned to his apartment, Paul maintained contact with his new-found friends from the church. In time, he made his way into their initiation process and was baptized, confirmed and shared Eucharist for the first time at the Easter vigil.

That vigil was like no other for Paul's friends. It carried a power they had never experienced, for they had never approached the celebration on a journey like this one. With his friends and other parishioners present that evening, Paul stated his renunciations of the prince of darkness and professed his faith in the Lord of light, familiar declarations for those who had gathered, but heard in a very different way this time. Many of them had witnessed the strength of evil in Paul's life and the struggle he went through to be freed of it. Now they were rejoicing with him as he declared his commitment to be a "child of the light."

You began by entering the forecourt of the baptistry. You faced westward, heard a voice commanding you to stretch out your hand, and renounced Satan as though to his face . . . "I renounce you, Satan." I will tell you now, for you need to know, why you face westward. The west is the quarter from which darkness appears to us; now the devil is darkness, and wields his power in darkness. So we look to the west as a symbolic gesture, and renounce the leader of shadow and darkness. . . . When you renounce Satan, you trample underfoot your entire covenant with him, and abrogate your former treaty with Hell. The gates of God's Paradise are open to you, that garden which God planted in the east, and from which our first parent was expelled for his transgression. When you turned from west to east, the region of light, you symbolised this change of allegiance. Then you were told to say: "I believe in the Father, the Son and the Holy Spirit, and in one baptism of repentance."[1]

Sue was a successful young lawyer working in a law

firm. At first appearance she had the world at her feet. She projected an image of self-confidence with an assurance about herself that proclaimed her satisfaction with who she was and how she lived her life. She was pretty, dressed well, drove a beautiful car, and lived in an exquisite condo.

Her friend Norma knew the hidden side of Sue. Despite all the things that were going well for her, Sue was struggling with an emptiness inside. For all that she had, she was beginning to see that it was not sufficient.

When she felt the time was right, Norma invited Sue to join her at a meeting of young professionals at her church. That evening, a whole new dimension of life was opened for Sue. She found herself among a group of people who had felt the same way she was feeling. But they were going beyond it by becoming involved in various projects which were aimed at reaching out to help the poor—volunteering their time to work at a soup kitchen in the inner-city and working with a local coalition of churches to provide shelter for the homeless.

After a few months of meeting and working with these other professionals, Sue began to inquire about their church affiliation. They invited her to "come and see" what their community of faith was all about. Eighteen months later, Sue celebrated the sacraments of initiation at the Easter vigil.

> First you fall on your knees. . . . You stretch out your hands to God in the attitude of one at prayer. For we have fallen into sin and the sentence of death has thrown us to the ground. . . . The rest of your body should remain upright, looking to heaven. By this attitude you present, so to speak, a request to God, asking him like a petitioner for liberation from your ancient fall and a share in the joys of heaven. . . .
>
> [After the bishop seals your forehead] immediately your sponsor stands behind you, spreads a linen stole over your head and raises you to your feet. You get up off your knees to show that you have abandoned your ancient fall, and have nothing to do with the earth and earthly affairs.[2]

The Process of Conversion

Contemporary journeys reflected in ancient rites portray what is at the heart of the R.C.I.A.: conversion, turning around one's life; metanoia, changing one's heart. It is precisely this that the document itself tries to convey to its readers:

> The rite of Christian initiation presented here is designed for adults who, after hearing the mystery of Christ proclaimed, consciously and freely seek the living God and enter the way of faith and *conversion* as the Holy Spirit opens their hearts. (#1, emphasis added)
>
> Before the rite of election is celebrated, the catechumens are expected to have undergone a *conversion* in mind and in action and to have developed a sufficient acquaintance with Christian teaching as well as a spirit of faith and charity. (#107, emphasis added)

The idea of conversion has for some time been viewed as an evangelical approach to faith. Because of some profound experience in life, a person comes to an acceptance of Jesus and is saved.

In recent years, however, mainline Christian churches are rediscovering the notion of conversion, not as a single event reality, but within the theme of pilgrimage of faith or the journey of conversion. This is due in part to the unfolding of various theories in the field of developmental psychology which have enabled our understanding of experiences of transitions in our lives.

I have heard the journey of conversion expressed in many different images; but the one that conveys what we are dealing with in the catechumenate best is the description given by Mark Searle in his article "The Journey of Conversion."[3]

Searle calls the whole process a "journey through crisis" in which the crisis is any experience which promotes change in one's life. This journey is characterized by three periods: 1) the setting out, 2) the adventure of crisis, and 3) the return.[4]

"Every human crisis, whatever its ultimate origin, calls that subjective world into question, causes a degree of disillusionment, creates a feeling of dissatisfaction, of being unable to continue with things as they are."[5] This experience stimulates the person to set out from where he or she is to discover a new way of being and acting, a new way of viewing the world and his or her own life. It prompts him or her to leave the familiar and secure so as to venture into the unknown. This then becomes the "adventure of crisis." It is movement out beyond the "tried and true" into a new realm. It is the willingness to enter into new dimensions of life, risking failure and the need to begin again in the honest search for what is truly right. Until at last the journey comes to fruition when "one becomes aware that new vision has been given, a new revelation has been granted, the grace of self-transcendence, of new life, of joy."[6]

A concrete example of this three-part experience is the familiar story of the exodus. While still enslaved in Egypt, the Israelites had a profound revelation of God in their lives. It opened to them a whole new way of thinking about themselves: as the people of God. It also presented some very exciting new possibilities. But for these possibilities to become real, they would have to make some changes. First and foremost, they would have to leave Egypt. They would have to venture forth into the unknown, trusting that God would lead them to the promised land. For forty years they wandered, being tested and being formed into a new people, until finally, they came to the land that God had promised to give them. It was there that their journey came to fruition. Now they were a free people, God's people, with a land of their own upon which to build a nation—no longer slaves and aliens; but a free people in a homeland.

This threefold description can easily be seen as an outline of the experiences of Paul and Sue mentioned earlier. It provides an understanding of what many others have gone through, although some with less dramatic changes, as they move into a deeper relationship with God in the midst of a believing community.

Other authors have also described the journey of conversion. In their research, Lofland and Stark identified seven elements in the conversion process. (They were specifically studying a religious cult group; and how this group went about initiating new members.)[7] For the most part, their schema is another way of expressing what Searle describes as the "journey through crisis." However, there are two elements in the Lofland and Stark study that are not mentioned in Searle's description of the experience: 1) affective bonds, and 2) intensive interaction.

When one is in crisis, quite often what enables the initial departure from the familiar is the strength of a relationship which either exists prior to the crisis or comes into being in the midst of it. This is an "affective bond." It is an interpersonal relationship through which the person receives the needed encouragement and support so that he or she will take the necessary steps to bring about change. It is important that this support be given throughout the process, and not just in the initial stages.

This need for support throughout the process is critical. But it need not rely solely upon the affective bond. It is enabled also through intensive interaction. The person needs to become involved on a regular basis with others who have achieved what he or she is seeking. Being involved with others who have successfully completed the conversion journey at least once themselves enables the new journeyer to persevere (especially in the periods of trial when the desire to return to the familiar is strongest), and to incorporate new ways of thinking and acting unto himself or herself.

If, as we saw above, conversion is what is at the heart of the R.C.I.A., then it is only appropriate that the rite seek to enable this kind of experience in the process it sets forth for the initiation of adults and ritually celebrate the various points of transition along the journey. A brief look at the rite will show that it does just that.

Conversion in the Rite

From the outset it calls for the two elements identified by Lofland and Stark: intensive interaction and affective bonds.

In its introductory paragraphs, the R.C.I.A. states:

The initiation of catechumens is a gradual process that takes place within the community of the faithful. (#4)

The rite makes it clear that there are a number of things that must go on as a part of this gradual process: "Opportunities should be provided for them to meet families and other groups of Christians." (#38) These gatherings with members of the community will be for catechetical sessions, prayer and liturgy, social events, and apostolic activities. (#75) These aspects are so vital to the experience that the bishop at the rite of election asks whether or not those seeking admission to the Easter sacraments have done these things: "Have they faithfully listened to God's word proclaimed by the Church? Have they shared the company of their Christian brothers and sisters and joined with them in prayer?" (#118B)

Throughout the entire process, which the rite envisions to be extended over a period of time (up to three years), there are numerous occasions when those seeking to be a part of the community are involved with the community itself. Although the rite never states it as such, it is suggesting experiences of intensive interaction with the faithful.

The rite also speaks of affective bonds, although not directly. In the section on ministries two ministries in particular qualify as affective bonds: that of sponsor and godparent.

A sponsor accompanies any candidate seeking admission as a catechumen. (#10)

It is the responsibility of godparents to show the candidates how to practice the Gospel in personal and social life, to sustain the candidates in moments of hesitancy and anxiety, to bear witness, and to guide the candidates' progress in the baptismal life. (#11)

These ministries are by their nature affective bonds. Through these ministries, a member of the community reaches out to a friend already known to them (as in the case of Norma and Sue), or establishes a relationship with someone new (as with Bill and Paul). Through their own commitment to and understanding of the Gospel message, they journey with the candidates, helping and supporting them each step of the way.

Throughout the text, the rite speaks of helping and supporting the candidates so that "with a purified and clearer intention they may cooperate with God's grace." (#38) It most certainly seeks to enable the conversion process.

It also provides the rituals to celebrate the various stages in this journey. The Rite of Acceptance into the Order of Catechumens begins with the candidates, their sponsors, and a group of the faithful gathered outside the church. The priest or deacon goes out to meet them. There is a dialogue with the candidates in which they essentially declare their belief in Jesus and their desire to be a part of this community. After their sponsors and the assembly affirm their willingness to help the candidates, they are signed with the cross, the sign of their "new way of life as catechumens." (#55) Then they are invited to come into the Church to share with the faithful at the table of God's word.

They who are not a part of this worshiping community gather outside of the community's place of worship. Only after they have declared their initial faith in Christ are they officially welcomed into the Church. The rite symbolizes the reality of what is happening in the candidates' lives. They are moving from one place in their life to another—from being "outsiders" to being "insiders." What seems to be an insignificant gesture to those of us who have been raised within this faith community resounds with immense meaning for the candidates. Many have stated that when they entered into the church during the rite, that walk down the aisle embodied their decision to move on in their life. It is the ritualizing of their "setting out."

The R.C.I.A. makes it clear that this first ritual is the celebration of the beginning of a long journey, not the conclusion.

The catechumenate is an extended period of time during which the candidates are given pastoral formation and guidance, aimed at training them in the Christian life. In this way, the dispositions manifested at their acceptance into the catechumenate are brought to maturity. (#75)

The time spent in the catechumenate should be long enough for the conversion and faith of the catechumens to become strong. (#76)

The Church seeks to help the catechumens during this "adventure of crisis" through minor exorcisms, blessings and anointings. Realizing the nature of this transitional period, the rite encourages using these special prayers and their accompanying gestures so that they receive "courage, joy, and peace as they proceed along the difficult journey they have begun" (#95) until

at last they reach that new shore where this call to conversion has come to completion.

This coming to maturity in faith is celebrated both in the rite of election and in the sacraments of Easter. In the rite of election, the bishop, assured by the godparents and members of the parish that the catechumens being presented to him have come to a mature faith, admits the catechumens to the initiation sacraments. At the Easter vigil, the Church celebrates baptism, confirmation, and Eucharist with these chosen ones.

Although not as dramatic as in the early Church, the vigil rites still proclaim what has been accomplished. With the formal rejection of Satan and his empty promises and the profession of faith in Christ, the candidates pass through the waters of baptism and are clothed in the white robe of the redeemed. Then they are led, for the first time, to the table of sacrifice so as to share in the Eucharist, the sacred meal belonging to those who are united to Christ.

The vigil celebrates the new life which the catechumens have entered into through their journey of conversion. With signs, gestures, and symbols it proclaims that they are born anew, that they are now fully united to Christ and to his people.

Thus we see that at the heart of the R.C.I.A. is conversion. It gives to us an outline for a process which enables and ritualizes the conversion process. If we are to be true to this vision of initiation given to us by the council, if we are to truly restore the catechumenate as our way of initiation, then we must recognize that the call to conversion is not just for those who come to the Church looking for something more in their life. It is also a call for the Church itself. For with the R.C.I.A. the Church proclaims that it has altered its way of initiation (not just the rituals, but its understanding of initiation as well). The promulgation of this rite calls us beyond the former ways of catechism instruction (in which initiation was seen as the teaching and learning of all the doctrines and dogmas of the Church). Although this passing on of our traditions and teachings is important (and an integral part of this rite), the R.C.I.A. is primarily about conversion. It is not sufficient to have learned all the dogmas—any atheist with an interest in organized religion can do that. The heart of the R.C.I.A. is enabling people to move out of their old ways into a new and deeper relationship with God within the Christian experience in such a way that they become not just disciples (believers in Jesus), but apostles (bearer of the good news to the nations).

The directive for this conversion in our understanding of initiation ministry and the consequent ritual changes was given by the Second Vatican Council in the Decree on the Missionary Activity of the Church:

The catechumenate is not a mere expounding

of doctrines and precepts, but a training period for the whole Christian life. It is an apprenticeship of appropriate length, during which disciples are joined to Christ their teacher. Therefore, catechumens should be properly instructed in the mystery of salvation and in the practice of gospel morality. By sacred rites which are to be held at successive intervals, they should be introduced into the life of faith, liturgy, and love, which God's people lives.[8]

In conclusion, the R.C.I.A. presents a real challenge to us and to those whom God leads to us. May we who are initiation ministers trust in God's guiding presence through these years of change constructing authentic conversion processes which serve those who come into our midst seeking the way of the Lord.

Notes

1. Edward Yarnold, S.J., *The Awe Inspiring Rites of Initiation*. England: St. Paul Publications, 1971, pp. 68–69, 73.

2. *Ibid.*, pp. 177–178, 187–188.

3. Mark Searle, "The Journey of Conversion," *Worship* 54:1 (January 1980), pp. 35–55.

4. *Ibid.*, p. 37, 39, 42.

5. *Ibid.*, p. 38.

6. *Ibid.*, p. 43.

7. John Lofland and Randy Stark, "Becoming a World-Saver: A Theory of Conversion to a Deviant Perspective," *American Sociological Review* 30 (1965) 863–874.

8. Walter M. Abbott, S.J., ed., "Decree on the Missionary Activity of the Church," *The Documents of Vatican II*. New York: Guild Press, 1966, p. 600.

ADVENT AND CHRISTMAS

The History of Salvation

By Eugene A. LaVerdiere, S.S.

The Gospel readings for Advent and Christmas-time outline the history of salvation and develop its dramatic tensions: the absence and presence of God, sin and divine love, the promise and fulfillment of salvation, yearning for the Lord and rejoicing in his presence. Even as the Gospel proclaims Jesus' birth, it announces his passion and death. These too are part of the events which have been fulfilled in our midst and which Luke has carefully ordered that we might come to a deeper knowledge of those matters in which we have already been catechized (Lk 1:1–4).

Salvation history is universal. It begins in the life of God with God's own inner word but then enters the world to be the Father's personal revelation, to give life and shed light, by dwelling among us as the Word become flesh (Jn 1:18). For a time, its story coincides with that of the Hebrew, Israelite and Jewish people (Mt 1:1–17), epitomized in the mission of John the Baptist and others (3:1–6, 10–18; 3:15–16, 21–22; 1:39–45), but then it opens up to all nations in the person of the magi (Mt 2:1–12), to climax one day in the Lord's definitive advent (Lk 21:25–28, 34–36). Most of the readings reflect on Jesus' identity, explore his life and meaning, and spell out their implications for his disciples and for all Christians who share in Christ's life and continue his mission to the ends of the earth.

Be On Your Watch

With the first Sunday of Advent we begin the new liturgical year. The reading is taken from Luke's account of Jesus' discourse on the fall of Jerusalem and the return of Christ as the Son of Man at the end of time (Lk 21:5–36). The passage selected deals with the events of the end (vv. 25–28) and the attitude of Jesus' followers toward these (vv. 34–36).

There is a major difference between Luke and Mark 13, which is his source for the discourse. In Mark, the siege and destruction of Jerusalem were very recent if not actually unfolding at the time the discourse was written. For many it seemed that the catastrophic events which marked the end had already begun. In Luke, the fall of Jerusalem had become an historical memory and clearly disassociated from the second advent. Luke and his communities looked to a long future

during which the life of the Church and salvation history would continue to unfold. Nevertheless Christians should live with the end in view. They should live under the sign of Christ's return. The return of Christ is presented as a cataclysmic event in which the very universe would be shaken to its foundations, so awesome would be the full manifestation of the Son of Man, the ultimate fulfillment of God's designs for humankind. Sobriety, watchfulness, prayer—those are the attitudes required of us. They are also the attitudes needed for good Christian living.

The Herald's Voice

On the first Sunday of Advent, we saw how Luke and his communities looked forward to a long history. Luke's sense of history is reinforced on this second Sunday with the introduction of John the Baptist (Lk 3:1–6) and the way John is carefully situated with regard to the Roman Empire and the religious and political context of Palestine. This is also the beginning of the history of the word. The same word which came to John would later reside in the ministry of Jesus and eventually ring out in the apostolic proclamation of the early Church. The history of the word, like the role of the Spirit, is one of the elements of continuity in the history of salvation.

John is a herald's voice in the desert of a new exodus. He is also a model for the historic role of Jesus' disciples and all future Christians. Just as John prepared his contemporaries for the coming of Christ in a first advent, we prepare our own contemporaries for his coming in a second advent. We too are called upon to prepare the way of the Lord.

Preparing the Way of the Lord

How then did John prepare the way of the Lord? We see it in his message. We see it in the way he addressed the ills of his time. On the third Sunday of Advent we see that John's work was prophetic and, more particularly, that it was a work of social justice, as we would call it today (Lk 3:10–18). We should note that, unlike Mark and Matthew, Luke does not emphasize John's baptizing activity. Instead he highlights John's prophetic message. If Luke were our only source, John would very likely be known as John the Prophet and not as John the Baptist.

John's message was very specific in both its contents and its addressees. He spoke to the crowds: they were to share their possessions, their clothing and their food with those who had none. He spoke to tax collectors: they were not to inflate the amount exacted from others to provide for themselves. He spoke to soldiers: they were not to bully or denounce people falsely to supplement their income. And finally, he himself had to be honest. He was not the Messiah, but merely the forerunner. The Gospel does not tell us how we must fulfill John's role today, but our need to do so and the approach is clear. It is not enough to speak in vague generalities when we deal with matters of justice. Like John, however, we must also be well-informed.

Jesus and John the Baptist

John the Baptist is the Advent prophet par excellence. As on the second and third Sundays of Advent, he is a central figure in the reading for the fourth Sunday (Lk 1:39–45). This time, however, he shares the stage with Jesus. The story is that of Mary's visit to her relative Elizabeth. On the surface, the theme seems to revolve about the two women, but in fact the central characters are the two unborn infants. At the approach of the unborn Jesus, John leaps in his mother's womb. He is filled with the Holy Spirit. John, the Old Testament, is quickened to life through contact with Jesus, the New Testament, and the Old Testament receives new meaning through its orientation to the New. As Elizabeth notes, Mary is blest for having trusted the word of the Lord, and this moment is the first expression of that word's fulfillment (1:45).

The passage also includes a second portion of the Hail Mary, "Blest are you among women and blest is the fruit of your womb" (1:42). The first was spoken by the angel Gabriel in the annunciation scene: "Rejoice, O highly-favored daughter (Hail, full of grace). The Lord is with you. Blessed are you among women" (1:28). The prayer should be approached in light of this biblical context.

Jesus Christ, Son of David, Son of Abraham

At the Christmas vigil, we read the entire first chapter of Matthew (1:1–25), which begins by recapitulating the biblical history of salvation in the form of a genealogy of Jesus (1:1–17). This genealogy (see also Luke 3:23–38) is a theological statement. It emphasizes Jesus' identity as the Christ (Messiah) and his relationship to David and Abraham. As the Son of David, Jesus is a messianic king. As the Son of Abraham, he fulfills

the promise that in Abraham's seed all nations would be blessed (see Gen 22:18). So it is that in the Gospel's conclusion Jesus commissions the eleven remaining disciples to "make disciples of all the nations" (Mt 28:18–20).

The second part of the chapter tells the story of how the birth of Jesus took place (1:18–25). Its central personage is Joseph, son of David, the husband of Mary, to whom the angel of the Lord appeared in a dream. His wife's child was conceived by the Holy Spirit. In him the prophecy of Isaiah 7:14 would be fulfilled. He would be called Emmanuel, which means "God is with us." In him God would be with his people. In this too the beginning of the Gospel looks to the conclusion when Jesus promises that he would be with his missionary Church always even to the end of the world (Mt 28:20).

Tidings of Great Joy

Matthew helped us see Jesus' relationship to the biblical history of salvation (vigil). At the Midnight Mass of Christmas, Luke helps us see his relationship to Caesar Augustus and the Roman Empire. It is through Caesar's decree that Jesus came to be born in David's city of Bethlehem, which did not provide hospitality at the time of his birth. Even the Roman emperor could be God's instrument in the unfolding of salvation history (2:1–7).

The shepherds were the first to hear the Gospel, the tidings of great joy that a Savior had been born to them, the Messiah and Lord. Here was the good news of salvation. It came from heaven, from God through an angelic messenger, just as Jesus himself was born Son of God through the power of the Holy Spirit. After they were given a sign in which they would be able to see the good news, a chorus of angels responded with a hymn of praise (2:8–14).

Seeing and Understanding

The shepherds had been given a sign: "In a manger you will find an infant wrapped in swaddling clothes" (Lk 2:12). In the Christmas Mass at Dawn, we read of how they went to Bethlehem, saw the baby lying in the manger and believed (2:15–20). A manger is a place where nourishment is given to the flock. The shepherds, who evoke the leaders of the early Church, saw how Jesus' life and person was offered as nourishment to the little flock (see Lk 12:32) of the Church. They saw, and on the basis of this concrete experience they understood the Gospel they had heard. The story ends with a series of reactions to the event and its Gospel.

Much of the same text, but without 2:15 and with

the addition of 2:21, is read on January 1, the Solemnity of Mary Mother of God. This second reading invites us to focus on how "Mary treasured all these things and reflected on them in her heart." Here is how we are to hear the Gospel. At the end of the passage, the circumcision is mentioned to introduce the naming of Jesus (2:21). Just as his very life came from God and the Gospel of salvation came from heaven through God's messenger, so also did his name, Jesus, which expressed his very identity (see Lk 1:31).

The Word Became Flesh

At Christmas Mass during the Day and on the second Sunday after Christmas, the magnificent prologue of St. John (1:1–18) is our Gospel reading. The basic form of this prologue is a hymn, which most likely was written independently of the Gospel. It sings the story of the word, a term which gathers up much of the biblical reflection on God's self-expression and communication from creation, and, even before, to the sharing of divine life. Although the Greek term used for this, *logos*, came from popular Greek philosophy, its meaning is closer to wisdom, *sophia*, as developed in works such as the Book of Wisdom.

The hymn opens with the first words of Genesis, "In the beginning" to introduce the Word in God's own life prior to creation (vv. 1–2). It then shows how the Word burst into creation (vv. 3–5), entered the world, the cosmos, a human reality (vv. 10–12), and even became flesh, taking on our human condition (vv. 14–16).

Several prose passages were added to the hymn when it became John's prologue. These verses speak of the person and role of John the Baptist (vv. 6–9, 15), explain the meaning of "children of God" in terms of virginal conception (vv. 12b–13), and comment on God's enduring love which came through Jesus Christ (vv. 17–18). The hymn had referred to the Father's only Son without actually naming Jesus. The prologue's editor named him directly. Jesus Christ, the only Son, is the revelation of the Father.

Journey to Jerusalem

For the Sunday after Christmas, the feast of the Holy Family, our reading is the story of the finding of Jesus in the temple (Lk 2:41–52). In telling of a relatively simple episode when Jesus was about the age of twelve, Luke sets out a major section of the entire story of Jesus, from the beginning of his great journey to Jerusalem (9:51) to the end of the Gospel (24:53). The journey to Jerusalem for the feast of Passover, the subsequent loss of Jesus, the search for him, the finding on the third day while he was teaching, and the necessity that he be with his Father (2:41–52) evoke the story of

his journey to Jerusalem, the final Passover, his passion, the visit to the tomb, the finding on the third day, his teaching first with the disciples of Emmaus and then with the whole community, and finally the ascension to his Father (9:51–24:53).

The story focuses on how Jesus' parents had to accept his going home to his true and ultimate parent. The early Christians had to let go of Jesus' earlier mode of presence among them if they were to discover him present in new ways. The same remains true with regard to the ways we have long known Christ among us. We must let go of the past to find him anew in the present. Such is the challenge of Christian growth and development.

Magi from the East

On the feast of Epiphany, we celebrate the manifestation of Jesus to the magi, who alone see the special star of Jesus at its rising among all the lesser personal stars in the heavens. King Herod and all Jerusalem, including the chief priests and the scribes, failed to see the star of Jesus.

The magi, religious Gentiles from the East, prefigure the eventual proclamation of the Gospel to the Gentiles, all the nations, after Israel's rejection of Jesus. Prostrating themselves before Jesus in homage, as they would before God himself, they offered the two gifts mentioned in Isaiah 60:5–6, gold and frankincense, and they added myrrh, an aromatic substance used in anointing a body for burial (see Jn 19:39). In Matthew 2:11, the myrrh may well symbolize the passion and death of Jesus. Jesus was offered gifts worthy of a king, but his kingdom was not of this world.

You Are My Beloved Son

Jesus was baptized by John (Lk 3:21–22), by one who proclaimed himself far his inferior (Lk 3:15–16). It was important for John, who prepared the way for Jesus' first coming, to recognize that he was not the Messiah. It remains important for us, who prepare the way for Jesus' second coming, to recognize the same. John models the life of Christians insofar as they are forerunners of his final advent.

Like the other Gospels, Luke is eager to present the origins of Jesus' mission, the proximate historical origins as well as the ultimate divine origins. This has influenced his story of the baptism of Jesus. Related to John, Jesus and his mission are nevertheless entirely distinct from John. That is why the descent of the Spirit and the proclamation of Jesus as God's beloved Son occur not at the time of the baptism but later while Jesus is communing with God in prayer.

Introduction to Advent and the Christmas Season

Each catechetical session in this section contains the following parts:
  Gathering Prayer
  Looking at Life
  Sharing Our Life
  Knowing Our Faith
  Making the Faith Our Own
  Living Our Faith
  Prayer

Each session begins with the "basic message" of the Sunday readings summarized in a few words. This focuses the session and assists the catechist in planning.

The dynamic behind each session is to juxtapose "your story" (experience) against the "Christian story" (tradition) and examine the difference. A decision is then solicited to do something about closing the gap (orthopraxis).

The *Gathering Prayer*, like a prelude, gives a taste of what is to come.

Looking at Life and *Sharing Our Life* focus on and clarify some human experience, personal or otherwise, which relates to the basic message.

Knowing Our Faith is an exploration, through teaching and discussion, dealing with a similar human experience in Scripture, history and theology. Suggestions for some further doctrinal study are usually made.

Making the Faith Our Own examines where the Church stands and where you stand.

In *Living Our Faith*, each person is challenged to decide what he or she is going to do about closing the discrepancy.

As an aid to *Prayer*, the responsorial psalm of the day is included at the end of each session. The catechist may wish to expand the prayer time by singing an appropriate hymn or engaging in some spontaneous prayer. Other prayers may certainly be used. After the prayer concludes, allow some time for socializing and informal discussion.

Further Reading and Resources

PREACHING THE LECTIONARY, Reginald H. Fuller, The Liturgical Press, 1984.

THE UNFINISHED IMAGE, George McCauley, Sadlier, 1983.

BANQUET OF THE WORD, Thomas Webbers, Resource Publications Inc., 1985.

THE DAILY STUDY BIBLE (The Gospel of Luke), William Barclay, G.R. Welch Co. Ltd. Toronto, 1975.

THE JESUS OPTION, Joseph G. Donders, Orbis Books, 1982.

JESUS, HOPE DRAWING NEAR, Joseph G. Donders, Orbis Books, 1985.

First Sunday of Advent

Jeremiah 33:14–16
1 Thessalonians 3:12–4:2
Luke 21:25–28, 34–36

BASIC MESSAGE

The pain of endings and beginnings.

GATHERING PRAYER

Let us pray. (silence)

Blessed are you, O Lord, our God. You fill our lives with many endings and beginnings. For all the doors you close in our lives, you open up new ones. In each transition you reveal some new dimension of yourself to us. Animated by your Holy Spirit, we follow the Lord Jesus on our journey toward the "fullness of life." Help us to be alert and strong enough not to refuse your invitation. In that way, not only do we come to know who you are, but we also come to know who we are. We make our prayer in the name of Jesus our Lord. Amen.

LOOKING AT LIFE

– Recall experiences of endings. This may be such things as:
  • a friend leaving for an extended holiday.
  • a loved one moving to a distant city.
  • a retirement.
  • a death.
  • explosion of nuclear bombs.
– Recall experiences of beginnings. This may be such things as:
  • entering into a marriage.
  • beginning a new job.
  • the birth of a first baby.
  • life without a spouse.
  • a move to an unknown city.
– How do you feel toward endings? toward beginnings?
– Are you fearful of endings? of beginnings?
– Did you try to stop the ending? the beginning?
– Was your life better or worse because of the ending? the beginning?
– To whom did you turn in those times?

– Were there signs of the coming of this experience or not?

SHARING OUR LIFE

Read the following statements, reflect, then discuss:

– Why were you fearful of the ending? the beginning?
– Why did you try to stop the ending? the beginning?
– Why did you promote the ending? the beginning?
– Why did you turn to the persons to whom you did?
– Why did you, or why did you not, turn to God at that time?

KNOWING OUR FAITH

Read, reflect, and dialogue about Luke 21:25–28, 34–36. Point out and discuss:

– After the death, resurrection, and ascension of Jesus, and the Pentecost experience, the early Christian community was involved in very challenging endings and beginnings. Their relationship with their Jewish community was ending and their relationship with the Gentiles was beginning.
– This pericope refers to two endings:
  • the destruction of Jerusalem by the Romans in the year 70 A.D.
  • the end of the world when Jesus will come in majesty and power.
– The majestic Jesus in all his glory is more powerful than all of creation.
– When Jesus comes, it will be a time of liberation.
– Times of transition are times to be careful.
– The pains which may be caused in times of transition may cause a person to turn to "debauchery and drunkenness."
– The sudden unexpected coming of Jesus may be like a trap.
– Times of transition are times to be prayerfully alert.
– You may wish to develop themes on eschatology.

MAKING THE FAITH OUR OWN

Read the following statements, reflect, then discuss:

Endings and beginnings are special times in which God can break into our lives.

– In what ways are you open to the unexpected coming of Jesus into your life in a new way?
– How are you ready to welcome the risen Jesus into your life?
– How do you avoid the occasion of sin?
– How do you pray at times of endings and beginnings?
– How does the Gospel challenge you to be more ready for unexpected endings and beginnings?

LIVING OUR FAITH

Read the following statements, reflect, then discuss and make a decision:

– What are you going to do to "stay awake"?
– When are you going to do it?
– Will you turn to Jesus at critical times?
– Will you stand with confidence when "your liberation is near at hand"?

PRAYER

Responsorial Psalm: Psalm 24 (25)

℞. To you, O Lord, I lift up my soul.

> Lord, make me know your ways.
> Lord, teach me your paths.
> Make me walk in your truth, and teach me:
> for you are God my savior. ℞.
>
> The Lord is good and upright.
> He shows the path to those who stray.
> He guides the humble in the right path;
> he teaches his way to the poor. ℞.
>
> His ways are faithfulness and love
> for those who keep his covenant and will.
> The Lord's friendship is for those who revere
>   him;
> to them he reveals his covenant. ℞.

Allow some time for socializing and informal discussion.

Doctrinal and Pastoral Issues: Advent, Conversion, Transformation, Eschatology, Death-Resurrection, Suffering

Michael Koch

Second Sunday of Advent

Baruch 5:1–9
Philippians 1:4–6, 8–11
Luke 3:1–6

BASIC MESSAGE

John preaches repentance.

GATHERING PRAYER

Let us pray. (silence)

Heavenly Father, we are sinners and always in need of your forgiveness. As John inspired sinners to repent and be baptized, so may your holy word touch us and help us to repent from our wayward and sinful ways. Fill us with humility to be attentive to the sacrament of reconciliation, and fill us with the joy of your forgiveness. We make our prayer in the name of Jesus our Lord. Amen.

LOOKING AT LIFE

- Recall experiences of repentance in your life.
- You may have lived a style of life incompatible with Jesus and his values. You feel you can no longer go on this way. You repent.
- You may be, by and large, living a life compatible with Gospel values, but, from time to time, you do something very foolish or sinful. You feel amends must be made. You repent.
- What values were you holding before you repented?
- How did you get to hold these values—selfishness, ignorance, peer pressure, etc.?
- What inspired you to repent—the Sacred Scriptures, a homily, the counsel of a friend, the pain of contradiction, the pain in the offended, etc.?
- How were you hurting before you repented?
- To whom did you go to express your repentance?
- How did you "mark" your repentance?
- Did you experience joy after repentance?
- Are you still unrepentant?

SHARING OUR LIFE

Read the following statements, reflect, then discuss:

- Why did you hold such second-rate values?
- Why were you not content with them?
- Why did you feel repentance was necessary?
- Why did you, or why did you not, go to someone to express your repentance?
- Why was it important to "mark" your repentance?
- Why are you still unrepentant?
- Why was it important for John to preach repentance?

KNOWING OUR FAITH

Read, reflect, and dialogue about Luke 3:1–6. Point out and discuss:

- For Luke, the emergence of John the Baptist was one of the hinges on which history turned. He dates the event in no fewer than six different ways.
- Five of these introductions are against a world background, the powerful Roman Empire and the Palestinian political situation. The sixth dating is against the local religious personalities, Annas (former high priest) and Caiaphas (current high priest).
- In the midst of these great powers, the word of God comes to ordinary John, son of Zechariah, in the wilderness.
- John was an itinerant preacher in the Jordan district.
- John's way of preparing for the Messiah was to proclaim a baptism of repentance for the forgiveness of sin.
- Verses 4–6 are a quotation from Isaiah 40:3–5.
- Whenever a king in the east proposed to tour part of his country, he would send a courier before him to prepare the road. Hence, John was regarded as the courier to the king.
- Discuss the pain of the Jews being forced into exile and the joy of the reunion (Bar 5:1–9).
- You may wish to develop themes on the sacrament of reconciliation.

MAKING THE FAITH OUR OWN

Read the following statements, reflect, then discuss:

- After John preached repentance, many people experienced conversion and marked it by being baptized by John.
- How are you ready to show repentance by making amends to the people you have injured?
- Do you believe you can show repentance by learning more about the sacrament of reconciliation or, if possible, to celebrate it?
- Do you believe you can show repentance by improving the quality of your prayer?
- Are you ready to show repentance by improving the quality of your charity?

LIVING OUR FAITH

Read the following statements, reflect, then discuss and make a decision:

- How are you concretely going to show repentance?
- When are you going to do it?
- To whom are you going to show repentance?
- To whom will you turn for help?

PRAYER

Responsorial Psalm: Psalm 125 (126)

℞. What marvels the Lord worked for us!
Indeed we were glad.

When the Lord delivered Sion from bondage,
it seemed like a dream.
Then was our mouth filled with laughter,
on our lips there were songs. ℞.

The heathens themselves said: "What marvels
the Lord worked for them!"
What marvels the Lord worked for us!
Indeed we were glad. ℞.

Deliver us, O Lord, from our bondage
as streams in dry land.
Those who are sowing in tears
will sing when they reap. ℞.

They go out, they go out, full of tears,
carrying seed for the sowing:
they come back, they come back, full of song,
carrying their sheaves. ℞.

Allow some time for socializing and informal discussion.

Doctrinal and Pastoral Issues: Repentance, Sacrament of Reconciliation, Healing, Conversion, Forgiveness

Michael Koch

Third Sunday of Advent

Zephaniah 3:14–18
Philippians 4:4–7
Luke 3:10–18

BASIC MESSAGE

Conversion—joy and justice.

GATHERING PRAYER

Let us pray. (silence)

Heavenly Father, we are always in need of conversion. You have created us out of nothing and have called us to everything. You have called us to make our home with you. Help us to be open and responsive to your invitation to new life. May we be willing to let go of the past and open to the future. May your word be alive in us as it was in John the Baptist. May we proclaim the good news to others in our times as John did in his. Hence, more people will believe in you. We offer our prayer in the name of Jesus our Lord. Amen.

LOOKING AT LIFE

Share with each other some of your conversion stories. You held a certain point of view or value. You had an unusual experience. After the experience, you were somehow changed. You now held a different point of view; you espoused a different value.

– What point of view or value did you surrender and what new point of view or value did you espouse?
– Who or what caused you to make that change?
– Are you living your life differently now than you did before?
– Did you support or fight this conversion process?
– Are you happier now that this conversion has happened?
– Do you now experience more contradictions between your new self and the people around you?
– Do other people notice the difference in you?
– Has this conversion alleviated or increased your suffering?
– Can you explain how this conversion came about or is it a mystery?

SHARING OUR LIFE

Read the following statement, reflect, then discuss:

– Why did this conversion happen in you?
– Why was your conversion beyond your control?
– Why do conversions give us more internal freedom?
– Why must conversions happen many times?
– Why are some conversions very dramatic and most very gradual?
– Why don't significant conversions happen more often?

KNOWING OUR FAITH

Read, reflect, and dialogue about Luke 3:10–18. Point out and discuss:

– It was John, powerfully preaching the word of God, who moved the hearts of his followers to conversion.
– St. Paul's teaching, "Faith comes by hearing."
– John's preaching reached everyone, the general public, the tax collectors, and soldiers. All asked what they must do.
– John's baptism of repentance was a plunging of oneself into something. The immersion into water was a sign of plunging oneself into a personal change of heart and way of life. It was the immersion of humanity into the full reality of God.
– John's message had three outstanding characteristics:
  • he demanded people share with one another.
  • he asked people to stay with their jobs, and work out their salvation in it—e.g., tax collectors should continue being tax collectors, but honest ones.
  • John made it clear that he was not the Christ, only a forerunner of the Christ.
– When the Christ comes, judgment will happen. He will separate the good from the bad. The Jews of the day felt that God would judge the Gentiles by a harsher standard than the Jews.
– You may wish to pursue the different kinds of conversion.
– You may wish to develop themes on the doctrine of grace.

MAKING THE FAITH OUR OWN

Read the following statements, reflect, then discuss:

- Do you believe that the conversions resulting from John's preaching were the work of the word of God?
- Do you believe that conversion will bring more joy and peace into your life?
- Do you believe that conversion is primarily the gratuitous work of God?
- Do you believe that for conversion to happen in your life, you must pray and be open to the Holy Spirit?
- Do you believe that conversion should be marked by some kind of celebration?
- Does this session help you to love Jesus more?

LIVING OUR FAITH

Read the following statements, reflect, then discuss and make a decision:

- How do you desire to experience a deeper conversion in your life?
- How do you intend to learn more about the different kinds of conversion?
- How will you pray that a deeper conversion to Jesus will take place in your life?
- When are you going to begin doing the above?
- To whom will you turn for help?

PRAYER

Responsorial Psalm: Isaiah 12

℞. Sing and shout for joy
for great in your midst is the Holy One of Israel.

Truly, God is my salvation,
I trust, I shall not fear.
For the Lord is my strength, my song.
He became my savior.
With joy you will draw water
from the wells of salvation. ℞.

Give thanks to the Lord, give praise to his
name!
Make his mighty deeds known to the peoples!
Declare the greatness of his name. ℞.

Sing a psalm to the Lord
for he has done glorious deeds,
make them known to all the earth!
People of Sion, sing and shout for joy
for great in your midst is the Holy One of Israel. ℞.

Allow some time for socializing and informal discussion.

Doctrinal and Pastoral Issues: Conversion, Grace, Surrender, Justice, Baptism, Judgment, Christian Living

Michael Koch

Fourth Sunday of Advent

Micah 5:1–4
Hebrews 10:5–10
Luke 1:39–45

BASIC MESSAGE

Mary—Bearer of Good News.

GATHERING PRAYER

Let us pray. (silence)

Our Father in heaven, in your love for us, you sent us good news. Your angel Gabriel announced the good news to Mary in Nazareth. Through her "yes," her "fiat," your Son entered into human history. We thank you, Lord, for Mary, your mother, for her yes, and for being the bearer of good news. Help us today to rejoice with Elizabeth and to accept the Lord Jesus more deeply into our own lives. May our hearts leap because the Lord is within us. Help us, in our turn, to be bearers of the good news to others. We make our prayer through Christ our Lord. Amen.

LOOKING AT LIFE

Recall experiences in your life in which someone brought you excitingly good news. Share your stories. Examples might be a graduation, winning a sweepstake, a promotion to a unique job, being vindicated from an accusation of serious crime, a serious illness was arrested, a healthy new baby was born.

– When was the good news brought to you?
– Where were you when the good news was brought to you?
– How did you feel when you heard the good news?
– Who brought you the good news?
– Who was with you when you heard the good news?
– Who was the first person to whom you told the good news?
– How soon did you tell that person?
– How did you feel toward the person who brought you the good news?

SHARING OUR LIFE

Read the following statements, reflect, then discuss:

– Why were you not expecting to hear good news?
– Why were you so excited when you heard the good news?
– Why were you attracted to the person who brought you the good news?
– Why did you feel a need to tell someone?
– Why did the good news make a difference in your life?
– Why did you, or did you not, give thanks to God?
– Why were Mary and Elizabeth both so excited about the good news of the new babies?

KNOWING OUR FAITH

Read, reflect, and dialogue about Luke 1:39–45. Point out and discuss:

– Since there are only two annunciation stories in the Gospel, Matthew and Luke, which are read on the fourth Sundays in Cycle A and B, Cycle C switches to the story about the visitation.
– Mary's journey may have been for several reasons:
  • to visit and care for Elizabeth, an outstanding act of charity.
  • the human need to share the good news with Elizabeth.
– Mary, the new ark of the covenant, brings Jesus, the new presence of God, to Jerusalem.
– Elizabeth calls Mary blessed three times in the pericope.

There are several reasons for calling her blessed:
  • Mary's faith (see verse 45).
  • Mary was bearing the Christ child.
– Mary is so blessed not because of what she is in herself, but because of her relationship to the incarnate Christ.
– Luke does not operate with a pre-existent Logos-Christology as John does. Hence, the conception of Jesus is the sign that he is the one who will perform the eschatologically unique role in salvation history. Isaac, Moses, and Jeremiah are lesser Old Testament examples.
– Elizabeth's great joy is that Mary brought good news into the house of Elizabeth and Zechariah.

– A teaching on the rosary could follow.

MAKING THE FAITH OUR OWN

Read the following statements, reflect, then discuss:

– Mary, in visiting Elizabeth, brought good news into her life. It made Elizabeth ecstatic.
– Why do you believe that Mary should be honored and blessed?
– What does Mary's "yes" to God's invitation mean for you?
– Do you believe that you, like Mary, can be the bearer of the good news?
– Why should Catholics pray the Magnificat?

LIVING OUR FAITH

Read the following statements, reflect, then discuss and make a decision:

– What does Mary mean for your life?
– What effort will you make to pray the Magnificat?
– What efforts will you make to pray the "Hail Mary"?
– What efforts will you make to learn how to pray the rosary?
– When will you start doing this?
– To whom will you turn to help you to do this?

PRAYER

Conclude your study with the Magnificat.

Gospel Canticle: Luke 1:46–55

> My soul proclaims the greatness of the Lord,
> my spirit rejoices in God my Savior
> for he has looked with favor on his lowly ser-
> vant.
>
> From this day all generations will call me
>   blessed:
> the Almighty has done great things for me,
> and holy is his Name.
> He has mercy on those who fear him
> in every generation.
>
> He has shown the strength of his arm,
> he has scattered the proud in their conceit.
>
> He has cast down the mighty from their
>   thrones,
> and has lifted up the lowly.
>
> He has filled the hungry with good things,
> and the rich he has sent away empty.

> He has come to the help of his servant Israel
> for he has remembered his promise of mercy,
> the promise he made to our fathers,
> to Abraham and his children for ever.

Allow some time for socializing and informal discussion.

Doctrinal and Pastoral Issues: Mary, Incarnation

Michael Koch

Christmas

(At Midnight)

Isaiah 9:1–6
Titus 2:11–14
Luke 2:1–14

For a catechumenal session on Christmas Day, please refer to "Breaking Open the Word of God" Cycle A, page 27. Either session would be appropriate for a dismissal on Christmas Day.

BASIC MESSAGE

The Birth of Jesus: The Incarnation.

GATHERING PRAYER

Let us pray. (silence)

Lord God, Creator of heaven and earth, we never cease to marvel at your great love for us. You have created a beautiful world through which you reveal yourself. But more profoundly, you have revealed yourself through your Son Jesus in the incarnation. You have made human life sacred. In your humanity, you eat and love, suffer and die with us. You have become human so that we may really and truly touch the divine. Help us, Lord, in this session to grow in understanding your greatness. We make our prayer in the name of Jesus the Lord. Amen.

LOOKING AT LIFE

Recall some experience in your life concerning birth. This may be the birth of one of your own children, of a brother or sister, or the baby of a relative or friend.

- When and how did you first find out that this little one was on its way?
- How did you feel about the news?
- Where was the child born?
- When was the child born?
- What were the feelings associated with the birth?
- Who was in attendance?
- Where in the family was this child? (e.g., 1st, 3rd, etc.)
- Who were the first people who were informed about the birth?

SHARING OUR LIFE

Read the following statements, reflect, then discuss:

- Why did you feel the way you did about this new baby?
- Why was the baby born where it was?
- Why did you first inform the people that you did?
- Why do we celebrate Christmas today?
- Why was Jesus born in such primitive circumstances?
- What does Christmas mean?

KNOWING YOUR FAITH

Read, reflect, and dialogue about Luke 2:1–14. Point out and discuss:

- The secular circumstances of Jesus' birth—i.e. the Roman Empire, Caesar Augustus, and Quirinius.
- The census was taken primarily for two reasons:
  • for accurately assessing taxation.
  • for compulsory military service.
- The journey from Nazareth to Bethlehem, about eighty miles, was very difficult. Reflect on the difficulty of journeying in faith today.
- The anguish in Mary and Joseph because, in their time of greatest need, there was such a lack of hospitality. Reflect upon where you experience welcome in the Church, or the lack of it.
- Through Jesus, because of his great love for us, God takes on human flesh and becomes one of us. Reflect upon how you experience God's immanence in your own daily life.
- The significance that the shepherds were the first to hear the good news. Shepherds, like tax collectors and prostitutes, were outcasts. Shepherds were poor and often thieves. Who are the outcasts in Church and society today who proclaim good news?
- You may wish to develop the doctrine on the incarnation.
  • Make connections between Christmas and incarnation. Avoid historicism.

MAKING THE FAITH OUR OWN

Read the following statements, reflect, then discuss:

– When Jesus was born, the world did not welcome
   him. What can you do to welcome every person—
   young and old? How do you care for the poor and unwanted?
– Why do you believe that it was because of God's great
   love for us that he gave us his Son Jesus?
– Why do you believe that God is on the side of the
   poor, the lowly, the underdog?
– What does God becoming our flesh mean to you?

LIVING OUR FAITH

Read the following statements, reflect, then discuss and
make a decision:

– What efforts will you make to welcome Jesus into
   your own life?
– In what way are you on the side of the poor and the
   underprivileged?
– What efforts do you make to care for the poor, the
   alienated, the unwanted?
– How does your lifestyle reflect a life-giving presence?
– How do you reveal the presence of God to others?

PRAYER

Responsorial Psalm: Psalm 95 (96)

℟. Today a Savior has been born to us;
    he is Christ the Lord.

   Oh sing a new song to the Lord,
   sing to the Lord all the earth.
   Oh sing to the Lord, bless his name. ℟.

   Proclaim his help day by day,
   tell among the nations his glory
   and his wonders among all the peoples. ℟.

   Let the heavens rejoice and earth be glad,
   let the sea and all within it thunder praise,
   let the land and all it bears rejoice,
   all the trees of the wood shout for joy
   at the presence of the Lord for he comes,
   he comes to rule the earth. ℟.

   With justice he will rule the world,
   he will judge the people with his truth. ℟.

Allow some time for socializing and informal discussion.

*Doctrinal and Pastoral Issues: Incarnation, Christol-
ogy, Christmas, Care for the Poor, Presence of God,
Value of Life*

Michael Koch

Holy Family Sunday

Sirach 3:2–6, 12–14
Colossians 3:12–21
Luke 2:41–52

BASIC MESSAGE

Christian Family Life.

GATHERING PRAYER

Let us pray. (silence)

Be with us today, Eternal God, as we reflect upon family life, an image of the Triune God. In your wisdom you have created the human family in which we can learn how to live. You have given us the Holy Family as a model to imitate.

Give us the strength, O Lord, to believe that the Holy Family is possible to imitate. We are able to identify with the Holy Family, not because they were so extraordinarily holy, but because they too experienced harmony and conflict, joy and suffering, confusion and peace. Their strength was that they remained faithful to the Lord God. Bless us in the name of the Holy Family, Jesus, Mary, and Joseph. Amen.

LOOKING AT LIFE

Share with each other some of your experiences with family life. Include experiences of harmony and conflict, joy and suffering, health and sickness, permanence and brokenness.

- How do you evaluate the quality of family life today in Church and society?
- Do the majority of people today trust family life?
- What causes harmony in your family?
- What causes conflict?
- How do you celebrate joy in your family?
- How do you bear up under suffering?
- Do you believe in the permanence of marriage?
- Are children important in a marriage?

SHARING OUR LIFE

Read the following statements, reflect, then discuss:

- Why are there so many broken families today?
- Why do you have trouble maintaining harmony?
- Why do you find celebrating in your family difficult?
- Why can suffering be relation-building?
- Why do you, or why do you not, believe in the permanence of marriage?
- Why are children important in a marriage?
- Why is the Church interested in family life?
- How can the Holy Family serve as a model today?

KNOWING OUR FAITH

Read, reflect, and dialogue about Sirach 3:2–6, 12–14. Point out and discuss:

- This reading is a commentary on the fourth commandment, "Honor your father and your mother."
- In the Old Testament, obedience and respect for parents was considered a way for atoning for your sins. For Christians, atonement for sins is made through Jesus alone.
- Long life was considered a reward for those who respect and honor their parents.
- The monition to take care of one's parents in their old age, regardless of their condition.

Read, reflect, and dialogue about Colossians 3:12–21. Point out and discuss:

- The heart of this passage is the first verse—"You are God's chosen ones; now live accordingly!"
- "Clothe yourselves" reflects the catechumen coming out of the baptismal pool and putting on the white baptismal garment. The new Christian "puts on" the virtues mentioned in verses 12–13.
- Verses 18–21 refer to Christian family life.

Read, reflect, and dialogue about Luke 2:41–52. Point out and discuss:

- That Mary and Joseph are very committed Jews is shown by their going to Jerusalem every year for the Passover.
- This first journey of Jesus to Jerusalem as a legal adult

(twelve years of age) foreshadows his final journey for his passion and death.
– The anguish of Mary and Joseph over the lost Jesus.
– The search for Jesus in Jerusalem and finding him in the temple with the teachers and doctors.
– The normal family life in Nazareth after this incident.

MAKING THE FAITH OUR OWN

Read the following statements, reflect, then discuss those most appropriate:

– How do you believe that Christian life is possible today?
– How can the Holy Family serve as a good model for family life today?
– What do you intend to read of today's Church teachings on family life?
– What do you do to nurture and enrich your marriage—spiritually? emotionally? relationally?
– Would you consider making a Marriage Encounter?
– Do you intend to celebrate some of your family events?
– Do you believe in daily family prayer?

LIVING OUR FAITH

Read the following statements, reflect, then discuss and make a decision:

– When will you start celebrating family events?
– When will you read some of the Church's documents on family life?
– What effort will you make to find out more about Marriage Encounter and then to make one?
– How and when will you reinforce your family prayer?
– To whom will you turn for help?
– How do you improve your family relationships?

PRAYER

You may wish to conclude with spontaneous prayer, a song, or the responsorial psalm.

Responsorial Psalm: Psalm 127 (128)

℞. Oh blessed are those who fear the Lord
and walk in his ways.

Oh blessed are those who fear the Lord
and walk in his ways!
By the labor of your hands you shall eat.
You will be happy and prosper. ℞.

Your wife like a fruitful vine

in the heart of your house;
your children like shoots of the olive,
around your table. ℞.

Indeed thus shall be blessed
the man who fears the Lord.
May the Lord bless you from Sion
all the days of your life! ℞.

Allow some time for socializing and informal discussion.

Doctrinal and Pastoral Issues: Christian Family, Parenting, Christian Love, The Fourth Commandment

Michael Koch

January 1—Solemnity of Mary, the Mother of God

Numbers 6:22–27
Galatians 4:4–7
Luke 2:16–21

BASIC MESSAGE

Mary, Mother of God.

GATHERING PRAYER

Let us pray. (silence)

Eternal God, in your great love for us you sent your Son into our midst, born of a woman, born of flesh. In entering time, he did not cling to his equality with God, but emptied himself to become one of us. We thank you, Abba, for raising him up, and us with him. Today we honor your Son by honoring Mary as Mother of God. In her lowliness you raised her up so that all generations will call her blessed. We make our prayer through Jesus Christ, our Lord and liberator. Amen.

LOOKING AT LIFE

Recall experiences in your life where you or someone else put someone on a pedestal. This could be Miss America, a sports or political personality, a saint who is canonized, someone from your local community, or somebody in your personal life.

– How do you feel about putting someone on a pedestal?
– How do you think the person put on the pedestal feels?
– Did you know the person put on a pedestal?
– Did the person's personality change after being put on a pedestal?
– Did you become a better person because of the person on the pedestal?
– What happened to the ordinary life of the person on the pedestal?
– How does the media put people on pedestals?

SHARING OUR LIFE

Read the following statements, reflect, then discuss:

– Why do we put some people on pedestals?
– Why do our values change because of the person on the pedestal?
– Why is the person on the pedestal an inspiration to what we want to achieve?
– Why can our preoccupation with the person on the pedestal be an escape into a dream world and away from real life down to earthly life?
– Why can a person on a pedestal be a cause of hope?
– If the gap between the person on the pedestal and ordinary life is too great, it can cause indifference. Why?
– Has the Church put Mary on a pedestal by calling her the Mother of God?

KNOWING OUR FAITH

– In order for God to redeem or liberate all humanity, God chose to be conceived by an ordinary woman. The purpose of the incarnation was the liberation of human beings from the law so that they might become children of God. The purpose of the incarnation was to make God immanent. Discuss: Why are we so threatened by a God who becomes immanent?
– Pious practice has distanced Mary from our humanity. She is made extraordinary at the expense of her ordinariness; she is put on a pedestal.
Discuss: When we make Mary too extraordinary, the average Christian can no longer identify with her.
– Jesus is divine, but he does not cling to his equality with God; he empties himself to become human, even to death, death on a cross. But God raised him up. When God raised him, he took all humanity with him. Mary is the paradigm of the lowly raised to the level of Mother of God.

MAKING THE FAITH OUR OWN

Read the following statements, reflect, then discuss:

– What does "Mary, Mother of God" mean to you?

– How do you believe that in emptying yourself completely (surrender to God) God will fill you?
– How do you treasure the fact that Jesus took on humanity to liberate all humankind?

LIVING OUR FAITH

Read the following statements, reflect, then discuss and make a decision:

– How will or do you show reverence to Mary, Mother of God?
– How will you come to a deeper understanding of Mary's role in salvation?
– When are you going to do this?
– To whom will you turn for help?

PRAYER

For your closing prayer, you may sing a Marian hymn, have some spontaneous prayer, pray the Hebrew blessing (Numbers 6:24–26) (1st reading) or pray the responsorial psalm.

Responsorial Psalm: Psalm 66 (67)

℞. O God, be gracious and bless us.

> O God, be gracious and bless us
> and let your face shed its light upon us.
> So will your ways be known upon earth
> and all nations learn your saving help. ℞.

> Let the nations be glad and exult
> for you rule the world with justice.
> With fairness you rule the peoples,
> you guide the nations on earth. ℞.

> Let the peoples praise you, O God;
> let all the peoples praise you.
> May God still give us his blessing
> till the ends of the earth revere him. ℞.

Allow some time for socializing and informal discussion.

Doctrinal and Pastoral Issues: Jesus in Ordinary Life, Incarnation, Mary Mother of God, Salvation, Liberation, Christology

Michael Koch

Epiphany

(Sunday between January 2 and January 8)

Isaiah 60:1–6
Ephesians 3:2–3, 5–6
Matthew 2:1–12

BASIC MESSAGE

Light for the Gentiles.

GATHERING PRAYER

Let us pray. (silence)

Holy and generous God, in your great love you have
revealed yourself in creation. But you have done even
more—you have revealed yourself in your Son, our
Lord Jesus. By believing in and following him, we are
led to eternal life with you. Help us not to be like King
Herod, who, threatened by your revelation, tried to kill
Jesus. Help us to be like the magi so that when we see
your revelation, we will be filled with delight. We
make our prayer in the name of Jesus our Lord. Amen.

LOOKING AT LIFE

Recall experiences in your life in which you came from
darkness to light. This could be physical darkness and
light, but it would be better to use experiences of coming from darkness to insight.

- What was the new insight or revelation that came
  upon you?
- Was it a delightful or painful experience?
- Who or what caused this insight or revelation to hap-
  pen?
- How was your life changed because of it?
- Did you grow in any virtues because of it—e.g., un-
  derstanding, patience, gentleness, peace, love, etc.?
- With whom did you first share this revelation?
- What was his or her reaction?
- Would you want to go back to your former way?

SHARING YOUR LIFE

Read the following statements, reflect, then discuss:

- Why do you think this insight or epiphany happened
  to you?
- Why can such insight be delightful or cause us fear
  and pain?
- After the revelation has occurred, why is it not possible to return to the former darkness?
- Why did you share this revelation with the person
  you did?
- Why did that person react the way he or she did?

KNOWING YOUR FAITH

Epiphany means revelation or manifestation. Epiphany
was originally an Eastern Church celebration. It was
originally and primarily a celebration of baptism, the
first epiphany or manifestation. As the celebration
moved westward, it took on the meaning of the revelation of Jesus to the Gentiles. The central point of this
pericope is that God's salvation is intended not only for
the people of Israel, but for all people.

Read, reflect, and dialogue about Matthew 2:1–12.
Point out and discuss:

- Jesus was born during the reign of King Herod.
  Herod was very paranoid about someone taking his
  throne from him.
- The wise men or magi from the east came to Jerusalem inquiring about the "infant king of the Jews."
  This potential usurper greatly upset the paranoid
  King Herod.
- Herod called together his advisors to inform him
  where the Christ was to be born. They informed him
  that it was in Bethlehem in Judea.
- Herod's deceit in calling the wise men to disclose the
  whereabouts of Jesus so that he might pay homage to
  him. His true intent was not to pay homage to him,
  but to kill him.
- The effects of this epiphany or revelation—Herod was
  perturbed, the wise men were filled with delight.
- The star (light), the fear of Herod, the quest for dis-
  covery, the adoration of Christ by the magi, were
  signs which manifested Jesus as the epiphany or revelation of God.
- The offering of the gifts of gold, frankincense, and
  myrrh were symbols to manifest their acceptance of
  Christ as king, priest, and prophet.

- God revealed in a dream to the magi that they should not go back to Herod.
- Read Isaiah 60:1–6 from the point of view of a revelation.
- Read Ephesians 3:2–3, 5–6 from the point of view of a revelation.
- A teaching on the nature of revelation could follow.

MAKING THE FAITH OUR OWN

Read the following statements, reflect, then discuss:

- What is the connection between your story and the biblical story?
- Do you believe that Jesus is God's most profound and fullest revelation to humanity?
- Do you believe that God's revelation is meant for all people?
- Do you believe that, for some people, God's revelation can be very threatening and painful while others are filled with delight?
- Do you believe that some people, like Herod, will do evil to block God out of their lives?
- Do you believe the Church's teaching on revelation as described in Vatican II's Dogmatic Constitution on Divine Revelation?

LIVING OUR FAITH

Read the following statements, reflect, then discuss and make a decision:

- How will you be open to God's revelation as it happens to you in your daily life and in the Church?
- How will you take the time to prayerfully reflect on how God is daily being revealed to you?
- How much of an effort will you make to learn more about the nature of revelation?
- Will you daily read the Scriptures to come in touch with God's revelation?
- Are you willing to point out God's revelation to others?
- To whom will you turn for support?
- How has your faith in Jesus increased because of this session?

PRAYER

Responsorial Psalm: Psalm 71 (72)

℟. All nations shall fall prostrate before you, O Lord.

O God, give your judgment to the king,
to a king's son your justice,

that he may judge your people in justice
and your poor in right judgment. ℟.

In his days justice shall flourish
and peace till the moon falls.
He shall rule from sea to sea,
from the Great River to earth's bounds. ℟.

The kings of Tarshish and the sea coasts
shall pay him tribute.
The kings of Sheba and Seba
shall bring him gifts.
Before him all kings shall fall prostrate,
all nations shall serve him. ℟.

For he shall save the poor when they cry
and the needy who are helpless.
He will have pity on the weak
and save the lives of the poor. ℟.

Allow some time for socializing and informal discussion.

Doctrinal and Pastoral Issues: Revelation, Epiphany, Inspiration, Prayer, The Constitution on Divine Revelation

Michael Koch

Baptism of the Lord

Isaiah 42:1–4, 6–7
Acts 10:34–38
Luke 3:15–16, 21–22

BASIC MESSAGE

Empowered for Ministry

GATHERING PRAYER

Let us pray. (silence)

Eternal Creator, you have revealed yourself to us in many ways. Your most delightful revelation is in your Son Jesus. Through him you have revealed yourself as Trinity; Father, Son, and Holy Spirit. Through your Holy Spirit you have empowered Jesus to engage in his mission with commitment unto death. Help us, O God, to be docile to your Holy Spirit so that we too, in the imitation of Jesus, will be empowered to carry out the ministry to which you have called us. We make our prayer in the name of Jesus Christ our Lord and Savior. Amen.

LOOKING AT LIFE

Share with each other some of your experiences regarding motivation.

– What was it that needed to be said or done?
– What motivated you to say or do it—self-preservation, someone's nagging, financial gain, honor, principles, inspiration of the Spirit?
– Were you slow or fast in responding?
– Did you have to fight against laziness, tiredness or fear?
– Was your motivation hampered by lack of knowledge, doubt, or tradition?
– Did enough insight free you to act?
– Did you have enough faith to act?

SHARING OUR LIFE

Read the following statements, reflect, and discuss:

– Why was it necessary to say or do what needed to be said or done?
– Why did you hesitate so long in doing it?
– Why can doubt or tradition hinder motivation?
– Why does faith contribute to motivation?
– Why does it sometimes require power from the Spirit to motivate us?

KNOWING OUR FAITH

Read, reflect, and dialogue about Luke 3:15–16, 21–22. Point out and discuss:

– The basic message in this reading is that God has empowered Jesus for ministry.
– John baptized with water but Jesus, who is greater than John when he comes, will baptize with the Holy Spirit and fire.
– What was unique about Jesus' baptism was the inclusion of the Holy Spirit and the Father's affirmation "You are my Son, the Beloved; my favor rests on you."
– Note the revelation of the Trinity in this epiphany.
– Read and enjoy Isaiah 42:1–4, 6–7. Notice that much of the imagery that Luke uses comes from this reading. The commissioning for service is found in "I have endowed him with my spirit that he may bring true justice to the nations." Verses 6 and 7 describe some of the ministries.

Read and enjoy Acts 10:34–38. Point out and discuss:

– Peter's new insight. Originally, Peter believed that salvation was limited to the Jews. After his vision, he was motivated by the Spirit to expand evangelization to the Gentiles.
– Peter, in his new insight, sees that salvation is for all persons, but it has come through the people of Israel, brought to them by Jesus Christ.
– Jesus is empowered for ministry through his baptism in which "God has anointed him with the Holy Spirit and with power."
– Because God was in Jesus, he was motivated to do the work of God—that is, teaching, healing, and exorcising.
– In this session, you could introduce the Church's teaching on the Trinity and the sacraments of baptism and confirmation.

MAKING THE FAITH OUR OWN

Read the following statements, reflect, then discuss:

– Why do you believe that God desires the salvation of all people?
– Why do you believe that Christians are the people through whom God wishes to reveal himself to the people of the world?
– Why do you believe that Christians need to be motivated and empowered by the Holy Spirit to accomplish this mission?
– How do you believe that through our baptism we are empowered by the Holy Spirit to build up the body of Christ and engage in its mission?
– How do you believe that you can be motivated by the Holy Spirit?

LIVING OUR FAITH

Read the following statements, reflect, then discuss and make a decision:

– What will you do to pray that the Holy Spirit empower you?
– How will you learn all you can about baptism, and, if you are not baptized, long to celebrate this sacrament?
– In what ways are you open to accepting all non-Christians as worthy of God's salvation?
– What will you do to heal broken Christianity?
– In what ministry will you engage in your parish?
– When are you going to do this?
– To whom will you turn for support?

PRAYER

You may wish to end your session with the prayer to the Holy Spirit, the responsorial psalm or spontaneous prayer.

PRAYER TO THE HOLY SPIRIT

Come, Holy Spirit, fill the hearts of your faithful, and kindle in them the fire of your love.

V.   Send forth your Spirit and they shall be created.

R.   And you shall renew the face of the earth.

    Let us pray.
    O God, you have taught the hearts of the faithful by the light of the Holy Spirit; grant us, in the same spirit, to have a taste for what is right, and to rejoice always in his consolation. Through Christ our Lord. Amen.

Responsorial Psalm: Psalm 28(29)

℟.   The Lord will bless his people with peace.

    Oh give the Lord, you sons of God,
    give the Lord glory and power;
    give the Lord the glory of his name.
    Adore the Lord in his holy court. ℟.

    The Lord's voice resounding on the waters,
    the Lord on the immensity of waters;
    the voice of the Lord, full of power,
    the voice of the Lord, full of splendor. ℟.

    The God of glory thunders.
    In his temple they all cry: "Glory!"
    The Lord sat enthroned over the flood;
    the Lord sits as king for ever. ℟.

Allow some time for socializing and informal discussion.

Doctrinal and Pastoral Issues: Baptism, Ministry, Faith and Doubt, The Holy Spirit, Christian Unity

Michael Koch

LENT

The Work of Redemption

by Eugene A. LaVerdiere, S.S.

Lent is a very special season in which we look at Jesus' teaching and all of his activities in the light of his passion and death. We also see what his passion and death meant for our redemption and how by learning from his life and by following his teaching we fulfill our baptismal commitment and progress toward salvation.

The Gospel readings begin on Ash Wednesday with a call to enter into the season devoutly and generously as people willing to translate the first-century demands of the Gospel into those of the twentieth century (Mt 6:1–6, 16–18). On the first and second Sundays of Lent, we begin by approaching the great tests of Jesus' life and how he responded to them (Lk 4:1–13). We then reflect on his glorious manifestation in the transfiguration (Lk 9:28b–36). Together these readings recapitulate the entire life of Jesus and anticipate his passion, Jesus' ultimate test, and resurrection, his definitive entry into glory.

From the third to the fifth Sundays, we reflect with Luke on the need and urgency of reform (Lk 13:1–9) and the need to forgive and be reconciled (Lk 15:1–3, 11–32) and then with John on the need to help and correct without condemning one who sins (Jn 8:1–11). Together these readings describe the life of those who chose to live under the sign of Jesus' passion-resurrection. Finally, on Passion Sunday, we accompany Jesus into Jerusalem (Lk 19:28–40) for the unfolding of the events of the passion, death and burial (Lk 22:14—23:56).

To appreciate the deeper implications of the message, however, we need to note its context. The previous verse, Lk 3:38, which marked the conclusion of the genealogy of Jesus, ended with the words, "son of Adam, son of God." Later in the temptation episodes, when the devil says to Jesus, "If you are the Son of God . . ." we should recall the conclusion of the genealogy. Jesus does not deny, of course, that he is the Son of God, but his response reaffirms his being son of Adam. He is Son of God in a way which does not contradict his being son of Adam. Jesus affirms the fullness of his humanity, something which Adam had not been able to do.

The Transfiguration

The first Sunday of Lent, with its story of Jesus'

temptations, anticipated the celebration of the passion of Jesus. Both deal with the testing of Jesus. The second Sunday, when we focus on the transfiguration (Lk 9:28b–36), anticipates the celebration of Jesus' glorious Easter manifestation. Although the accounts of the transfiguration in the Synoptic Gospels are quite similar, each includes special emphases.

In Luke's Gospel the special focus is on the subject of the conversation that Moses and Elijah hold with Jesus. They speak with him of his passage, literally his exodus, which he was to fulfill in Jerusalem. They thus prepare us for Jesus' great journey to God, a journey to Jerusalem, which begins in Lk 9:51 and continues, thematically if not geographically, to the very end of the Gospel (24:53). It also describes that journey as an exodus, a theme introduced on the first Sunday of Lent with the story of Jesus' triple response to temptation.

A Chance To Try Again

The third, fourth and fifth Sundays of Lent are closely related. All three deal with the theme of reform and repentance. On the third Sunday, the reading warns against jumping to conclusions and judging by appearances (Lk 13:1–9). Reform is possible. First of all, the Gospel speaks of something which is just as important today as it was in New Testament times. When people suffer misfortune, it is not because they have sinned. Nor can one conclude that because some are fortunate it is because they are good or virtuous. So, concludes the Gospel, do not count on your present situation, which now may be very good, to guarantee you life and prosperity in the future!

We then have a parable about a fig tree which has not borne any fruit for at least three years. The master or owner of the vineyard, where the fig tree was growing, orders it cut down. The vinedresser, however, asked for another chance to work at it. Perhaps next year it will bear fruit. There is no giving up on what seems hopeless. Of course we do not know what happened the following year. Was the tree again barren? Did the vinedresser ask for still another chance?

The Prodigal Son

Over and over again, Luke's Gospel returns to the

theme of the banquet and how Jesus was constantly welcoming and eating with people whom the righteous considered objectionable. This is the setting (Lk 15:1–3) for one of Luke's best remembered parables, that of the prodigal son (15:11–32), the third of three parables. The parables of the lost sheep and the lost coin which precede prepare the ground for it. In those two parables, attention focuses on the one who has lost a sheep and the one who has lost a coin. So also here. In the story of the prodigal son, it focuses on the one who has lost a son. Once the son is found, everything shifts to the call to celebrate because what was lost is now found. For the sheep and the coin, however, nothing further was said. In the third parable, there is resistance. The older brother, who had been faithful all along, does not want to join in the celebration. Luke has placed his finger on a big problem in the Christian community. How difficult it is to welcome one who has strayed and to join in reconciliation. Did the older brother eventually yield before his father's pleading? It is for us to finish the story.

Sin No More

There is much discussion about whether John 8:1–11, the story of a woman caught in adultery, is a misplaced chapter in John's Gospel. Be that as it may, it is not out of context in the fifth-Sunday Lenten celebration for the year of Luke.

The scribes and the Pharisees, the same group which had accused Jesus in Luke 15, approach Jesus to test him with a case of adultery. Moses said the woman should be stoned! What does he, the Teacher, say? Jesus does not respond. He ignores his questioners by writing on the ground. It is not what Jesus wrote which is important but that he wrote. When they persist in their questioning, he redirects the test at them. Which one of you is without sin? It is one thing to accuse someone else of sin. It is quite another to proclaim oneself sinless. When all go away and there is not one to condemn the woman, Jesus, the only one who in fact was sinless, refuses to condemn her but gives her the admonition to sin no more. There is much here to reflect upon. Jesus does not condemn the sinner. He simply asks that sin be avoided in the future.

Almsgiving, Prayer and Fasting

The Lenten season begins on Ash Wednesday with a Gospel reading on the three practices characteristic of a good religious person in the cultural world of the New Testament. The passage is taken from Jesus' sermon on the mount (Mt 5—7). It includes a general principle (v. 1) and its application to almsgiving (vv. 2–4), prayer (vv. 5–6) and fasting (vv. 16–18). The close parallel structure

of each of these sub-units indicates that they formed a rhetorical whole before they were included in Matthew's Gospel, when 6:7–15 was inserted, with the result that the parallel pattern is now less obvious. The same three practices are referred to in the Old Testament's Book of Tobit (12:8–10).

The purpose of the passage is to warn against inappropriate attitudes and behavior in each of these areas, where public display and self-aggrandizement are a danger. Alms should be given discreetly, not in order to be applauded by others. Prayer should be done quietly or privately, not in order to be noticed. Finally, one's fasting should not be advertised to draw attention to oneself.

Jesus' Response to Temptation

In Luke's Gospel, a much simpler tradition (Mk 1:12–13) concerning the temptations of Jesus has been replaced by a highly developed one (see also Mt 4:1–11). We read this tradition (Lk 4:1–13) on the first Sunday of Lent. It speaks to us of the tempting of Israel during the years of exodus, and it shows how Jesus responded to these temptations in the course of his life. The passage shows how Christians should respond to temptation in the economic (bread), political (power), and religious (testing God) spheres.

Approaching the End of the Journey

On Passion Sunday, the Gospel reading for the procession with palms is drawn from the final stage of Jesus' journey to Jerusalem (Lk 19:28–40). Jesus has been on that journey since Lk 9:51, when he determined to make his way to Jerusalem, the place where he would ascend to his Father. His entry into the city of David is not that of a conqueror. Astride an ass, he enters humbly only to be exalted with "Blessed is he who comes as king!" The crowd's canticle echoes that of the angels at Bethlehem (Lk 2:14). This is no ordinary crowd that welcomed Jesus. It is the crowd of his disciples. As usual, the Pharisees object. Few passages show so well how Jesus would reign in the kingdom of God. Jesus' entry into Jerusalem has nothing to do with earthly power.

The Story of the Passion

The Gospel for Passion Sunday is the story of the passion according to St. Luke (22:14—23:56). On the surface, it resembles the other accounts in the New Testament, but like each of the others it is unique.

One of its characteristic features is the presentation of the Last Supper of Jesus (22:14–38) with its clear distinction between the Last Supper and the Lord's Supper. It is a final supper: "I will not eat again until it is fulfilled in the kingdom of God" (v. 16; see v. 18). It is the Lord's Supper: "This is my body. . . . This cup is the new covenant in my blood" (vv. 19–20).

Perhaps the most striking feature is the way Jesus continues to be the reconciler until the end. He forgives the thief crucified along with him (23:42). He even forgives those who crucified him: "Father, forgive them; they do not know what they are doing" (23:34).

Then there is Jesus' dying word: "Father, into your hands I commend my spirit" (23:46). For Luke, Jesus' last word was a prayer.

Introduction to Lent

Regarding the presentation of materials in the sessions within this segment of the book: each session is structured in an outline, consistent throughout the season. This outline is only a format that facilitates provision of some background and process recommendations for you. Your study of the material here, and, more importantly, your adaptation of it is what will make the gatherings with your group truly beneficial.

Typically, the session begins with Opening, a song or prayer, some vehicle to focus the energy and thought of the group once all have settled into the place of meeting. I trust you will use or change the suggestion according to your wisdom. In selecting one recommendation, I had to not write a dozen other good alternatives. As you prepare your session, other suggestions and possibilities may come to you. The opening can truly be a powerful part of the session. I value it as a unique step in the session, not just a sort of "forethought."

The second step is the Thematic Framework. This reflection on the liturgical theme sets a focus for reflection on the readings. Drawn and adapted from a variety of sources, this section attempts to give you some background for developing discussion on the Scriptures themselves, often in connection with the catechetical focus of the day, or with our daily lives. They are meant for your reflection during your preparation time. They are not designed as a "lesson plan," for each group will have a quite different set of needs, questions and responses, requiring the personalized preparation of the parish team.

The third movement is the Reflection on Life. In preparing these sections I looked deeply into the Scriptures and probable catechetical themes and asked myself, "What does this mean in my life? What's happening here?" These sections trace, in some way, a personal conversion story, landmarked by the themes of the days. These reflections are offered as a stimulation to you, to reflect on your own life in relation to the themes and questions. Your stories, questions and responses will be different. So will they be for each member of the group. But it is the process of asking and reflecting that is important. Your life, the lives of the team members, elect, sponsors, inquirers/catechumens, whoever may be meeting with you each week—these lives deserve attention and drawing forth. Catechumenate ministry and conversion blend knowledge, wisdom

and spiritual development—these are life issues, not just head knowledge.

The next section as outlined is titled Knowing Our Faith. Here I have tried to elucidate and filter a catechetical theme or topic that seems to flow from the Scriptures and reflections. The topics here may overlap previous sessions. You would discern whether additional enrichment or perspective is of value, or whether your group would deal with a completely different topic. Often there are questions and issues that arise from within the group which require extended time. The group, in truth, sets the agenda, balancing their personal and shared concerns with our efforts to share with them the spiritual and catechetical heritage of the faith community they seek to know and join. It is important for all involved to understand that the fullness of that heritage will be an on-going learning, not completed during the time of catechumenate proper, but continuing through the mystagogical period and the months and years following. Because learning is enhanced through well-planned media use, I have occasionally recommended that you preview and select some resource to supplement your presentation and to stimulate understanding. Again, your wisdom, creativity, and the availability of high quality resources will shape the actual use of such materials.

In the section designated Integration I have set out a few questions that most likely will be incorporated into the process of your session, rather than held for the very end. The group discussion, in large or small groups, might mix catechumens and sponsors with team members or others. Typically there is some need for some quiet time, a few moments to gather thoughts before launching into discussion. By the time the group has come through the catechumenate into the Lenten season, they have probably formed a close community, enabling open discussion to happen more easily. If your dismissal group includes inquirers or catechumens not as familiar or comfortable with the process, you and the team will necessarily adapt.

A word about Journaling. There is a certain wisdom in encouraging participants to spend personal time reflecting and writing. We own more fully what we spend personal time and care with. Journaling, as given here, is an informal way to invite participants to track their questions, insights, reflections, prayers, and growth. Journals may be utterly private or may be springboards for discussion with sponsors (or elect), or with spiritual companion or spiritual director. More than anything, the *process* of journaling is our discipline in focusing what we have seen/heard/felt and not losing it as the rest of life crowds in after the session. There are many books, articles and tapes on the styles and advantages of journaling that may be helpful to you, the other team members, sponsors and elect. Different persons may prefer different styles.

Besides the more structured disciplines of Ira Progoff (Intensive Journal), and George Simon (Personal Journal) there are increasingly more resources that help us through booklets or notebooks. In a recent issue of *Weavings*, May–June 1987, Anne Broyles outlines briefly journaling as a spiritual discipline. The title indicates to me its value: "One More Door into God's Presence."

Anne gives some suggestions as ways of journaling: journaling from daily life, in response to Scripture, as recording dreams, in response to quotes, as recording conversations. These too serve as a beginning. She quotes Edward Farrell from *Prayer Is a Hunger*, "Writing is a way into what is going on and developing within ourselves. It can become a powerful way of prayer, a key to self-understanding and inner dialogue. The power in writing stimulates the very inner process that is engaged in describing, drawing the process further inward."

So the questions provided here are suggestions that we nurture a continuing discipline of reflection, deepening and integration of the spiritual journey.

The Closing, like the Opening, is not simply an additional thought. How we conclude our time together leaves a sense of welcome, enjoyment, prayer, holiness, and acceptance. It is what we create as we send our people forth. Again, these are only single, simple suggestions, meant to be included with shared prayer, planned or spontaneous, quiet or spoken or celebrative. Different members of the group may want to plan or lead an opening or closing prayer. A variety of experiences and formats would be strongly advised. Let the Spirit flourish, even through the end of the session.

So with this resource in hand, and your awareness of the needs of your group, the input of the rest of the team, and a creative, adaptive style, you now begin planning and reflecting on the season of Lent.

Ash Wednesday

Joel 2:12–18
2 Corinthians 5:20—6:2
Matthew 6:1–6, 16–18

OPENING PRAYER

Song: "Ashes" by Tom Conry (Glory and Praise, #84).

THEMATIC FRAMEWORK

(Since this is not a Sunday, there will be a special effort to have the catechumenate community gather at the parish Mass and celebration of Ash Wednesday with dismissal or a gathering after Mass if there is no dismissal.)

Within each of us is a failure to live up to the Gospel values. Evil does exist in and around us. We are not as steadfast as we are called to be. During the season—and today in particular—we acknowledge our weakness and our need for grace and strength, for mercy and blessing in order to grow. Now is the time to take a step, or two, in our conversion journey. We look toward a new—or renewed—mission at Pentecost.

Ashes, signifying dust, old ways, former sin, are used as a reminder that our old sinfulness is done away with through forgiveness and conversion. Our actions particularly during these next weeks of Lent will reinforce our resolve to become a new person.

Every Ash Wednesday the same readings are proclaimed. The prophet Joel calls his people and us to repentance. He calls us to a life focused on the spiritual. In much of the Church's history it was literally a call to undertake specific and serious penance, a real change of heart and action. The response and fidelity of God's people assure them (and us) of his concern.

Paul's plea to the people of Corinth stirs in us a realization that it is through one another that we are called to holiness, that others are the ambassadors of God, that it is God who saves us. And through us God reaches out to others. Through us he calls to conversion and reconciliation.

The Gospel reading comes directly after the Sermon on the Mount, continuing Jesus' outline of building the kingdom, of living a life in the Spirit of God. Action and contemplation are called for—give alms to the poor (service), fast and pray. We have some wonderful guides for prayer. The traditions of Lent call us to prepare and specifically focus on a renewal and conversion of life.

The blessing and giving of ashes is a tradition with roots and symbolism that are rich in meaning. The ashes are typically from the burned blessed palms of the previous Lent. Ashes, in former times, were a sign of the penitents—those who were undertaking a season of self-denial and purification. The ashes on our forehead will have as much meaning as we give them. Make this symbolism a significant beginning to a time of penance, preparing to celebrate the paschal mystery of our Lord's death and resurrection. Here at the opening of Lent we are looking toward our own new life at the Easter season.

REFLECTION ON LIFE

Take time. Break out of routine. Step back and take a look at your life. What is there that needs some attention?

Although each day should be lived consciously, attentively, we become routinized quite easily. We are, you know, creatures of habit. It seems that New Year's Eve and Ash Wednesday are the two times we are willing to look at ourselves and make a resolution or two to do something about self-improvement. In spiritual language, it is our time of conscious conversion, a time when we evaluate our progress and status in spiritual growth and decide how we can grow.

In most areas of my life it is easy to take so much for granted. We observe holidays, holydays, birthdays, anniversaries and special memory days to help us be alerted to special people and events. Special days give us a chance to stand back and remember so that we can step forward and appreciate.

How practical and caring of the Church to offer us this Ash Wednesday, not only for itself but also as a pointer to the Lenten season and the Easter season following it. It is a brave step to receive ashes on our forehead and then go back into our daily life situations where other people may ask, tease or ridicule our attentiveness and efforts in spiritual growth. Several times over the years I had wiped off the ashes before going back to my workplace—more out of embarrassment than because of any professional prudence. But now, to wear the ashes seems a bit like a proclamation that I am who I am and that Ash Wednesday is important to me. We have had some very personal conversations about God, faith, life values, perhaps because, without words, someone can see a bit more clearly what I am trying to do with my life.

KNOWING OUR FAITH

According to scriptural traditions, both Moses on Mount Sinai and Jesus in the desert spent forty days in intense spiritual work. As Christians, we prepare to celebrate the paschal mysteries by a penitential season of forty days.

When the catechumenate/inquiry group includes members who may not be familiar with our customs, additional time for explanation and discussion of the Lenten season may be needed. If there has not yet been information shared on the liturgical year, it may be most opportune now to do so. There are generally helpful explanations found in missals or in special booklets. There are several filmstrips which can give excellent background as well as current information on the celebration of the liturgical seasons.

Penance and penitential practices are part of the Christian way of life. The customs themselves may change, but the idea has always remained present. Penance is about the reality of sin and conversion, about our experience of them. Through penance we strengthen our adherence to good; we turn from evil in and around us; we turn toward God more fully.

Practices or customs which have traditionally been emphasized during the Lenten season are prayer, fasting and charitable works. They are not outdated. There has been a shift toward emphasizing action, doing, rather than "giving up." Whatever we each decide to do during Lent is a personal decision, but it should be related to our unique effort in spiritual growth, a conscious choice to deepen ourselves. It may mean doing less—taking quiet time for prayer. It could be simply doing more attentively what we already do, with renewed motivation. We become holy the more fully we respond to the Gospel message. Our special efforts may best be the beginning or renewal of a commitment that continues long past the Easter season—a facet of our on-going conversion toward wholeness and holiness. Making an effort in living simply, in sharing what we have, in tak-

ing a stand for a peace/justice/human issue—the Gospel imperative for holiness touches each of us differently, calls us on a unique path toward a common goal: fullness in Christ Jesus.

INTEGRATION

Questions for Discussion

1. If media are used, discussion should follow that use, as outlined in the media guide.

2. If you were able to celebrate liturgy and receive ashes, how did you feel as you sensed the ashes being pressed onto your forehead? How do you feel about wearing your ashes in public?

3. What is your main hope for yourself during this Lenten season?

Journaling

1. What does it mean to me to hear: "Remember, you are dust and to dust you shall return"?

2. The Lenten season calls us to turn from sin and to be faithful to the Gospel. What does that really ask of me?

3. What is my main hope for myself during this Lenten season?

CLOSING PRAYER

Song: "Earthen Vessels" by John Foley, S.J. (*Glory and Praise*, #13).

Pastoral and Theological Issues: Lent, Temptation, Christian Witness, Liturgical Seasons, Penance

Clare Colella

First Sunday of Lent

Deuteronomy 26:4–10
Romans 10:8–13
Luke 4:1–13

OPENING PRAYER

Song: "Here Is My Life" by Joe Wise (album, *Take It For Gift*)

THEMATIC FRAMEWORK

What is central at the Easter season will largely determine what is central now:

All three cycles include a version of the temptation story on the first Sunday of Lent. This Sunday is a special time for a profession of faith—a statement of purpose, direction, intention. Each reading gives an insight into a progression of faith. In the first reading from Deuteronomy, the Hebrews—and we—reflect upon God's continual protection of and presence among his people. Already in the opening prayer of today's liturgy the theme is our awareness of and response to God's constant fidelity and care for us. The story within the story is the capsule retelling of the Hebrew heritage—from Abraham to Moses to the settling in the promised land.

The responsorial psalm seems to be a dialogue—God's promises and our reply—a mutual covenant.

This segment from Paul's Letter to the Romans reminds his listeners and the continuing community of believers that the heart, the core, of our belief is that God raised Jesus Christ from the dead (foreshadowing Easter at the opening of Lent) and that our belief in the Lord calls us to proclaim our faith by our very lives.

So it is with Jesus himself in the Gospel episode. This tradition about Jesus describes the temptations, the challenges, of the early Church community: Where does our true strength and fidelity lie? What is most important to us? In what direction will we focus our Lenten (and on-going) efforts in spiritual growth? The three "categories" of the temptations are "bread"—material provisions and comfort; "power"—independence, self-sufficiency and pride; "vanity"—testing the fidelity of others, testing God.

REFLECTION ON LIFE

The special preface of today's liturgy, the prayer over the gifts, and the Communion prayer, focus on our lives, the contemporary struggle with temptation, our personal journey of faith. As puzzling as it may seem, temptation is a measure of our human freedom. If we can make a decision, we have a choice. To have choice means there are alternatives—we can say yes or no; we can be tempted, swayed. The free person has a choice. That very privilege is also a responsibility.

The central values of faith and fidelity come into play. In our lives we have each made at least one cornerstone decision, a lifestyle, a vocation, a profession, perhaps a decision to marry. That one decision does not really take away our freedom. It gives us a firm direction, purpose or covenant. But daily, sometimes several times within a single day, we affirm (or perhaps move away from) that pivotal decision. We can be tempted to deny our covenant. We may not feel like being faithful. It may appear easier to become lax. Our freedom makes us susceptible to temptation in many forms.

We take a lot for granted. Even the most "special" persons or relationships or gifts become commonplace after a while. It seems that our faith may be subject to that phenomenon. Our spiritual heritage becomes vague or neglected. Perhaps even with inquirers or catechumens (now the elect) the regular gatherings for spiritual growth and knowledge may become routine. Expectations and attention could be getting dull. So the Lenten season offers each of us—the baptized community and all those in the catechumenate process (at whatever stage)—a change of pace and focus.

The atmosphere of Lent takes its keynote partly from today's Gospel—we are invited to spend time "apart with the Lord." Customs of Lenten fasting, almsgiving, sacrifice and prayer are designed to help us keep before our mind's eye our spiritual journey and the quality of fidelity to our decisions and covenants.

KNOWING OUR FAITH

The very questions of the Rite of Election provide the self-examination we need to evaluate our "state of the heart" at the beginning of Lent: Have we listened to the word? Have we begun to translate it into action? Have we sought the fellowship of believers and joined with them in prayer? How, we might ask, is our Spirit?

The wonderful traditions of Lenten penitential practices are ways to loosen ourselves from the grip of concerns and habits that may diminish our fidelity to Jesus Christ and the Gospel message. The movement toward positive practices offers ways to strengthen the good we do, to deepen our goodness and charity.

If there has not been an opportunity on Ash Wednesday or previously to explain the liturgical year and the significance of the seasons, this may be an ideal time.

Extended explanation of the traditional customs of Lent—fasting, prayer, charitable works, abstinence from meat on Fridays—would help acquaint the group with our Catholic heritage. Information on the commemoration of the stations of the cross or special traditions/opportunities in spiritual growth may be very helpful. Again, for each of these topics print and audiovisual resources are usually available through your parish or diocese.

Remember that much of what we take for granted in our liturgical seasons is unknown to our inquirers and catechumens. Even active Catholics like the sponsors may appreciate a "refresher."

INTEGRATION

Questions for Discussion

(select one or two questions as appropriate):

1. Regarding the Rite of Election: What has been asked of the elect and their sponsors? What has the community of the parish been asked to do in response? Why is the participation in a diocesan Rite of Election, with the bishop, so special a step at this time? How did the elect and their sponsors feel about both the questions and the witnessing within the Rite? How do inquirers feel about watching others go through the Rite?

2. What core of faith did the Hebrews express in the first reading? What core of faith did the apostolic community (early Church) express in the second reading? What core beliefs did Jesus live by in dealing with the temptations depicted in the Gospel?

3. What might be some core, central beliefs in my life right now?

4. How do I want to grow during the Lenten season?

Journaling

1. How do I feel about the experience and message of this Sunday's liturgy?

2. What concrete steps will I take toward intentional spiritual growth during Lent?

CLOSING PRAYER

Song for listening; reflection (Choose one)

"Isaiah 49" by Carey Landry (Album: I Will Not Forget You)

"Anthem" by Tom Conry (Album: Ashes)

Pastoral and Theological Issues: Temptation, Salvation History, Conversion, Lenten Customs

Clare Colella

Second Sunday of Lent

Genesis 15:5–12, 17–18
Philippians 3:14—4:1
Luke 9:28–36

OPENING PRAYER

Song: "All That We Have" by Gary Ault (Glory and Praise, #82).

THEMATIC FRAMEWORK

The importance of the great Hebrew ancestral covenant between Abraham and Yahweh, his God, is linked in each liturgical cycle on the second Sunday of Lent to a narration of the transfiguration story. Each Lenten season also precedes "Transfiguration Sunday" with the telling of the episode about the temptations of Jesus. There is a clear wisdom in opening the chief penitential season of each year with a consideration of our susceptibility to temptations as we undertake a deliberate refocusing of our conversion journey. A week after our reflection on the temptations of Jesus and our weaknesses, we, the Church community, gather to hear and reflect on the long-standing covenant of care and fidelity between God and his people. As far back in our religious heritage as Abraham, even further back than Abraham, our God has proclaimed his covenant. He invites us into that covenant—individually and as a people. We are asked to step out in faith. Abraham, as yet in this episode without a son, hears the words of God and believes that indeed he will have descendants as numerous as the stars. The acceptance of the sacrifice was, as it were, God's affirmation and renewal of the covenant.

The Gospel event of the transfiguration continues the dialogue between God and man. In the person of Jesus Christ we are called to prayer, to acknowledge our relationship with God. As Jesus was transfigured through his relationship with God, so are we called to enter into a spiritual transformation, a relationship with God that leads us into a life of prayer. That is what the season of Lent is about—taking a deliberate turn away from temptations and patterns of sinfulness and making a conscious effort to deepen our relationship with God, the transforming power in our lives.

REFLECTION ON LIFE

Transfiguration is a word so powerful that we tend not to relate the experience to our own lives. Yet spiritual, personal transformation is what we are called to, particularly through the Lenten season—a time to look at our lives and make some conscious evaluation of our spiritual growth and fidelity to Gospel values. We easily slip into patterns of behavior. This is the time to take note of what is happening. This season is focused on "purification" and "enlightenment." It is a time for change—as the spring season with its own new life exemplifies. The cyclic changes and our own on-going growth (change) do not mean discontinuity. Change is itself the basis of our continuity as persons. Only inasmuch as we grow, change, do we sense our vitality. Following the pattern of Abraham and Jesus Christ, as well as our personal mentors of faith, we expand our horizons, deepen our awareness of God. In a way we open ourselves to the surprises of God's presence and action in our lives. We open our horizons to discover even more the holy in all that is around us.

The goodness and beauty we discover, the awesome transforming insight, lead us, at times, to want to camp there, to build tents and stay in the new glory. But we are a pilgrim people; we "come down from the mountain." Having been transformed (again and again) we continue the mission journey. As Paul tells us in today's reading from the Letter to the Philippians: "He will give a new form to this lowly body of ours and remake it according to the pattern of his glorified body. . . . For these reasons . . . continue to stand firm in the Lord." It is not just our body in the simple physical sense Paul is speaking of. Our body is the expression of our lives. It is we ourselves who will be remade according to the glorified Jesus.

Are we really ready for transformation and transfiguration according to Jesus Christ? Do we believe that we have been given the vision of our potential and the grace to become the faith-filled disciples sharing in the vision, living it out in our very lives?

What is it in our lives that needs to be opened to the brightness of transfiguration?

KNOWING OUR FAITH

Continually throughout the readings of the liturgy we find linkages of persons and events of the Hebrew Scriptures with persons and events of the Christian Scriptures.

Today's readings offer us an opportunity to deepen our insights and appreciation of our Jewish faith heritage and roots. Look again at the Rite of Election which asks the elect to examine their lives and see whether they—and we—have found those lives to be converted to spiritual values. Do we live lives of faith? Abraham's story, glimpsed today in a covenant ritual, tells us of a man who, time and again, was led by the Lord to change his life—to move his family from one place to another, to become a father at a very old age, not only to one son, but to descendants who would be as numerous as the ther in faith, is a man of simple, deep belief in God. Our Hebrew (Jewish) roots bring us models for our own life. Two other models are presented in the Gospel story as companions with Jesus: Moses and Elijah, men of prayer whose whole lives were changed because they heard the call of God and responded in faith.

How well do the elect understand the Hebrew roots and heritage of our Christian faith? How well do we attend to these mentors of conversion and faith-filled living? To understand the Jewish background of Jesus and the apostolic community is an important step in appreciating the context of today's readings. Moses and Elijah, even Abraham, could speak of the passage, the journey, ahead for Jesus because they each lived out a unique passage event—the journey to the land promised to Abraham, and his descendants, the exodus event and forty-year journey of Moses and the Hebrew people, the flight of Elijah towards Mount Horeb and thence to Palestine to the prophet Elisha. Elijah also figures in the tradition story of being taken to heaven in a fiery chariot.

Spending some time deepening the awareness of our Hebrew roots could be facilitated by selecting appropriate media on the Hebrew Scriptures, why readings from the "Old Testament" (better terminology: "Hebrew Scriptures") are included in the liturgy, or on how the Bible was written. Media producers like Chaning L. Bete, Roa-Brown, Franciscan Communications/Teleketics and Paulist Press are some reliable sources of such media. There are certainly others.

As always, plan far enough in advance the time you need as facilitator/catechist to preview available resources and select what is most appropriate for your group at this time. With a topic as broad as our Hebrew heritage and the formation of the Bible, more time than one session may be planned. These topics may have arisen earlier or need to be expanded upon later. In any case, today's readings do provide a timely opportunity to deepen awareness and appreciation of the connection between Jesus and the Hebrew people's heritage—his own Jewish roots.

INTEGRATION

Questions for Discussion

1. Have there been any important experiences of religious/spiritual traditions in our personal faith journey? What are our own roots?

2. If media are used, follow or adapt the print discussion guide/resources that accompanies such use. Typically, producers try to provide integrative and developmental materials with films/filmstrips and other media.

3. What do we know about the Hebrew roots of our Christian faith?

Journaling and Meditation

1. How do I perceive my spiritual roots?

2. Who/what has brought me to this point in my spiritual journey? Who might be standing with me as my spiritual guides?

3. What does transformation of my own life ask of me at this time?

CLOSING PRAYER

Selection from second reading: Philippians 3:20—4:1

Song: "Beginning Today" by Balhoff and Ducote (*Glory and Praise,* #183)

Pastoral and Doctrinal Issues: Transfiguration, Transformation, Journey of Salvation, Prophets, Spiritual Journey

Clare Colella

Third Sunday of Lent

Exodus 3:1–8, 13–15
1 Corinthians 10:1–6, 10–12
Luke 13:1–9

This is the first of the Scrutiny Sundays. If you and your parish opt for Cycle A readings, please refer to your Cycle A resource. The next three weeks in this volume are written based on Cycle C readings.

OPENING PRAYER

Song: Gather Us In by Marty Haugen

THEMATIC FRAMEWORK

As a Sunday of Scrutiny, we look today for critical questions and insights with which to evaluate our spiritual progress and conversion. Have the lives of the elect—and our lives—given clear evidence of their intent and purpose? The questions of the first reading center on Moses, shepherding flocks, as he is caught up in the mystery of a burning bush, conversation with God, and his learning of God's name "I Am Who Am." The God who is linked to us is linked to Abraham, Isaac, Jacob and Moses. Where do we find God? Are we open to seeing him in the midst of daily tasks? Do we recognize that all ground can be (is) holy ground? When God names himself "I Am Who Am" he immerses himself in all of life. Are we growing in our personal spiritual lives? The Lenten season is a time of paying particular attention to that growth. Today, as a community with our elect, we are confronted with Moses who experienced God in the desert, we hear Paul's warning to his people in Corinth to stand upright, to be reformed in their lives, and we hear Jesus' admonition to his listeners to reform their lives. Reform is an action work—the fig tree had better show results. Our lives must give evidence of our lived faith.

The opening prayers of today's liturgy specifically mention our conversion, overcoming sin through fasting, prayer and works of mercy, sharing with others. How are we doing in these efforts?

Words of strength and comfort assure us of the love and compassion of the Lord. "The God of your fathers sent me." Do we truly believe that? Do our lives show our trust and hope? Is our repentance sincere enough to create renewed fidelity? Are we indeed willing to reform our lives? Lent is a time for us to look intently at the Scriptures and at our lives. What do we see? What is to be done? What is required in order to be fruitful?

REFLECTION ON LIFE

Twice in today's Gospel story we hear, "You will come to the same end unless you reform." Paul's message to the people of Corinth and to us is that we must be alert and "stand upright" before the Lord. What is it in our lives that keeps us from being a fertile and fruitful tree? When we look at our own lives, what needs to be pruned? What needs nurturing? The first reading opens the whole horizon in our lives of where we see/hear God, what we reverence as "holy ground," and our closeness to God who is ever present.

The Scrutiny: in preparing for a celebration of the scrutiny based on today's Scripture, a good amount of advance work needs to be done. Perhaps an effective way to create and personalize the scrutiny experience would be to work with the elect, their sponsors and a few other parish members including the homilist/celebrant during the previous week. Read each Scripture selection; spend time reflecting on the word itself. Then focus on the questions posed above: What in our lives needs reform? What keeps us from being fruitful? What are the personal and societal patterns and priorities that require being uprooted so that society and we may more truly be faithful to the word? Reflect on our personal lives, on our society, our country, even our world. What forces and priorities are non-human, violent, selfish, power-hungry, domineering, unjust, oppressive?

The first reading is so powerful. A man shepherds his flock; we do simple everyday tasks. He sees a burning bush, "a remarkable sight"; we encounter persons and places that can speak to us of God if we only look and listen. We may not hear a voice outside. But surely there is an inner voice that calls us to encounter the holy, to discover and to cherish the extraordinary within the ordinary. How can we develop an awareness for the holy within the ordinary tasks, relationships, events of our days? In his book *Tales of the Hasidin: Later Masters*, Martin Buber quotes a teaching of Rabbi Moshe of Kobryn: "God's words to Moses, 'Put off your shoes from your feet,' apply to us all: 'Put off the habitual which encloses your foot, and you will know that the place on which you are now standing is holy ground.' For there is no rung of human life on which we cannot find the holiness of God everywhere and at all times." That insight is followed by another story in the editorial page of *Weavings*, May–June 1987, about a rabbi and his son: "One day the young boy came in from a game of hide-and-seek with tears streaming down his face. His father asked what was wrong. The son explained that when he had hidden himself no one had come seeking him. The rabbi embraced his son tenderly and said that perhaps now the boy could understand better how the Lord felt. For God is hidden in our midst, still waiting for us to begin the search."

How do we break away from our habitual perceptions, our patterned responses and actions? Where are we called to see and hear more deeply? How do we begin to cherish what we have taken for granted? How do we see "I Am Who Am" in the midst of the familiar?

What are the experiences and insights of your people as you search for personal and communal reform? How can these be turned into litany and petition for the scrutiny and liturgical prayer? In breaking open the word for the whole parish community how can the homilist bridge the insights of the preparatory group for the whole community?

KNOWING OUR FAITH

This ground is holy ground. We celebrate that truth with fruitful prayer along the way in the daily routine. It is a rich part of our faith heritage to incorporate many forms of prayer into our spiritual growth. A part of this week's development may be a reflection on some of the forms and formats of prayer—in the personal lives of the members of your group, in the life of the Church community. The Church offers us the liturgy of the Mass with its intrinsic variety of prayer—ritual action, psalmody, scriptural readings, music, quiet, communal prayer. Each sacramental celebration offers adapted and ritual prayer, with availability of spontaneous prayer. The Liturgy of the Hours, traditional devotions and prayers are all a part of our heritage. Awareness of the sacred within the ordinary is a natural foundation for personal spontaneous prayer. The more we become familiar with the prayer of the Church, the better we can balance the various experiences and opportunities of prayer. Prayer might be considered as the fertilizer offered to the sterile tree in an effort to make it fruitful. Prayer is the stuff in our life that can help us make of it something beautiful for the Lord.

If during the past week you have gathered people to look at their lives in preparation for the scrutiny, you have led them in a prayer form that bridges daily reality into liturgical and ritual prayer. Read from a missal or missalette the prayers of today's liturgy and note the scriptural heart of prayers formulated to suit the theme of the Mass. Good prayer speaks the truth of our reality. If we are beginning to gather, asking forgiveness, celebrating the proclaimed word, offering gifts, the words of our prayer express the reality.

One delightful example of prayer out of our human reality is the movie "Fiddler on the Roof." In several scenes, the people, Tevye in particular, talk with God about their pain, joy, questions—they pray out of their real lives. They—and we—balance ritual or communal prayer with personal prayer from the heart. Other forms of prayer include meditative prayer, relaxation and imagery, prayer of listening to readings or song that lead us actively into the presence of the Holy. Prayer is celebrated, expressed, in countless art forms and actions. It is also at times simply held in our hearts, intimately.

During the weekly sessions with the catechumenate group, it would be beneficial to plan a variety of prayer experiences, perhaps with the help of members of the group who would like to share some of their experiences or insights. Exposure to non-common prayer forms and less familiar devotions (e.g., stations of the cross) is recommended as well.

Discussion would include a "debriefing" of the variety of prayer experiences in the Church, particularly those that the group has encountered. It is important to facilitate appreciation of the variety and to help individuals develop a comfortableness with several prayer forms. Other prayer forms, like the scrutiny, are confrontative and challenging. They are good for our growth, because they also lead us beyond the familiar and easy, stretching us into growth and change.

INTEGRATION

Questions for Discussion

1. What has been a comfortable or familiar prayer style for me?

2. What form of prayer do I feel called to explore, to become more aware of? Why?

3. How can I bring conversion and "reform" in my life into prayer?

Journaling

(Perhaps choosing the most appropriate one for reflection)

1. What in my life prevents me from being a fruitful tree? What needs scrutiny and reform?

2. How well do I perceive and celebrate the holy within the ordinary in my life? What steps will I take to deepen my awareness of God's presence within my daily life and surroundings?

3. What is my present experience of prayer? How can I broaden or deepen my prayer life? Who can help me with that growth?

CLOSING PRAYER

Song: "We Remember" by Marty Haugen (Album: *With Open Hands*)

Pastoral and Theological Issues: Repentance, Social Justice, Prayer, God's Presence

Clare Colella

Fourth Sunday of Lent

Joshua 5:9, 10–12
2 Corinthians 5:17–21
Luke 15:1–3, 11–32

OPENING PRAYER

Song: "Remember Your Love" by the Dameans (Glory and Praise, #134).

THEMATIC FRAMEWORK

Second Scrutiny—Reconciliation and Mercy.

(As with last week, if you and your parish choose the Scripture readings from Cycle A, please refer to your resources for that cycle. Today's session and scrutiny are developed from the Liturgy of Cycle C.)

The prayers of the Mass, the responsorial psalm as well as the Scripture readings, cluster on a wonderful Lenten theme of mercy and reconciliation. How timely to focus at this season on this presence and action of God in our lives.

The first reading from Joshua assures us of God's continuing care and providence for his people. For the years of the exodus and the desert journey, on through the first settling in the promised land, the Lord provided manna as the staff of life. It is only when the people were able to provide from their own new harvest that the manna ceased. God's provision simply took a different form, appropriate now to the abilities of his people to grow their own crops. A feast of Passover was the significant time when they recognized that they were no longer a nomadic people as they had been during the years of their desert trek. In a real sense, they were home, free from the reproach of Egypt.

Paul's message to the Corinthians and to us is that in Jesus Christ the world and all people have been reconciled to God. Transgressions have been forgiven and we have been called to be a new people, aware of our reconciliation and being a new creation of holy people. We have been forgiven, welcomed and cared for.

The Gospel story of the merciful father continues to unfold the overwhelming tender mercy, love and forgiveness of our God.

REFLECTION ON LIFE

However we perceive and image God, we cannot escape the powerful experience of this story, a parent who patiently, persistently waits at the gate, watching down the path for the return of one who was lost; as we develop the scrutiny for this week, again ideally with members of the parish and catechumenate group during the previous week, we can explore and identify with several different scriptural characters.

The early Hebrew community, wandering through the desert toward some unknown promised land, relied on God for food and water. They may have come to take that for granted. They may have, and did, turn away from him at times. Yet he continued to nourish and care for them. Paul's Corinthians seem to have been aware of their transgressions, so imperative was it for Paul to assure them of their forgiveness and reconciliation. The Gospel story is, of course, full of persons we can identify with in different ways. For me the discussion ought to highlight the "audience" to whom Jesus was speaking as well as the characters within the parable. More than the "prodigal son," this is the story of the merciful father, compassionate for his lost son. The son who stayed home is a key character—he forces us to look at our own willingness or reluctance to offer forgiveness, to celebrate the reconciliation of others and their welcome back to the loving community.

Perhaps it is our personal and social sense of sinfulness with regard to self-righteousness, vindictiveness or unforgiveness that needs to be scrutinized. In a society that incarcerates and at times condemns to death those who have sinned, where do we stand as heralds of forgiveness, reconciliation and hope? In a family or neighborhood experiencing pain and rejection, how do we deal with those who have hurt us?

How do we affirm those who are steadfast and struggle to be faithful while we welcome and forgive those who have run away, spurned us, or been caught up in sinful, harmful patterns? How do I forgive myself for my own wrongdoing? Do I accept God's reconciling love and depend on it to reform my life? How can I—we—be supportive and welcoming to others on this same journey homeward?

There is much rich material here for a personal and

powerful celebration of the scrutiny, again adapting the words of the ritual itself to incorporate this Gospel story, but keeping the simple, striking litany form, petitions, and laying on of hands. Again, the dismissal of the elect is a strong message to the rest of the parish that there is more here than what first meets our eyes and ears. While they continue with the liturgy of the Eucharist, the need for on-going scrutiny and conversion is not settled here.

KNOWING OUR FAITH

In a Church that celebrates and sacramentalizes reconciliation and forgiveness we often take for granted—or are ignorant of—the far-reaching implications of the experience of self-study, self-revelation, forgiveness, reconciliation. Reconciliation is not only a sacrament. It is an attitude that shapes our life-style of openness, welcome and acceptance. It is a strength and commitment to be honest with ourselves and others as we work out our life's path. Reconciliation is an experience as simple and intimate as apologizing sincerely to a family member or friend we have hurt, or accepting the apology of another who has sensed brokenness in his or her own life in relation to us and others. It is as heartening as the renewed promise to befriend and support another.

Reconciliation may be as demanding as requiring the ceasing of a harmful pattern of behavior, as wrenching as a change in an aspect of our life-style. Living out our trust in a forgiving and reconciling God may call some of us to speak out against legal decisions that are oppressive to human beings, that minimize potential for conversion and growth. Our faith in a forgiving God may cause some of us to minister to those who are imprisoned, particularly, perhaps, those who are condemned to death by a legal system that comprises the worst of our social fears and deals with the poorest of our societal experiences.

There are statements published by the National Council of Catholic Bishops that help give a perspective on capital punishment, on issues of oppression and injustice. As members of a faith community, we need to know the issues of human and social justice that call us to proclaim forgiveness and reconciliation. From knowledge and proclamation, we are called to act upon those beliefs.

We are especially called to deepen our awareness and experience of reconciliation in our own lives. At this time, that may mean study of the sacrament of reconciliation and perhaps a paraliturgical celebration of reconciliation or prayer service. During the Lenten season, there may be a parish penance service that could be adapted for the elect, or they may choose to join, in a special way, the parish service, understanding the difference between their participation and that of the baptized community.

The Sunday catechumenate session may focus on a media piece to help clarify the meaning and ritual of the rites of penance as currently celebrated by the Catholic Church.

INTEGRATION

Moving from the Scriptures into the present Church understanding and celebration of reconciliation will provide multiple opportunity for participants to reflect on their own experiences of reconciliation (or rejection), of forgiving and being forgiven.

In small groups, have group members share an experience of reconciliation in their own lives.

Reread Luke 15:1–3, 11–32 (the missing segments are the parable of the good shepherd and the woman searching for her lost coin). In the story of the merciful father, with whom does each participant identify at first? Discuss with the groups the attitudes and experiences of that character. How can we learn from one another about reconciliation, even through this discussion? A large group feedback time may help share some insights.

Perhaps the group would like to plan or participate in a special reconciliation service. It would be probable that those who are to be baptized at the Easter vigil may celebrate their first sacramental reconciliation during the mystagogy period. If so, some connection could be made now to that forthcoming event.

Journaling

Choose a character in the Gospel reading with whom you feel some familiarity. Dialogue with that character about reconciliation or rejection. What have you to learn from their insight? What is God saying to you about reconciliation in your own life?

CLOSING PRAYER

Song: "Love Is Forever" by the Dameans (Album: Remember Your Love) or "Take All the Lost Home" by Joe Wise (Album: Take All the Lost Home)

Pastoral and Theological Issues: Forgiveness, Reconciliation, Mercy, Justice, Rites of Penance

Clare Colella

Fifth Sunday of Lent

Isaiah 43:16–21
Philippians 3:8–14
John 8:1–11

OPENING PRAYER

Song: "How Can I Go?" by the Dameans (Album: Day of the Son)

THEMATIC FRAMEWORK

In the midst of the Lenten season, we continue to find assurance of God's care, presence and forgiveness. In process of purification, we are called to be a new creation: Isaiah's "See, I am doing something new." We are reminded by Paul that while we are still running the race, our attention is on the goal: life with Jesus Christ. We are purified and enlightened through the Gospel episode in which, with very few words and a simple action, Jesus teaches us about forgiveness, honesty, conversion.

With the third scrutiny at hand, we may need to look at our lives, searching for those sometimes hidden areas of selfishness, pride, and oppression that prevent us from greater holiness. Let us look, whether we identify with the "one caught in sin" or with those seeking retribution for the wrongdoer. What does Jesus say to us? The questions of the scrutiny reflection in preparation for Sunday's celebration might probe our willingness to face up to our sinfulness, to put it behind us, to walk on as new and forgiven persons, and to forgive one another truly. How much baggage do we carry about our past and the wrong-doing we have not forgiven ourselves? Are we reluctant to become the new creation? Do we hesitate to claim life with Jesus Christ, life as fully alive Christians, as the goal we strive for? Why?

For Paul who writes from prison to his beloved Philippians, this present moment is the time to let go of the past and face forward. He seeks to "know Christ and the power flowing from his resurrection, likewise to know how to share his sufferings by being formed into the pattern of his death." Do we seek to know the living Christ with anywhere near that intensity? Do we want to share in the power of his saving actions? Do we recognize in our sufferings the likeness of the suffering of Jesus? Do we minimize the call to go on, to be converted? All this is new to us, perhaps, or we may have thought about some of it and are moving along the path with Paul. There is matter here for reflection and scrutiny.

Again, the litany and petitions of the scrutiny rite need to reflect our personal and shared reflection on these questions, and more, opening for the rest of the community the doors to insight and deeper conversion based on today's readings.

REFLECTION ON LIFE

In my life, I do not let go easily of all the events of the past, particularly some that have caused pain or that I do not yet forgive myself. How about you? I do not always see—or want to perceive—something new God is creating. How is your perception? I hear and know, intellectually, that I am a part of the people God has formed for himself, to announce his praise. Usually I am so routinized and self-absorbed that I neglect *being* that person. How attentive are you? Sometimes I feel as though I am doing it all alone, so I forget that what I possess, who I am, is a gift shared with grace through Jesus Christ. I often don't race along toward Jesus Christ. It is more of a shuffle. There is an occasional burst or insight of illumination, yes, but I was caught today by Paul's intensity. How about you?

Sometimes I know I'd easily forgive the adulteress. Then I don't have to look at my own life quite so intently. I don't want to scrutinize—or to be scrutinized. Sometimes I wish Lent would just go away. I'm not going to look at the sand. In my heart I know what has been written there.

And then some Jesus comes into my life, waits wordlessly beside me, and eventually says, "Neither do I condemn you. You may go. But from now on, avoid this sin." Someone has helped me let go of all that past, to step out anew. Somehow my human dignity and sense of hope have been nourished with strength and tenderness. God is merciful, and we can work toward a better future. We have been grasped by Christ, perhaps in the form of some other person, perhaps in the experience of forgiving myself finally.

Our reflection on life, recognizing these experiences in

our own flesh and blood, leads us to pray again the responsorial Psalm 126: The Lord has done great things for us; we are filled with joy. We are glad indeed.

KNOWING OUR FAITH

The Christian is an alleluia from head to foot. When we claim for ourselves the gift of being Christian, we are on the path of encountering Christ Jesus. This encounter with this Jesus is a horizon that opens us to all sorts of growth. We are not condemned and then abandoned. Nor are we forgiven and then abandoned. We are loved and forgiven and loved and forgiven and loved and . . .

As Catholic Christians, we celebrate in many forms our basic belief in our redemption, our goodness, or our call to be like and with Jesus Christ. As the bumper sticker says: "Christians aren't perfect. Just forgiven." How fully do I recognize the truth of that? Are we ready to acknowledge, here in this community, in our families, in this Lenten season, even to ourselves, that we are good, that we are loved with an everlasting love? Do we accept others with that same frame of mind?

Let us spend some time reflecting on our faith which is built on our assurance that we are good, that we have been created good, that we are loved. This same faith is honest about our human weakness, ambiguities, faults and brokenness. Our Church fathers and mothers have shared in many ways their beliefs in our call to holiness, individually and communally. We have been formed by God for himself, to announce his praise, to celebrate his goodness, not to grovel in unforgiven guilt and shame for our lives. We are called to live lives of praise and goodness, mercy and compassion. We are called to high moral standards. We don't get off easily just because we are forgiven and loved. We have within us the yearning for goodness and the intimacy with a loving God as exemplified in our readings today. We celebrate the scrutinies to keep fresh our hunger for grace and growth; we look at our life's path forward and mark out the way we seek to go.

There are multiple means to help us evaluate our maturity, our progress in choosing the good, our motivations for the decisions we make. Some study and discussion of the stages of moral development and human/spiritual growth may be helpful as we sort out our values and focus on "the prize." Because "grace builds on nature," it is quite appropriate to incorporate insights on moral growth and development. In understanding ourselves, most of us need all the help we can get.

Whether it is through the resources dealing with Pi-

aget, James Fowler, Lawrence Kohlberg, and Malcolm Knowles, from filmstrips or books, or from workshops or symposia, we need to learn more ourselves in order to help others. I have found the book *Faith Development in the Adult Life Cycle* edited by Kenneth Stokes (Sadlier, 1983) helpful, though many resources and insights have been incorporated into spiritual reflections. For group input, media selection may be a simple and clear presentation of core materials which you can then develop according to the needs of your people.

INTEGRATION

Questions for Reflection and Discussion

1. Build on the material presented in media or discussion on growth in faith and moral development. Helping clarify stages or steps in growth with members of the group will give help in evaluating/integrating conscious growth.

2. Invite questions from the group about issues and concerns that relate to today's theme and topic. Possibly additional time may be needed to explore issues and questions that arise.

Journaling

In what way am I becoming a new creation for the praise of God? What is there in my life that holds me back from running the race toward fullness in Jesus Christ? What will I do about it?

CLOSING PRAYER

Song: "For You Are My God" by John Foley, S.J. (*Glory and Praise*, #16)

Doctrinal and Pastoral Issues: Redemption, Self-Awareness, Holiness, Faith Development

Clare Colella

Passion Sunday/Palm Sunday

Procession with Palms: Luke 19:28–40
Isaiah 50:4–7
Philippians 2:6–11
Luke 23:1–49

OPENING PRAYER

Song: "The King of Glory" (Traditional Israeli Folk Song)

THEMATIC FRAMEWORK

It is Palm Sunday. With the blessing of palm branches, the readings and the procession, something different is happening. What does it mean? It is important that those who may be new to our Church customs participate in both the celebration of the palm service and the procession and have a chance to learn more about their basis in Scripture. It is really quite ironic that just a few days before the crucifixion of Jesus, the Church emphasizes in its liturgical practice his triumphant entry into Jerusalem. We acknowledge that Jesus, like other great persons, was controversial. Even his close followers did not really understand during his lifetime who he really was or what he was doing or even his teachings. Clearer understanding came later. Certainly those who opposed him did not understand him.

Even the Church expresses a certain amount of ambiguity, calling this day both Passion Sunday and Palm Sunday. So what is it that we are doing today?

We look at the choice Jesus has made to fulfill the mission he came with—to go to Jerusalem to do his Father's work. That first happened in triumph—some of those who had heard him watched him, celebrated his arrival as a great and holy man, a prophet or messiah, a person coming in the name of the Lord. So he is. We bless palms, hear the Gospel reading and proclaim him as our Lord as well.

In the course of the liturgy, we are touched by the "suffering servant" of Isaiah, suddenly aware of the Hebrew Scriptures which foretold something of the mission of this chosen one of God. The responsorial psalm alerts us to the pain ahead. Its very last verse as given today moves beyond death and pain to praise and glory.

Paul's message to the Philippians assures us that because of and beyond his death on the cross, Jesus is Lord, the chosen of God. These first two readings are proclaimed every Palm Sunday. They are a transition into the passion and death to come.

The passion narrative from Luke lends itself to adaptation for dramatic proclamation by various readers. Note the special portions that only Luke recounts, for even in his passion, according to this Gospel, Jesus is there for the weary and downtrodden. Those in the courtyard with Peter, the episode of Jesus before Herod, those who accompanied Jesus as he carried his cross, the criminal crucified with Jesus asking forgiveness—all give particular focus on Jesus' care for the poor, even now.

REFLECTING ON LIFE

There is a unique perspective on the passion, death and resurrection that is explored by Henri Nouwen in the periodical *Weavings* (January-February 1987). Nouwen writes of active waiting, the spirituality of waiting. There are two aspects of waiting, he says. One is waiting *for* God, the other is the waiting *of* God. In the passion and resurrection of Jesus, we see God as a waiting God. At the turning point of his betrayal, Jesus was "handed over." From that point onward, he becomes the one to whom things are being done. He is no longer the active leader, preacher, doer, as in the first part of his public life. Here, now, things are being done to him. He allows it, the Father allows it, but it is the painful mystery of being passive, of waiting, the experience of passion. Our actions end in passion because the response to our actions is out of our hands. It is in the very waiting for response that the intensity of love is revealed to us. We realize that the glory of God bursts forth through Jesus' passion precisely when he is being the victim, because it is in the passion that the fullness of God's love shines through. It is supremely a waiting love, a love that does not seek control.

When we allow ourselves to feel how we are being acted upon, we can realize that a new life is within us that we were not even aware of before. Even in the midst of our suffering, we are in touch with resurrection.

Looking at ourselves and the world around us, we recognize the truth that although there is a small arena where we are active, there is a far greater portion of our life in which we are acted upon by people, events, society, other factors beyond our control. It becomes important for us to accept that a large part of our life is spent in waiting in the sense of being acted upon. In understanding that in Jesus Christ God is waiting for our response to divine love, we can discover a new perspective on how to wait in our own life. We learn that fulfillment can be found in waiting. Our service to others may include helping them see glory not only in acting but in being acted upon, in our creative, positive response of waiting.

Honesty with myself tells me that I will go on trying to balance the action and the passion in my life, that in the arenas where I can I will act with gentleness and fidelity to grace. In the arenas where I experience the passion, the waiting, I will need to be gentle and patient, active in creative passive ways, learning, loving, accepting. Probably I will spend a lot of time trying to sort out why being in waiting is so difficult. I've never really liked the stories of Jesus' passion and death. Even waiting for God to act seems endless at times. But I think there is a lot more than just a story of redemption once upon a time. Part of the redemption story is my accepting that something is happening to me. Redeeming goes on for all of us—it is the continuing story. Working our salvation is not only my *doing*—it is also my *accepting*, seeing, and reflecting.

There is a simple sculpture titled "Ad Sum," depicting a young woman, kneeling, resting back on her heels, holding her hands open, palm upward, in her lap, her back straight, her head bowed slightly, waiting. I've prayed in that position before, asking for the ability to accept a difficult reality. I have even prayed in that stature out of glad acceptance of a joyous gift. But as a frame of mind, I have yet to adopt active waiting. How about you?

KNOWING OUR FAITH

Today's liturgical celebration presents wonderful examples of ritual and simple pageantry. Themes of symbolism and sacramentals may flow well from a reflection on what we heard, saw, did, and felt in today's liturgy. As a Church, we value sacramentals and symbols—objects and actions that help us encounter the holy in a special way, creating an environment for response to God's presence.

During their time with the catechumenate community, the elect have seen abundant use of sacramentals—holy water, altar candles, statues, ashes at the beginning of Lent, perhaps rosaries, and now blessed palms. The group members may remember even more specific ones—and have questions about their origin and meaning in our expression of faith. You may want to field a few of these questions ahead of time and do a bit of research for your preparation. There will also be abundant use of sacramentals and symbols in the liturgies of Holy Week, which you may want to enrich beforehand—why a seder meal with its historical and spiritual roots, why a prayer service and reverencing the cross on Good Friday? Some groups also choose to prepare some discussion of the symbols used in the initiation sacraments as well.

If there is no scheduled retreat/prayer day before the Easter vigil, you may want to spend some brief time talking about the experiences of the catechumenate journey and introduce the variety of sacramentals and symbols that will be used in the forthcoming rites, not in detail, but enough to help give a spiritual framework to the actions and emotions of nervous elect. We have found that a few words of explanation in advance helped those receiving the sacraments to feel less nervous or self-conscious so that they could enter more deeply into a spiritual experience. Your group members may respond differently. By now you would have a good sense of what helps them to be most open to the ritual and spiritual experiences they will encounter.

It is a unique Catholic Christian heritage to be so rich in symbols and sacramentals, though group members may have insights or questions springing from their previous religious background. That we use sacramentals as reminders and path markers in our spiritual development (but do not worship statues, stained glass windows or holy water) is an important part of learning to see—and think—beyond the visible reality into a deeper spirituality. We not only act—use the sacramentals and symbols—we also let them act on us, drawing us into a deeper atmosphere or reflection on the holy. We might learn to be actively passive, waiting, watching, listening, and encounter God in a different way. To pray can be to wait, to listen as well, not just to speak. Understanding the role and impact of sacramentals and symbols can then enhance our spiritual growth.

INTEGRATION

Questions for Discussion

1. What have been some sacramentals that you feel comfortable with? How have they helped you pray or come closer to God?

2. Are there some sacramentals that are unfamiliar or confusing to you? Why?

3. Does the idea or experience of being quiet or passive in prayer or in life present difficulties to you? Why? Do you want to change?

Journaling

1. What am I to learn from reflection or being passive, letting things happen without always trying to be in control?

2. When am I uncomfortable with letting go of control? Am I afraid? Can I—do I want to—become more balanced in letting go? When I let go of power or control, what am I holding to as the greater value in my life?

CLOSING PRAYER

Song: "Seek the Lord" by Roc O'Connor, S.J. (*Glory and Praise*, #46)

Doctrinal and Pastoral Issues: Images of God, Sacramentals, Death and Resurrection, Holy Week

Clare Colella

EASTER

The New Creation

By Eugene A. LaVerdiere, S.S.

The Easter triduum is the highpoint of the liturgical year. It begins on Holy Thursday with an anticipatory celebration of the paschal mystery which will unfold on Good Friday and at the Easter vigil. On this first day of the triduum we focus on Jesus' Last Supper, his farewell to history in word and deed and the gathering up of the Church into the mystery of his death-resurrection. The second day is Good Friday, when we dwell on John's account of the passion and Jesus' glorious return to the Father. The triduum's climax is the Easter vigil, a celebration of the resurrection, an event which touched creation itself to the core and transformed all of history.

The Easter triduum is a transitional period. It can be viewed as the conclusion of Lent, but it is also the introduction to the season of Easter and its seven Sundays of Easter, together with the feast of the Ascension and Pentecost Sunday. Most of the readings are taken from John's Gospel for this season, and fittingly so, since the resurrection of Jesus permeates that entire Gospel.

The Last Supper

On Holy Thursday, the Gospel reading for the Mass of the Lord's Supper is John 13:1–15. Passover was approaching, and the decisive hour had come when Jesus would demonstrate the total gift of his love and return to the Father. The forces of treachery had not really triumphed (vv. 1–2). The body of the reading includes the washing of the feet (vv. 3–12a) and part of a brief discourse by Jesus (vv. 12b–15).

To appreciate the force of Jesus' action, we need to realize who participated: the disciples, an extremely varied gathering which still included Judas, and Jesus the Lord. Kneeling before each disciple in turn and washing their feet, the Lord not only showed humility but destroyed any claims to human status and social prestige among the disciples. When the Lord himself kneels before the powerful and the humble of the world, they have to recognize their equality as persons before God. So do Jesus' disciples. Peter's resistance when Jesus approaches him is an expression of pride, not of humility.

In the discourse, Jesus asked his disciples to do for one another and for others what he had just done for them. He thus showed the Church how to pursue its mission to the ends of the earth and gather all nations and peoples into one family of God.

The Glorification of Jesus

On Good Friday, we read John's account of the passion, death and burial of Jesus (Jn 18:1—19:42), an account quite different from that of Luke, which we heard on Passion Sunday. Luke's telling of the events, like that of Matthew and Mark, would have been incomplete without the resurrection account. Not so with John's, whose passion is the story of Jesus' glorious return to the Father. Unlike Matthew, John does not speak of the resurrection event. Like Mark and Luke, he presupposes it and focuses on the proclamation of the resurrection and on the disciples' experience of the risen Lord.

Throughout the passion and to the very moment of his death, Jesus is in full command of the events. John gives no hint of Jesus' anguished prayer at Gethsemane. The arrest takes place in the garden, and Judas is there with the others, but there is no need for a betrayal sign. Jesus steps forward and presents himself (18:4–5). Before Pilate, Jesus makes a solemn statement on the nature of the kingdom and the purpose of his life (18:36–37). Before dying, he shows how his death and passage to God transform our relationship to one another: "Woman, there is your son . . . there is your mother" (19:26–27). Finally, when Jesus sees that everything has been fulfilled, he declares it so and gives up his spirit. He has drunk the cup the Father had given him to drink (18:11).

Visits to the Tomb

At the Easter vigil, the Gospel reading is Luke 24:1–12, a story of two visits to the tomb, one by a group of women and one by Peter, on the first day of the week, which the early Christians viewed as the day of the new creation. At this point, however, that day has barely dawned. In Mark's Gospel, when the women enter the tomb, their attention is taken up entirely with the young man who addresses them. Only later at his initiative do they notice that the tomb is empty. In

Luke, when the women also enter into the tomb, their attention focuses immediately on the absence of the Lord's body. Only afterward do two men in dazzling garments enter the story to interpret what has happened. First, the women should be seeking the living one among the living, not among the dead! Second, they should remember how Jesus had once spoken to them about his passion, death and resurrection. With this they understood but were unable to convince the Eleven and the others.

Peter is singled out in this story. After the women's report, he personally went to the tomb and saw nothing but the wrappings inside. At the end of the account, we leave Peter filled with wonderment until the risen Lord appeared to him, an event whose story we are not told but which is referred to later in Luke 24:34.

From Darkness to the Light of Faith

On Easter Sunday, the Gospel is either John 20:1–9, which tells of two visits to the tomb, or Luke's account of the experience of a group of women (Lk 24:1–11) and of Peter (Lk 24:12) at the tomb, a reading which we have already heard at the Easter vigil.

Mary Magdalene went to the tomb on the first day of the week, literally on day one of the week, an expression which recalls Genesis and its account of day one of creation. Like the other evangelists at this point in the Gospel, John is announcing a new creation, a new beginning for the human race in Christ the Lord. The creative word of God was about to burst into the world and destroy all darkness, but when Mary went to the tomb it was still dark (Jn 1:4–5). For her the empty tomb was a sign of death and hopelessness.

Hearing of her experience, Peter and the disciple whom Jesus loved also went to the tomb. Early in the tradition, this disciple may have been an historical figure, but by the end of the first century he represented every Christian. Together the two saw not only that Jesus' tomb was empty but also that everything associated with Jesus' death, the wrappings, had been left behind. When the beloved disciple entered the tomb, something Mary Magdalene had not done, he saw and believed. The early Church thus presented the empty tomb as a symbol of resurrection, Christian hope, and eternal life.

The Breaking of Bread

The evening Mass for Easter Sunday presents the story of two disciples leaving Jerusalem in discouragement and going to Emmaus (Lk 24:13–35). On the way they met the Lord but were unable to recognize him. They presented their view of what had happened to him, a seeming stranger, and Jesus proceeded to expand their understanding of the Scriptures so that they might see in them a reflection of what they had experienced. With this, they invited Jesus, still a stranger to them, into their home. In the sharing of bread with Jesus the stranger, their eyes were opened in recognition, and they returned to Jerusalem to share the good news with the assembled community.

This reading is vital for understanding how to interpret the Scriptures in personal and pastoral situations. Sometimes they remain opaque because our approach to them is too limited and we fail to look at all the Scriptures. We also are taught that to recognize our risen Lord in the breaking of bread, we must be able to extend Christian hospitality to those who are strangers to us.

The Gift of the Spirit

The first day of the week, the day of the new creation and the day on which the early Christians first experienced the risen Lord, is also the day on which the Lord breathed the Holy Spirit on the Christian community (Jn 20:19–23) and on which the early Christians continue to experience the risen Lord, share their faith and proclaim it in the weekly assembly (Jn 20:24–29). On the second Sunday of Easter we thus learn much about the origins of Sunday as well as about the first Easter. We also learn that John's Gospel did not try to present all of Jesus' signs, but only as many as would enable us to have faith and life in his name (Jn 20:30–31).

We should note that Jesus came with the witness of his wounds to bring peace to disciples who were afraid of being wounded, and he sent them on their mission as he had been sent on his. As Lord, he could now breathe into them a Spirit of new life, his own, as God had breathed his life into Adam. Like him they were to be reconcilers, and this brought with it a serious responsibility. If they withheld Christ's peace, many would never be reconciled.

The appearance to Thomas and the disciples on the following first day of the week develops some of the same elements for Christians who were far removed from the first experiences of the risen Lord. With Thomas we are called to hear the voice of the risen Lord in the life and message of the Christians who preceded us in the Church and to experience his presence in our Christian assembly.

It Is the Lord

On the third Sunday of Easter, we join the disciples on a fishing expedition which is followed up by a meal on the shore of the Sea of Tiberias (Jn 21:1–19). The passage can be divided into three sections: the fishing episode (21:1–8), the meal on the shore (21:9–14), and the dialogue with Simon Peter following the meal (21:15–19). All of these are taken from an appendix to the Gospel, which originally ended with John 20:30–31.

The apostolic fishing story (see also Lk 5:1–11) reflects the experience of those who had become fishers of men. At first they caught nothing—they were fishing on the wrong side of the boat. Following Jesus' instructions, however, they tried on the other side and made an extraordinary catch which nearly overwhelmed them. Such was the missionary effort of the early Church. Back on shore, the disciples joined the risen Lord in a meal which consisted of bread and fish. We are reminded of the bread and fish shared with the enormous crowd on the occasion of the multiplication of loaves and fishes. As in the Eucharist, Jesus the Lord is the host at the meal they enjoyed. The reading ends with a dialogue in which Jesus asks Peter whether he loves him. As Jesus repeats the question a second and a third time and Peter stumbles through the answer, we are reminded of how Peter earlier had denied knowing Jesus three times. After Peter's third reply, Jesus announces how one who loved him and followed him would do so to the end and die like him.

The Gift of Eternal Life

John 10, the highly popular "good shepherd" discourse, is also one of the most challenging in the Gospel. It identifies Jesus as the good shepherd, presents the qualities of the good shepherd, and speaks of how such a shepherd was willing to lay down his life for his sheep. It shows how all those who shepherd the flock of Christ are to model their lives on that of Jesus the good shepherd. The chapter also speaks of those who follow Christ the good shepherd, the sheep who hear his voice and believe in him. As we hear in the Gospel for this fourth Sunday of Easter, those sheep are not to be confused with those who are not Christ's sheep and refuse to believe. Those who hear his voice follow him, and he guarantees them the gift of eternal life. They are in his hand as surely as he is in the Father's hand, and they shall never perish (Jn 10:27–30).

A New Commandment

On the fifth Sunday of Easter, we hear a short discourse of Jesus which is of tremendous significance. Like the long discourse which comes soon afterward, it is delivered at the Last Supper (Jn 13:31–35). Jesus already has washed the feet of the disciples. The meal proper is over, and Judas has left to betray Jesus. As the Gospel says, "It was night." In the midst of this night Jesus speaks to his disciples of his coming glorification and how he would no longer be with them as he had been. The Word made flesh was returning to his Father, and at least for now they could not follow him.

It is in this context of betrayal that Jesus asks his disciples to love one another. Jesus' disciples do not hate one another. They love one another, and this is how all can know that they are his disciples. Jesus calls this a new commandment, and it is. The quality of the disciples' love for one another is to be measured by that of Jesus who was laying down his life out of love for them and all who would come after them. He was laying down his life even for those who hated and betrayed him. Christian love was new in both its scope and its depth.

The Divine Indwelling

Jesus' farewell discourse, as presented in John 14—17, provides the Gospel with an opportunity to have Jesus address the problems of a later age. Such discourses enabled ancient writers, including the evangelists, to respond to the question, "What would Jesus say to us today?" The passage selected for reading on the sixth Sunday of Easter addresses some of those concerns (Jn 14:23–29).

First Jesus establishes a link between loving him and keeping his word. Such is the mark of true love. Given this, Jesus the Lord and the Father establish their dwelling in such a person. They make their home in the heart and mind of one whose love is genuine. Jesus then promises the disciples the Paraclete, the Holy Spirit, who also will be sent to reside in them. The Spirit's role will be to illumine them and stimulate their memory of Jesus' teaching when he would no longer be with them as he had been. With this Jesus gives them his peace as a farewell gift, a peace which would be renewed after his resurrection (20:19–23) and which they would share with one another in their assemblies for the Lord's Supper.

The Ascension

For the feast of the Ascension, our reading is taken from the conclusion of Luke's Gospel. Jesus has appeared to the entire assembled community of his disciples. Even those who returned from Emmaus are there. He also has enjoyed a meal with them (Lk 24:36–43), and he now turns to a final short discourse on their future mission to preach to all nations once they have been clothed with power from on high. In this, Jesus refers to Pentecost, whose story is told at the beginning of Acts.

The reading begins with the final part of this discourse, which provides the setting for the ascension itself. The ascension does more than provide a conclusion for the Gospel or mark the definitive end of an era, the period of Jesus in history, and the beginning of the new era of the Church. In blessing the disciples, we see fulfilled the promise made to Abraham that in his progeny all peoples would be blessed (see Acts 3:21–26). The ascension thus opens the way for the Church to fulfill its mission to all nations, to the ends of the earth. All is now ready for Luke's second volume, the Book of Acts, which shows how the promised blessing would unfold in the history of the Church.

A Universal Prayer

Jesus' final discourse in John ends with a long prayer (chapter 17) which unfolds in three parts. In the first part, Jesus speaks personally to his Father about the fulfillment of his mission and how his disciples recognize its source in the Father (Jn 17:1–8). In the second part, he prays for all his disciples, all those he has known and who have known him as the Father's Son (Jn 17:8–19). The first and second parts of the prayer are read as the Gospel for the seventh Sunday of Easter in Cycles A and B.

This year in Cycle C, we read the third part of the prayer, in which Jesus prays for all those who will believe in him in the future, once he is gone, through the word of those now gathered around him (Jn 17:20–26). In other words, he prays for us and for all Christian generations which link us to the first disciples. He also prays that we will be good bearers of the tradition of his life and word. Jesus' prayer is for unity among Christians, a unity which crosses the boundaries of every particular Christian community, a unity which bridges the generations and gathers all into the life and love of the Father.

Pentecost

We are accustomed to viewing Pentecost through the eyes of St. Luke and the episode he presented in the Acts of the Apostles (Acts 2:1–13). In the vigil celebration for Pentecost we learn to see it through John 7:37–39. The Spirit flows from Jesus, the one who has been glorified, as living water from which all who believe in Jesus can drink. The waters of Pentecost, which recall the water from the well at Samaria, are the waters of baptism. There is no Christian baptism apart from the gift of the Spirit, and the gift of the Spirit is inseparable from the presence of the risen Lord. Jesus, through the Holy Spirit and the baptismal waters, reaches out beyond his historical life, in order that none of those he had taught and none of those who would draw near to him later would ever be lost.

On Pentecost itself, the Gospel is John 20:19–23. The first day of the week, the day of the new creation and the day on which the early Christians first experienced the risen Lord, is also the day on which the Lord breathed the Holy Spirit on the Christian community. Jesus came with the witness of his wounds to bring peace to disciples who were afraid of being wounded, and he sent them on their mission as he had been sent on his. As Lord, he could now breathe into them a Spirit of new life, his own, as God had breathed his life into Adam. For John, there is no separating Pentecost from Easter. It is there that we see most clearly why it must be the last Sunday of Easter.

Holy Thursday

CHRISM MASS:
Isaiah 61:1–3, 6, 8–9
Revelation 1:5–8
Luke 4:16–21

EVENING MASS OF THE LORD'S SUPPER:
Exodus 12:1–8, 11–14
1 Corinthians 11:23–26
John 13:1–15

OPENING PRAYER

Opening prayer of Holy Thursday Mass (from Missal or Missalette).

THEMATIC FRAMEWORK

There are so many possible liturgical experiences for the catechumenate members that you will need to plan well in advance for your point of focus.

Chrism Mass

If it is possible for members of your parish group to participate in the diocesan Chrism Mass (which may be scheduled for a day other than Holy Thursday) there would be an experience of participation in the diocesan Church community with two special facets: the blessing of the holy oils—some of which will be used during the Easter vigil (holy chrism for baptism and confirmation)—and the renewal of commitment by the priests to their priestly service.

Most typically there would not be dismissal, since these two special events take place after the homily. Therefore some advance discussion of what will happen may be in order. It would also be appropriate to take some time after the Chrism Mass to reflect on the experiences, insights and questions of those who participated.

The candidates for initiation have journeyed with the parish community for quite a time and have proven themselves willing to take on the responsibilities of membership in the Church. Their initiation into the Catholic Church immerses them in a community that has broad (diocesan, national, international) reaches and deep roots. The custom of blessing the sacramental oils exemplifies those aspects.

Holy oil is abundantly used as a symbol of the realities we call "mystery" within the sacraments. The oil of catechumens is the "oil of salvation" which may strengthen the baptismal candidate with the power of Christ our Savior. The elect were most likely anointed with the oil of catechumens during the Rite of Acceptance into the Catechumenate. The "chrism of salvation" is an aromatic oil used both at baptism and at confirmation. We are anointed as Christ was anointed as "Priest, Prophet and King."

As Jesus Christ prayed over and blessed the sick with powerful symbolic action, so does the Church accompany the prayer for the sick with an anointing with holy oil which signifies healing and strengthening.

These three oils then are the ones blessed during the Mass, which the priests (or deacons) will take home to their parish for use in the sacramental ministries in the year ahead.

During this liturgy which the bishop celebrates with the clergy of the diocese, he speaks about priestly ministry, to which all renew their commitment. The bishop asks all those present to pray for the priests as well.

Mass of the Lord's Supper

If this Mass is celebrated in conjunction with the seder meal, it may be that dismissal after the homily seems not appropriate. Whether or not there is dismissal, this session material is based on the presumption that there will be a gathering with the elect that will spend some time in reflecting on the meaning of the Scriptures and the entire Holy Thursday liturgy.

Most uniquely, this day's liturgy reaches back to the origins of the Mass itself. The Lord's Supper with his disciples preceded his passion and death. The Eucharist was given to them—and to us—"the night before he was betrayed." It was in celebrating the Jewish Passover (seder meal) with his disciples for the last time that Jesus began a new meal—that which the Church remembers and renews at each Mass: "From now on I am the paschal lamb, the new sacrifice, that takes away the sin of the world. This is my body; this is my blood: Do this in remembrance of me." The heart of the liturgy we are familiar with is anchored in the events of this first Holy Thursday.

Another special ritual reaches back to that first "Lord's Supper," the re-enactment of the washing of feet. "Love one another as I have loved you." "Serve one another. You must wash each other's feet." With the liturgical renewal stimulated by the Second Vatican Council, this ritual was given to us as an image and experience of mutual ministry and servant leadership. As the Lord himself was a servant caring for the needs of his people, so too is the ideal and goal of our Church leadership.

Depending on local liturgical and pastoral practice, the transfer of the Holy Eucharist to a side altar or chapel and stripping the altar may be a part of this evening's experience. The power, simplicity and meaning of all these events will generate questions, insights and a deeper spiritual awareness of the sacredness of the triduum.

Be sure to consult with the liturgical planners so you know in advance what will be happening, in order to better maximize the experience with your catechumenate community.

All three readings trace the significance of this day—the Passover, Paul's proclamation of the new sacrifice, and the Gospel account of the Last Supper, focusing on the centrality of the holy meal in the life of the community.

REFLECTION ON LIFE

As members of the Catholic faith community, we find the variety and richness of today's liturgy full of insights into who we are as Church.

We are those who gather and pray not only to remember the past and retell the stories of our roots. Even more, we are bringing the reality of the Eucharist alive in our midst as Jesus celebrated with his disciples at the first Eucharist, the Lord's Supper. Today we are reminded as well that our lives in the community are to be characterized by compassion and service, as in the ceremony of washing the feet of guests. Our love for one another finds expression in many ways, but seldom are we challenged or invited to this kind of service, this depth of awareness of others.

It is relatively easy to become routine about the prayers and the mystery of the Mass, our Eucharist. "Eucharist" means thanksgiving. Celebration of the Eucharist is not to lull us in routine, but to reawaken us and nourish us as we become more fully today's disciples of Jesus. It is our opportunity to link our total lives in gifts, offering the joy and pain, hopes and hard work, our questions and ourselves. Eucharist is our action of bringing ourselves, welcoming one another, and, in hearing the words of Scripture, letting ourselves be re-

fashioned into the forgiving, celebrating people of God. Jesus is with and within us. From this Eucharist we emerge nourished and strengthened by Jesus and by one another, as we continue our Eucharist—"thanksgiving"—in the context of daily life.

In those parish communities who are developing the "re-membering Church" ministry to welcome back alienated or marginated Catholics, this day's liturgy may be the special celebration of their return to the active community. If that is to happen it would be advisable to have alerted the catechumenate group in advance so they can understand better the meaning and power of re-entry into the eucharistic community. Much has happened in the lives of these returning Catholics; those elect (and inquirers or catechumens who may be present) who are seeking membership in the community may understand better than we do how difficult and how rewarding the journey of a seeker may be.

KNOWING OUR FAITH

The variety of Scriptures, rituals and events within today's liturgical experience is so full that reflecting on them is its own focus.

If there has been a group participating in the Chrism Mass, some sharing and reflection on that experience is suggested. More appropriately that "breaking open" would be done at the gathering of the catechumens/ elect as close to the event as possible. (In our diocese, the Chrism Mass is celebrated a few weeks early so that, by this time, we have already debriefed that event and explored its meaning for us.)

The seder meal, if celebrated, deepens our awareness of the Hebrew/Jewish roots and connections we have as Christian Church. The "Last Supper," the Lord's Supper, was not an isolated event for Jesus and his disciples. It is the bridge into the new creation of his community of believers, a step in the formation of the Christian Church—not by itself complete, for the events yet to come all take us toward Pentecost with its powerful sending forth to be and become Church. But through this meal/sacrifice together, the disciples are bonded together as the new community.

The Scriptures and rituals of this liturgy almost break themselves open. The questions and insights of the group tend to cluster around the actual events they have experienced—seeing the feet of community members being washed. One of the group may have been asked to participate in the ritual and would have a different perspective and experience to share.

Welcoming the returning Catholics will unfold its own questions about faith journey, reconciliation, welcoming and accepting, the significance of being a sacramental participating member of the Church.

Follow the process of "What did you hear? What did you see?" "What does it mean?" "What does it ask of you?" (or whatever process questions you have typically formulated to deepen and draw forth the experiences and insights of participants). Together with your reflections and information their input will create a powerful Spirit-filled gathering time.

INTEGRATION

Reflection and small group discussion:

1. Choose one of the events or rituals of today's liturgy and reflect on its meaning for us now.

2. What is being asked of me through this liturgy?

3. Who is with me in this on-going growth?

CLOSING PRAYER

Pray together the antiphons of the washing of the feet: John 13:4, 5, 15; John 13:6, 7, 8; John 13:14; John 13:35; John 13:34 and 1 Corinthians 13:13.

Doctrinal and Pastoral Issues: Eucharist, Seder Meal, Ministry Sacrifice, Christian Service

Clare Colella

Good Friday

Isaiah 52:13—53:12
Hebrews 4:14–16; 5:7–9
John 18:1—19:42

OPENING PRAYER

First prayer of the Good Friday liturgy (from Missal or Missalette).

THEMATIC FRAMEWORK

Today's worship service comprises three parts:

1. The liturgy of the word (renewing our faith in the power of the passion death of Jesus and the general intercessions).

2. The veneration of the cross (honoring the symbol of the redemptive death of Jesus).

3. Holy Communion (according to the ancient tradition, Mass is not celebrated today).

The setting of the church itself is stark, bare, forcefully making us aware of the day's events. The style of the service itself is quiet and solemn. Before the new life and joy of resurrection we must go through the darkness and pain of passion and death. What Jesus experienced in his life—the suffering, death, then new life and glory—is a model for our lives as well. In the anticipation and participation for the Easter vigil and celebration of initiation, we must not neglect our identification with suffering as well.

Through dramatic proclamation of the passion of Jesus (today's Gospel) and the veneration of the cross, we come to realize that suffering is not the dark end of the road, but part of the unfolding journey of salvation, of spiritual growth. For it is in these times of pain that we can come to deeper realization of our inner strength. In reflection on the passion of Jesus we see that we are not alone in our own suffering.

There is a theology of suffering that surfaces today in the first two readings. From Isaiah we hear that the suffering servant (foretelling Jesus) was innocent; his pain was because of all of us and redemptive of us all. The writer of the Letter to the Hebrews draws forth the parallels, comparing Jesus with the Jewish high priest, offering sacrifice to God in behalf of the community, serving as mediator. The early Christians were far more familiar with this imagery and experience than we are. Our consideration of the readings moves us from the ancient times to our own lives—it is our sins that are laid on the suffering servant; it is we who must hold fast to our faith, who receive mercy and favor, who find help in time of need.

With these readings and particularly the passion, we are not just observers. Our response is personal and faith-filled in the general intercessions and the veneration of the cross, and in the Communion service (for the baptized community) we claim our participation in the paschal mysteries.

REFLECTION ON LIFE

In a world of competition, in strivings for power, in a society of predatory activity and domination, with heartlessness and oppression on all sides, the only hope we have—or the only hope we can give—is an act of compassion, mercy and liberation, a way of doing and being which is rooted in our awareness of and participation in the on-going process of redemption.

Today is a prime time for reflection on what we have been given—what Jesus has done for us, in his own life/ death and what he continues to do for us today. When we acknowledge that we are identified with Jesus Christ, we give ourselves over to God to work in our lives. We become active—and also passive. We take part in the passion of Jesus not by fighting our circumstances but by trying to discern and follow God's will and purpose in our lives. We do not simply acquiesce to God's presence in our lives; we incarnate it. We take on the labor of love that Jesus undertook in advance of us. We do, and yet we wait. The fears and pains of not being in control are real. The urge to fight for control is real. Anger and despair weave themselves into our lives. They are the finite perspective on an infinite reality. The pain and suffering are the temporary actualities. We do not give life without giving of our own life; we do not bring God's spirit to new life without suffering, without giving out of the very substance of who we are. As dark and foreboding as all this may sound, the new life and infinite perspective provide a hope-filled, peace-giving foundation to the very processes themselves.

So we are not simple observers in the passion narrative. We are part of the timeless event of suffering-death-resurrection. We are believers and people who hope. Corazon Aquino, in her presidential acceptance speech, said that faith "is not simply patience which suffers passively until the storm is past. Rather, it is a spirit which bears things—with resignation, yes, but above all, with blazing, serene hope."

We are a people who have, in our spiritual life which touches all aspects of life, a sense that beyond the present moment, the pain, the finite, there is something greater which undergirds us—the kingdom, the Father's will, the infinite context.

KNOWING OUR FAITH

Death, where is your sting?

In the commemoration of Jesus' passion and death, the Church gives us also a dynamic prayer in the general intercessions and the veneration of the cross. Strengthening our awareness of the universal Church, all members of the Christian and Jewish communities and those who do not express belief in God or Jesus Christ, the prayers also reach out to those in public leadership and those who are in special need. Our identification with the suffering Messiah leads us outward, not inward. Redemption is for all, not an elite group. We move beyond our personal concerns. Through the death we remember, we look beyond to a new and better life for all.

The cross itself then represents not death/despair but the outpouring of selfless love, the ultimate gift of oneself for the salvation of others: death/life. By our personal and communal veneration of the cross, we affirm our hope and faith in the resurrection.

The unique reception of Holy Communion in a solemn service outside Mass again affirms our belief in the continuing life of Jesus Christ and the vitality of the Church which celebrates his eucharistic presence. All the prayers are threaded with references to the resurrection. We look beyond. But we are to endure a solemn waiting time, the vigil. The burial of Jesus brought on a painful, doubt-filled time for his followers. They did not have the advantage we have of a time perspective. We know about the resurrection. They did not. And yet, in our own lives, do we always believe in a triumphant outcome? Are not our dark nights as real as theirs? Do we not sometimes feel overwhelmed or lost? Abandoned? Confused?

Does resurrection refer only to Jesus? Not if we are really believers. If all of life is holy, then all of life has been redeemed, touched by the grace and reality of the infinite, capable of new life from dying.

We do not stop with the passion narrative; we do not close with Good Friday. We continue the journey through this time to the vigil, the waiting/watching hope in the resurrection.

INTEGRATION

Questions for Discussion

1. Which of the events of today's liturgical service speak to you most strongly? Why?

2. What is your feeling or insight about Jesus' suffering and death? About his followers during the time of his passion, death, and burial?

Journaling

1. What "death" have I experienced in my life—death of a loved one, an abrupt and painful change, having to let go of someone or something I cherished? What do I remember about the "dying"?

2. Did some sort of new life or deeper growth evolve from that experience? Was there some person who walked with me through that dark time, who stood by my side, waited at the tomb?

CLOSING PRAYER

Song: "Wood Hath Hope" by the St. Louis Jesuits (Album: Wood Hath Hope)

Doctrinal and Pastoral Issues: Death and Resurrection, Theology of Suffering, Compassion, Grief

Clare Colella

Introduction to Easter to Corpus Christi

The format for these sessions is divided as follows:
Opening Prayer
Reflections
Closing Prayer
Each parish will have to adapt the local situations such as scheduling coffee breaks or the arrival of sponsors (if they join the session after the Mass).

The prayer sessions are designed to offer a variety of models and experiences to the catechumens. Some are taken from the Rite of Christian Initiation of Adults, others from the Sacramentary and the Liturgy of the Hours. Some of the prayers from the Mass or from the repertoire of traditional Catholic prayers (such as the Act of Charity) could be printed on good quality paper so that each member of the group could be given a copy. These could be collected in a folder for each catechumen. Another type of prayer is a litany of petition or thanksgiving. The leader will usually be a catechist; however, sometimes another minister such as a deacon or cantor is suggested. A leader of music would be an excellent addition to the team, at least for part of the time. This is a feasting season and an Alleluia acclamation would add a celebrative character to the sessions.

The environment of the gathering room should also reflect the season and echo the sanctuary in color, light (candle), and texture. An arrangement of flowers, if this is done in the main assembly area, would be good. The room should appear welcoming, comfortable, and hospitable. It should be prepared for the Breaking Open of the Word. There should be a nice copy of the Lectionary, open to the readings of the day. It should be placed in a fitting location.

The reflection section is divided into three or four themes, each of which is explored in two ways. At the beginning there is a statement of the theme. The catechist should introduce the theme in his or her own words, or by reading the statement.

The second portion of each theme suggests a variety of ways to begin the discussion and sharing. Catechists can start by relating an experience of their own and then ask for stories of similar situations, or a question can be asked directly. A significant amount of time should be spent in this sharing. Adults come to faith by integrating their personal experience with mystery. No one can do this for them. The catechist is the guide. The catechist can make connections and can relate the experience of the local church, the immediate neighborhood, and the people who are known to the catechumens and candidates.

After the sharing by the members of the group, the catechist should summarize the theme. If needed, the catechist can move the exploration of the theme to a deeper or broader level. For example, after rooting and grounding the theme in personal experience, thought can be given to historical or contemporary situations beyond the immediate experience. Catechists should research these areas ahead of time. At the end of each reflection section several issues of doctrine, morality, or ecclesiology are suggested. These can act as guides or chapter headings for the catechist during the preparation time. The presentation of these should not be academic and detached, but should always be framed in the reflection of the people present, the living Church.

Easter Sunday

Acts 10:34, 37–43
Colossians 3:1–4 or 1 Corinthians 5:6–8
John 20:1–9

OPENING PRAYER

Leader: Grace and peace be with you.

All: And also with you.

Leader: With the celebration of Easter we again pray the Gloria. We began this on Holy Thursday. This hymn of praise is filled with words and images that are particular to this Easter season. Let us pray this again this morning in one voice.

(Have copies of the prayer available—see the introduction to this section for an idea for the format.)

All: Glory to God in the highest,
and peace to his people on earth.
   Lord God, heavenly King,
   almighty God and Father,
   we worship you,
   we give you thanks,
   we praise you for your glory.
Lord Jesus Christ, only Son of the Father,
Lord God, Lamb of God,
you take away the sin of the world:
have mercy on us;
you are seated at the right hand of the Father:
receive our prayer.
   For you alone are the Holy One,
   you alone are the Lord,
   you alone are the Most High,
   Jesus Christ,
   with the Holy Spirit,
   in the glory of God the Father.
Amen.

REFLECTION

1. One evening news program goes by the title "Eye-witness." What weight do we give to an eyewitness account? Is it more believable? Have you ever been an eyewitness to an event that even you yourself would not believe if you hadn't seen it? The Scriptures this morning are full of eyewitness accounts.

    Are the accounts of the resurrection of Jesus from the dead familiar to you? Reread the Gospel. Who saw what?

2. We call the death/resurrection of Jesus the salvation event, the act of redemption, the paschal mystery. Christ means the anointed one. When is it that the followers of Jesus recognize him and call him Lord, the Christ?

    How is it that you recognize the Christ, the risen Lord, in our midst today? Are we tempted to look only for the historical Jesus? If you hear someone say "If Jesus were alive today . . ." can you distinguish between the life of Jesus and the presence of Jesus Christ in the world today?

3. What does Peter believe? Perhaps it is unclear from the Gospel passage, but return to the first reading. The presence of the risen Jesus is attested to by Peter in no uncertain terms. The selection from Acts is an abstract of the Easter season. Spend some time on the words of the passage: anointed, power, healing, good works, raise up, chosen, ate and drank, commission, preach, judge, believes, forgiveness.

    (Each of these words will lead into the themes of the following weeks. You will have opportunity to return to them with more time for reflection and integration.)

    Why do you believe in the resurrection? How do you believe in the resurrection and the living presence of Jesus Christ? Concentrate on the catechumenate process of the triple-pronged pattern of story telling: the story of the Scripture, the Church, and the individual.

4. What are the traditions of your local church for the celebration of Easter? Explain them to the catechumen.

CLOSING PRAYER

A member of the team reads the Easter Sequence (prose or poetic text). All could sing an Alleluia!

Doctrinal and Pastoral Issues: Paschal Mystery, Resur-
rection, Belief, Easter Celebrations and Traditions

Elizabeth Lilly

Second Sunday of Easter

Acts 5:12–16
Revelation 1:9–11, 12–13, 17–19
John 20:19–31

OPENING PRAYER

Leader: Grace and peace be with you.

All: And also with you.

Leader: Let us pray.
Lord Jesus Christ, you said to your apostles:
I leave you peace, my peace I give you.
Look not on our sins,
but on the faith of your Church,
and grant us the peace and unity
of your kingdom
where you live for ever and ever.

All: Amen.

(This prayer is part of the Communion rite of the Mass. The response to God's word is always to be drawn ever closer in union with the Lord. The breaking open of the word is a communion with the Lord.)

REFLECTION

1. What is belief? What is believable? How does one come to faith?

    Richard P. McBrien, in his book *Catholicism* (pages 24–27), defines Christian faith as "personal knowledge of God in Christ", "the perception of God in the midst of life." Faith is, by nature, always in search of expression, in search of a form of description. Theology, he states, is the reflection, the bringing to consciousness of faith. "Theology is that process by which we bring our knowledge and understanding of God to the level of expression." He defines belief as "a formulation of the knowledge we have of God through faith."

    Faith in the risen Christ is different than knowledge of the historical Jesus. Thomas distinguished the two and then moved into faith. Do we? Where do we see, in Jesus, the wonder of God revealed?

    Name some examples of coming to faith in your life, in the local community, in the world. Think of the people who carry out the mission and ministry of the life of Jesus. What are the signs and wonders of our day?

2. What is the Church? Think about this definition: The Church is the community where the risen Christ is at work. Just how this work is made concrete, made visible, can and does change from time to time, from place to place. Do you know this Church? Do you see this changing Church? How are you part of this Church?

    Two aspects of the paschal mystery could be explored. The first is that each member of the Church is given the power of the presence of God. The other is that each individual church or particular church is one with the universal Church. This is a sign of the unity of all in Christ.

3. Why do fear and doubt persist in our lives? Why the lack of peace? Can we face our own doubts and fears?

    Do you recall Peter's denial of Jesus during the trial? Today we hear another account of separation, of the distancing of a disciple from Jesus. How have we distanced ourselves from the Lord? How have we distanced ourselves from the Church?

    In the opening prayer we acknowledged our lack of faith and unity with the Lord. This is recognized by all members of the Church. Doubt and fear are with us. We together, as Church, grow in faith. How often are we Thomas? Do we recognize that we are part of the Church even in the midst of our fears and questions?

4. The images in the reading from the Book of Revelation are perhaps not as familiar to us as images such as Christ, the light of the world. At some convenient time, point out the Greek letters on the paschal candle, the First and the Last, the Alpha and the Omega.

CLOSING PRAYER

Leader: Let us pray.
Lord, you are present among us.
Hear our fears and our doubts.
Through your Church,

through those who believe in you and trust
    in you,
increase our faith and hope.
Change our doubt to trust.
We thank you for your gift of peace.
We now offer each other a sign of your
    peace.

Quietly, the leader embraces or takes the hand of each catechumen. After a moment, speak the words: "The peace of Christ be with you, (name)." Catechists then can follow suit. Depending on the size of the group and the arrangement of the room all could greet each other. It is important that the ritual manner of the greeting and exchange be maintained.

Leader: Go in peace to love and serve the Lord.

All: Amen.

All: sing Alleluia!

Doctrinal and Pastoral Issues: Belief and Doubt, History of Creeds, Paschal Mystery, Church

Elizabeth Lilly

Third Sunday of Easter

Acts 5:27–32, 40–41
Revelation 5:11–14
John 21:1–19

OPENING PRAYER

The following prayer is the alternate opening prayer from the Mass of the day.

Leader: Grace and peace be with you.

All: And also with you.

Leader: Let us pray.
Father in heaven, author of all truth,
a people once in darkness has listened to
your Word
and followed your Son as he rose from the
tomb.

Hear the prayer of this newborn people
and strengthen your Church to answer
your call.
May we rise and come forth into the light
of day
to stand in your presence until eternity
dawns.
We ask this through Christ our Lord.

All: Amen.

REFLECTION

1. We continue to hear the story of the meetings of the disciples with the risen Christ. At first those who knew Jesus express anxiety and frustration. These are feelings and reactions that each of us can recognize, are they not? How often do we want to be in control, to accomplish something all on our own?

    What experience have you had of turning a problem or project over to another, recognizing your own limitations? Have you heard the expression, "Let go, let God"? How does this fishing story illustrate this phrase? When have you "let go" of an anxiety or doubt? Are there areas in your life now that you could release?

2. We come to faith through the combination of the word and the Spirit. Through the Gospel witnesses we hear of the action of God in our midst, in the life of Jesus and the community of followers. Through the Spirit we are empowered to respond with the community of faith to come to know God in Jesus. To follow Jesus is to act.

    How did you come to hear the words: Follow me? How do you recognize Jesus in the Church?

    A dramatic presentation of the lives of the four women from the United States who were killed in El Salvador in 1980 has been written. It is called "Guilty of the Gospel." Can you think of other contemporary examples of the acts of Christians where the established order is shaken to try to silence them? In the 1980's, the United States Catholic bishops wrote two letters to their church; one on peace and one on the economy. What is the Church called to do now to follow Jesus? What are you called to do? Do you see the work of the Spirit in calling and guiding you?

3. The community of believers gathers together to praise God. When you entered the catechumenate, you expressed your choice to enter this community, this Church. You entered into the order, the discipline, of the way of life and way of worship of the Church.

    The Book of Revelation, as we said before, is written in image language. Can you describe your choice to become Church in images? For example, can you imagine the Christian life bringing order out of chaos (a creation image)? There are other images in today's alternate opening prayer. What are your images?

CLOSING PRAYER

There are many areas of our lives where we could be anxious, overwhelmed, or fearful. The Church prays daily to experience God's freedom and peace. Invite all to bring those things to prayer. As a sign of letting go, also invite all to open their hands and turn them upward.

Leader: Let us pray.
Mighty God,
you call us to life, to live in your light.

	Hear these obstacles, these walls, these anxieties, which hinder us . . .
All:	(Each one can name something. The leader and catechists can begin. There should be pauses.)
Leader:	Deliver us, Lord, from all anxiety and grant us your peace. We ask this through Christ, our Lord.
All:	Amen.

Doctrinal and Pastoral Issues: Vocation, Pastoral Letters on Peace and Economy, Social Justice

Elizabeth Lilly

Fourth Sunday of Easter

Acts 13:14, 43–52
Revelation 7:9, 14–17
John 10:27–30

OPENING PRAYER

The following is the alternate opening prayer of the Mass of the day.

Leader: Grace and peace be with you.

All: And also with you.

Leader: Let us pray.
God and Father of our Lord Jesus Christ,
though your people walk in the valley of
    darkness,
no evil should they fear;
for they follow in faith the call of the shep-
    herd
whom you have sent for their hope and
    strength.
Attune our minds to the sound of his voice,
lead our steps in the path he has shown,
that we may know the strength of his out-
    stretched arm
and enjoy the light of your presence for
    ever.
We ask this in the name of Jesus the Lord.

All: Amen.

The leader could then play or sing one of the local community's hymns related to the image of the good shepherd or to the theme of dependence on God such as "Only in God" (Glory and Praise, Vol 1, North American Liturgy Resources, 1977).

REFLECTION

1. Security is something that occupies a good part of our time. The number of ways to lock up, protect and defend our health, income, nation, way of life, belongings, etc., seems to increase every year. And yet, we know that all of these things can be "snatched out of our hands."

   If we recognize our need for security, can we also recognize our need for salvation? When do we acknowledge our dependence on the power of the risen Christ? What gives us true security? How can the image of the "good shepherd" have impact for twentieth century disciples?

2. The work of the Word and the Spirit is the work of transformation.

   When we examine our values, our time, our relationships, what are we saying about our trust in God? How are we changing any part of our lives in this process of coming to follow the Lord?

   When are we tempted, like some of the people of Antioch, to "expel" from our lives the invitation to change?

3. Each of us holds an image of God. Today's readings give an image of the shepherd who will never let his flock know hunger or homelessness.

   Compare and contrast this image of God with other images. What is attractive about the image of shepherd even in an urban environment? Perhaps, especially in the inner city, we are aware of the numbers of homeless and the need for shelter.

CLOSING PRAYER

Reread the Gospel. If a deacon is a member of the group, he could do this. Pause for a few moments of silence at the end of the passage.

Deacon: This is the Gospel of the Lord.

All: Praise to you, Lord Jesus Christ.

Deacon: Go in peace.

All: Thanks be to God.

Doctrinal and Pastoral Issues: Hierarchy, Pastoral Leadership, Catholic Worker Houses, Image of God, Trust

Elizabeth Lilly

Fifth Sunday of Easter

Acts 14:21–27
Revelation 21:1–5
John 13:31–33, 34–35

OPENING PRAYER

The following prayer is adapted from the concluding prayer of the Rite of Becoming a Catechumen.

Leader: Grace and peace be with you.

All: And also with you.

Leader: Let us pray.
God of heaven and earth,
keep your servants joyful in hope
and faithful in your service.
Lead them, Lord, to the waters of baptism
that give new life.
May the eternal joy you promise
be the reward of all
who spend their lives in good works.
We ask this through Christ our Lord.

All: Amen.

REFLECTION

1. Recall the definitions proposed in the reflection for the second Sunday of Easter. What is faith? Do we have it? Do we need reassurance like the Christians of Antioch?

   In his book *Catholicism*, Richard McBrien states three components of faith: conviction, trust, and commitment. Throughout the accounts from the Acts of the Apostles we have heard the conviction: "Jesus is Lord." We have heard accounts of the trust that the apostles had in the Lord, and by their own testimony and travels we learn of their commitment.

   In the Rite of Becoming a Catechumen, you were instructed in these or similar words:

   You have followed God's light.
   Now the way of the Gospel opens before you,
   inviting you to make a new beginning
   by acknowledging the living God
   who speaks his words of truth to all.
   You are called to walk by the light of Christ
   and to trust in his wisdom.
   He asks you to submit yourself to him more
      and more
   and to believe in him with all your heart.
   This is the way of faith
   on which Christ will lovingly guide you
   to eternal life.

   Share some of the signs of conviction, trust, and commitment that you have noticed in the past several months. People can speak for themselves or for another member of the group, giving reassurances.

2. Church, the community of believers, sharing the common faith, giving on-going encouragement and instruction, with "prayer and fasting" is what we are about.
   What have you seen in the parish, the diocese, the universal Church that shows the Church being about its work? Where can you challenge the Church to be about its work, its mission?

3. Entering the reign of God is the mission of the Church. The discipline for this is the commandment: Love one another.
   What are some examples of dying to self that each of us encounters in our family or workplace? How do we balance the tension between the need for personal time and the commitment to serve others? How did Jesus? Share times when this has been easy or difficult, anticipated or unexpected for you. When have these times of dying to self brought about a healing or a wholeness? How do you experience loving another and being loved by another? Which is more comfortable?

CLOSING PRAYER

The following prayer, the Act of Charity, should be available for each person to have a copy to keep.

Leader: Let us pray.

All: O my God,
I love you above all things,
with my whole heart and soul,
because you are all good
and worthy of all my love.
I love my neighbor as myself for the love of
    you.
I forgive all who have injured me
and I ask pardon of all whom I have in-
    jured.
Amen.

Doctrinal and Pastoral Issues: Theological Virtues, Parish Life, Social Justice, Conviction, Commitment

Elizabeth Lilly

Sixth Sunday of Easter

Acts 15:1–2, 22–29
Revelation 21:10–14, 22–23
John 14:23–29

OPENING PRAYER

This prayer is modeled after the opening prayers of the ritual Mass of Confirmation.

Leader: Grace and peace be with you.

All: And also with you.

Leader: Lord,
   send us your Holy Spirit
   to help us walk in unity of faith
   to become more Christ-like
   and to discern your will
   as we seek your truth.
   Grant this through our Lord Jesus Christ,
   your Son,
   who lives and reigns with you
   and the Holy Spirit,
   one God, for ever and ever.

All: Amen.

REFLECTION

1. Today we face some of the apparent paradoxes and contradictions of the Church. Jesus gives the gift of his peace to the disciples, yet in the first reading we hear of differences within the early Christian communities. We also hear that a particular difference in understanding is resolved. Reread the words of the resolution: "It is the decision of the Holy Spirit, and ours too." The gift of peace and the presence of the Holy Spirit are one.

   Prayer is our way of discerning the will of God, the direction of the Spirit, the way of Jesus, in our lives. When we engage in prayer, formal or informal, in word or action, we are opening ourselves to God's presence. Prayer is necessary for discernment. Types of prayer vary from praise and thanksgiving to forgiveness and petition. The Mass includes all of these.

Identify these forms as we experience them in the Mass. Reflect and share how these types of prayer are lived, in word and action, by the Christian. How do we open ourselves to the presence of the Spirit?

2. The second reading continues to give an image of order and harmony, or completion and balance.

   When, faced with apparent chaos and imbalance, disorder and disharmony, have you relied on a dream or vision of wholeness to choose your course of action? What is your image of wholeness or harmony? Can you call this the kingdom of God? Can you discern the action of the Spirit in your choices?

3. Last week we spoke of the need for instruction and reassurance within the Church. In today's Gospel it is the Holy Spirit who "will instruct you in everything, and remind you of all that I told you." Discernment of the will of the Spirit, the way of truth, is tricky business. Traditionally, the Church seeks to know the truth through prayer, through the gathering of the Church in councils and synods, and through the common understanding of the Church or the sense of the faithful.

   For an individual, there is a responsibility to form a conscience in tune with the Spirit in the Church. Our conscience acts when we make moral decisions. A Christian conscience will base decisions on the values of the Gospel.

   Share some examples of conscientious decisions that one might make. These could be related to war and peace, to family life, to death. In reality, we make conscientious decisions on a daily basis. Identify these and share them in the group.

CLOSING PRAYER

Invite each person to reflect for a moment and recall something for which to give thanks and something which needs healing or forgiveness or strength.

Leader: Let us pray in thanksgiving for graces received, and in petition for our needs and the needs of others.

All: (After each prayer) Lord, hear our prayer.

Leader: Lord,

we give you praise
and we place our needs before you
with faith in your love and care for us.
We pray in the name of Jesus,
who lives with you and the Spirit.

All: Amen.

*Doctrinal and Pastoral Issues: Prayer, Conscience,
Heaven, Discernment*

Elizabeth Lilly

Ascension Thursday

(Thursday after Sixth Sunday of Easter)

Acts 1:1–11
Ephesians 1:17–23
Luke 24:46–53

OPENING PRAYER

The following litany of petitions is taken from the Letters of Paul. They should be read slowly, with time between the entreaty and the invitation to pray which is followed by the response.

Leader: Grace and peace be with you.

All: And also with you.

Leader: Let us pray.
God of our Lord Jesus Christ,
Father of glory,
hear our prayer.

Reader: Grant us the spirit of wisdom
and insight to know you clearly.

Leader: We pray to the Lord.

All: Lord, hear our prayer.

Reader: Enlighten our innermost vision.

Leader: We pray to the Lord.

All: Lord, hear our prayer.

Reader: Grant us hope.

Leader: We pray to the Lord.

All: Lord, hear our prayer.

Reader: Fill us with your power.

Leader: We pray to the Lord.

All: Lord, hear our prayer.

Leader: We ask these things
in the name of Jesus Christ, our Lord.

All: Amen.

REFLECTION

1. Power: the word is strong. What words do you associate with it, or what adjectives do you join with it? Did "power corrupts" come to mind?

   In today's readings, power is an attribute of God and a gift of God: "full authority has been given to me."

   Name some of the areas in our lives, personal or communal, where we need to be empowered by God to live into the kingdom of God? What areas of injustice need to be made just? What areas of violence need to become peaceful? What areas of fear need to turn to trust? What areas of despair need to be filled with hope? Continue with your own areas of need.

   What kind of conversion is needed for power to move in the way of the Lord?

   Can you imagine the difference between power for its own sake and power for the sake of the kingdom? Have you experienced either or both kinds of power?

2. Another name for the Church is the body of Christ. Today's feast is not a commemoration of the risen Christ leaving his followers. Rather, it is a feast of the union of Christ with the Church of all time and eternity.

   As the Easter season comes to an end, how, in your judgment or experience, is the Church the body of Christ? What criteria do you use? Does the Church give glory to God? Is the Church servant? How is the Church shepherd? The Church can be described by many models or images. Each one will speak to us at different times and in different situations. Which model or aspect of the Church is most attractive to the members of the group?

3. There is work to be done to follow Christ. Where can you become involved? All of you could look in the ordinary everyday places and situations of your lives. In the Easter stories, the apostles returned to familiar places. Where do we encounter the risen Lord in our everyday lives?

CLOSING PRAYER

Introduce, briefly, the core of liturgical prayer: to give thanks and praise. The following prayer is the Preface of Ascension (I). If possible, the Holy should be sung. A musician could be present, or a tape of the Holy best known in the parish could be played once and then repeated so that all could join in the prayer.

Leader: Let us pray.
Father, all-powerful and ever-living God,
we do well always and everywhere
to give you thanks.
The Lord Jesus, the king of glory,
the conqueror of sin and death,
ascended to heaven
while the angels sang his praises.
Christ, the mediator between God and
man,
judge of the world and Lord of all,
has passed beyond our sight,
not to abandon us but to be our hope.
Christ is the beginning, the head of the
Church;
where he has gone, we hope to follow.
The joy of the resurrection
and the ascension renews the whole world,
while the choirs of heaven sing
for ever to your glory:

All: Holy, holy, holy Lord,
God of power and might.
Heaven and earth are full of your glory.
Hosanna in the highest.
Blessed is he who comes in the name of
the Lord.
Hosanna in the highest.

Doctrinal and Pastoral Issues: Models of Church, Body of Christ, Liturgical Prayer, Power, Authority, Kingdom of God

Elizabeth Lilly

Seventh Sunday of Easter

Acts 7:55–60
Revelation 22:12–14, 16–17, 20
John 17:20–26

OPENING PRAYER

Today's Gospel is a prayer, the prayer of Jesus. Invite all to listen to it again, and to focus on the personal message: "I pray for you."

Leader: Reread the Gospel.

REFLECTION

1. We are nearing the end of the Easter season. We began with Jesus giving his disciples the power to forgive sins. We have grown to see that power is a gift of God, that it is received through the Holy Spirit. This is a power that dwells in the church.

   How has the Church, the Christian community, brought you to choose the way of God? How has the Church called you to continue to adapt your course in order to grow closer and closer with the will of Christ? In what ways can you name a turning, a choosing, that you are doing as part of your conversion journey? How are you empowered to do this? How are you gifted by the presence of the Holy Spirit?

2. The prayer of Jesus is a prayer for unity. The Church is one in Christ. Traditionally, the Church claims four signs of unity: one, holy, catholic, and apostolic.

   What are the signs of the Church in the world today that are signs of unity? How is the Church holy, for example? Reflect upon the difference between union in Christ and uniformity?

   What are the human times when we experience unity or oneness? Think how often sharing and remembering an experience brings this about. Another way to experience unity is through a common action or behavior—a mannerism, or family trait, for example.

3. In Lent, eight Sundays ago, we heard from Isaiah, "For I put water in the desert and rivers in the wasteland for my chosen people to drink, the people whom I formed for myself, that they might an-

nounce my praise." Today, in the passage from the Book of Revelation, we again have the image of water: "Let him who is thirsty come forward; let all who desire it accept the gift of life-giving water."

   Thirst is a healthy sign of our need for God. Thirst is a good metaphor. How is God forgiving and life-giving? In what ways do you thirst? Is it difficult to accept the gifts of God?

CLOSING PRAYER

The following prayer is modeled on the intercessions from Morning Prayer for the Seventh Sunday of Easter.

Leader:	In the company of all who have been reconciled with God through the action of the Spirit, we pray: Lord Jesus, may we be guided by the Spirit, and walk in the light of God's truth.
All:	Come, O Spirit of God.
Leader:	Through your Spirit may we be worthy to receive what you promise.
All:	Come, O Spirit of God.
Leader:	Open our hearts, that we may care for the good of all.
All:	Come, O Spirit of God.
Leader:	Teach us to know God, that we may come into your kingdom.
All:	Come, O Spirit of God.
Leader:	O God, help us remember that Jesus Christ lives with you in glory and remains with us for all time. We ask this in the name of Jesus.
All:	Amen.

Doctrinal and Pastoral Issues: Ecumenism, Second Vatican Council, Signs of the Church, Deaconate and Ministry, Unity, Forgiveness

Elizabeth Lilly

Pentecost Sunday

Acts 2:1–11
1 Corinthians 12:3–7, 12–13
John 20:19–23

OPENING PRAYER

Reread Psalm 104, the psalm response. If a cantor can be with you, this could be sung. Or copies could be available and the group could read the psalm antiphonally.

Leader: Let us pray.
Lord, send out your Spirit,
and renew the face of the earth.

All: Lord, send out your Spirit,
and renew the face of the earth.

Or the group could sing one of the hymns of the Holy Spirit of the Church. One suggestion would be to repeat the opening song used in the entrance rite.

REFLECTION

1. Renewal. Throughout the last seven weeks we have had a hope of newness. The hope is imaged in visions and offered as gift. This gift is freely given and yet not fulfilled. Why? Why do we have difficulty accepting?

   Talk about the process of giving and receiving. Which is easier? Why is the other difficult? Both require a certain graciousness to be done well. When there is a lack of grace, are questions of trust, fear, worthiness, and indebtedness involved?

2. The gift of peace, Christ's peace, is accompanied by a mission, a sending. We usually think of peace as a restful state, linked with security. What is peaceful about being sent to an unknown destination?

   Can you recall any time in your life that you could describe a sense of inner peace in the midst of action or even disruption?

3. This is the same Gospel that we heard on the second Sunday of Easter just six weeks ago. Why do we hear it again? Why are we invited again to examine the gift of forgiveness?

   If sin is a rejection of God and peace a gift of God, could not forgiveness be related to how well we receive that gift? In accepting (or rejecting) the gift of peace, we are turning toward (or away from) God. Turning toward God is a sign of the forgiveness of sin.

   Recall times when you have experienced an acceptance by another, a peace between two people, a forgiveness.

4. The gift of peace and the forgiveness of sins are signs of unity with God. They are the action of the spirit of God already at work within us. These gifts are not limited to individuals, but are for all of creation, for the common good. The Church, as a whole and in all its members, is gifted with the presence of the Spirit and sent to do the Lord's work. This work is the continuing transformation of all into the realization and acceptance of the company of God.

   Pentecost is sometimes called the birthday of the Church. This is a good time to reflect on the mission of unity of the Church. Where do you see signs of unity? How is your awareness of coming into communion with God enhanced in the Church?

CLOSING PRAYER

Sing a song about the Holy Spirit.

Doctrinal and Pastoral Issues: Renewal in the Church, Work of the Spirit in the Church, Vatican Council II, Authority in the Church, Forgiveness of Sins, Mission, Gifts of the Spirit, Holy Spirit, Pentecost, Peace

Elizabeth Lilly

The Trinity and the Body of Christ

By Eugene A. LaVerdiere, S.S.

Between the Easter season, which ends on Pentecost, and the resumption of Sundays in Ordinary Time, we celebrate Trinity Sunday, Corpus Christi, and the Sacred Heart of Jesus. Every other feast in the liturgical year celebrates an event. These three feasts are unique in that they celebrate a mystery. Liturgically, this is somewhat awkward, but it does provide an opportunity to reflect on some very important aspects of Christian belief.

The Trinity

The Trinity as such is never mentioned in the New Testament. It entered our Christian vocabulary through the theological and doctrinal reflection of the early Church. To appreciate what it means, however, it is good to get behind the term "Trinity" and examine its background in the New Testament, where we find the Trinity in reflection on the life of the Father, the Son, and the Holy Spirit, their relationship to one another, and the way they enter human experience. On this Trinity Sunday, the Sunday after Pentecost, the Church invites us to do this with John 16:12–15.

The reading is from John's presentation of Jesus' farewell discourse. In it, Jesus is looking to the future when he no longer will be with his disciples (v. 16). Once Jesus will have gone, the Spirit will come to the disciples. As the Spirit of truth, he will guide them to all truth. He will enlighten them in matters which they cannot yet understand (vv. 12–13). What the Spirit will reveal is in continuity with what Jesus has already taught them. Indeed the Spirit will teach only what it hears from Jesus the Son (vv. 13–14). Further, all that Jesus has to share comes from the Father, and that means that the Spirit's teaching also ultimately will come from the Father.

There is then one source of truth and all teaching, namely, the Father, and there are two personal ways in which the truth is communicated. First, it was communicated through the Son in the person of Jesus. Second, it is to be communicated through the Holy Spirit in a new and mysterious experience which is nevertheless continuous with that of Jesus the Son.

The Body of Christ

On the second Sunday after Pentecost we celebrate the feast of the Body of Christ, Corpus Christi. All over the world, Christians focus on the mystery of Christ's presence in the Eucharist and through the Eucharist in the Church itself. Unlike the expression "Trinity," the "body of Christ" is found in the New Testament, where it is associated with both the assembly and the eucharistic nourishment. Its context, which is broader and more experiential than the much more highly focused doctrine highlighted by the feast, helps us keep the doctrine in perspective. For the feast, we turn to a reading from Luke 9:11–17, one of the accounts of what is popularly described as the multiplication of loaves.

The setting is a city, Bethsaida, and Jesus has welcomed a large crowd, which he is teaching. He is also healing all who are in need of it. The immediate occasion for the event is the disciples' reaction to the crowd. How could they possibly nourish such a large crowd? Besides, all these people needed a place to stay. The disciples ask Jesus to dismiss the crowd. Instead he asks them why they cannot give them something to eat. Jesus then shows them that when they share the little they have, all are wonderfully nourished. The story also evokes the eucharistic liturgy: Jesus raises his eyes to heaven, pronounces a blessing, breaks the bread and gives it. Such is the body of Christ and such is the Eucharist: a community happy to share the little it has, a bread generously shared with all, a community united in one meal.

Trinity Sunday

(Sunday after Pentecost)

Proverbs 8:22–31
Romans 5:1–5
John 16:12–15

OPENING PRAYER

A copy of this prayer could be available for each one to keep.

Leader: Glory be to the Father,
            to the Son,
            and to the Holy Spirit.

All: As it was in the beginning,
         is now and ever shall be
         world without end. Amen.

REFLECTION

1. We listened first to a reading from Proverbs, a creation story, a delightful, spirited, and playful creation story. Here we do not have the numbered days of the account in Genesis. How are we to reconcile different accounts of the same reality—the relationship of the Creator and the creation?

   We can look to the Gospel, the promise of the Spirit of truth. For several weeks we have dwelt upon the gift of the peace of Christ. Is the peace the same as the Spirit of truth? Recall that the image language of the Book of Revelation was a way to express a truth that was beyond ordinary words.

   Should there be only one correct way of expressing truth? Catholic tradition says "no." The truth of the creation story, for example, is God's initiative, God's presence, God's life in the creation.

   Can you think of examples where misunderstandings have developed just because people had different, correct ways of describing one event? Some are funny to look back upon. But ponder now for a few moments if there isn't some area of your life where, in defending a particular way of expression, you may be losing sight of the truth. Anyone in the group could share examples of this.

2. For many weeks we have been reflecting upon the peace of Christ. This we understand to be the peace and harmony of the existence of God, an existence in perfect relationship with itself. Peace, whether personal or between people or nations, is a harmony of members. The way Paul describes this is in and through the communion or the community of God, Jesus, and the Holy Spirit.

   Reflect upon your relationships. Where is there harmony and peace and where is this lacking? Reflect also on your style or method of praying, of being in union with God. Can you describe any times of prayer as times of peace? You can ask for God's peace.

3. Father, Son, and Spirit—Creator, Redeemer, and Sanctifier. This is our way to open our understanding to God. The underlying principle is the unity of God, one God in three persons.

   We name God in three persons when we make the sign of the cross. We open and close our prayer with this sign. How is the sign of the cross a sign of unity and of hope?

   In fact, how is hope crucial to the Christian belief? How is hope connected with our manner of professing our faith in the power of God?

CLOSING PRAYER

A very traditional prayer of praise and glory to God may be prayed aloud together or may be sung to the traditional tune.

> Praise God, from whom all blessings flow;
> Praise him, all creatures here below;
> Praise him above, ye heav'nly host;
> Praise Father, Son, and Holy Ghost.

Doctrinal and Pastoral Issues: Trinity, Creed, Inclusive Language, Theological Virtues of Faith, Hope, and Love

Elizabeth Lilly

Corpus Christi

(Second Sunday after Pentecost)

Genesis 14:18–20
1 Corinthians 11:23–26
Luke 9:11–17

OPENING PRAYER

The following litany of invocations is modeled on the form of the penitential rite with the response "Blessed be God."

Leader:	Let us pray. Lord Jesus, you healed the sick.
All:	Blessed be God.
Leader:	Lord Jesus, you fed the hungry.
All:	Blessed be God.
Leader:	Lord Jesus, you give us yourself to heal us and bring us strength.
All:	Blessed be God.
Leader:	Lord Jesus, you satisfy our hunger and thirst.
All:	Blessed be God.
Leader:	Lord Jesus, you raise us to new life.
All:	Blessed be God.
Leader:	Lord Jesus, you show us the way to the kingdom.
All:	Blessed be God.
Leader:	May God bless us all and bring us to everlasting life.
All:	Amen.

REFLECTION

1. Blessings are important aspects of today's readings.
   Melchizedek blesses Abram, and he blesses God. Jesus blesses loaves and fishes, and bread and wine. Blessings are our recognition of God in created things; they express our desire to be united with God, and our recognition of God at work within us. Blessings are related to the creative Spirit of God ever transforming all of creation into the life of the kingdom. Blessings are prayers to consecrate or make holy. To be blest, to be anointed, to be Christened, is to be in communion with God.
   Recall and share events, people, and actions which we call blessings. Have you ever heard of a "blessing in disguise"? How easily do we accept blessings? Do we recognize our own blessedness? Do we recognize that we are the body of Christ in the world?
   (Other references to blessing are in the Gospels for the Feast of the Assumption, the Magnificat, and for All Saints Day, the Beatitudes.)

2. Food images are associated with the kingdom of God throughout the Gospel. Often there is a dinner or banquet. This selection extends the "banquet," the abundance and absence of hunger and want, to thousands.
   How does this challenge us today to extend the abundance of God? When have we felt that we have reached our limits, like the apostles, wanting to dismiss whatever is left?

3. "In remembrance of me." The great prayer of the Mass is the thanksgiving prayer, or the Eucharist (which means thanksgiving). When bread and wine are brought to the altar, blessed, broken, and shared in remembrance of Jesus, they are made holy. The word sacrifice, from the Latin "sacra face," means just this—to make holy. Those sharing the bread and wine come into union with each other and the Lord. This ritual action is the Communion, the most profound sign of the Church.
   This Communion in meal or in banquet is also a sign of the kingdom. Experiencing this ritually, each one is touched by the truth of the presence of God. Ritual is only one way to participate in the kingdom. Jesus continually combined speaking about the kingdom with actions of healing. This impacts the whole of the life of the Christian.
   What signs of Communion, outside of the formal ritual prayer, do you see? What acts of Communion, of living the kingdom, of feeding the hungry, of healing, of praising God, are you practicing now? What have you shared with your sponsors and with your parish community?

CLOSING PRAYER

The prayer suggested below is one of the blessings encouraged by the RCIA. Examples are found in numbers 121–124, and 374.

Invite the catechumen to kneel (or stand, depending on local custom). The faithful present (catechists, sponsors) place their hands on the head or shoulders of the catechumen.

Leader: Let us pray.
Lord,
look with love on your servants
who reverence your holy name
and bow in worship before you.
Help them to accomplish all that is good;
touch their hearts
so that they may always be mindful
of your mighty works and your commandments
and so give themselves wholly to your covenant of love.
Grant this through Christ our Lord.

All: Amen.

Leader: Let us greet each other in blessing.
(Hug, embrace, or greet with a hand-
shake.)

All: God bless you!

Doctrinal and Pastoral Issues: Eucharist, Sacrament, Social Justice and the Hungry, Kingdom, Anointing, Body of Christ

Elizabeth Lilly

ORDINARY TIME

Jesus and His Disciples

Part I: Origins of the Church in the Ministry of Jesus

By Eugene A. LaVerdiere, S.S.

In this first series of Sundays in Ordinary Time, all but one of the Gospel readings are taken from Luke's Gospel. More specifically, with the exception of Luke 1:1–4, which forms part of the reading on the third Sunday, all the readings are taken from the story of Jesus' ministry in Galilee (4:14–9:50). The focus of this part of the Gospel is on how Jesus presented his basic message, called the first disciples, constituted them as a new Israel, formed them, and sent them out on mission.

The readings include the preface for Luke's Gospel, where the author introduces his work and sets out his purpose and method (1:1–4), Jesus' inaugural presentation in the synagogue at Nazareth (4:14–30) and the call of Peter and his partners (5:1–11). There are also excerpts from Jesus' Sermon on the Plain, a discourse on the way of life of those who enter into the new Israel (6:17, 20–26, 27–38, 39–45), as well as a story of healing (7:1–10), of raising from the dead (7:11–17), and of forgiveness (7:36–8:3). This first set of readings ends with Peter's profession of faith in Jesus as God's Messiah and its implications for Christian discipleship (9:18–24).

For the first Sunday, see the last Sunday of Christmastime, the Baptism of the Lord (Lk 3:15–16, 21–22), with which it coincides. The second Sunday, with its reading from John's Gospel, presents the first of Jesus' signs, the wedding feast at Cana, which gave meaning and provided the context for all the other signs (Jn 2:1–12).

The First of Jesus' Signs

For the first Sunday in Ordinary Time, see the Sunday after Epiphany, the Baptism of the Lord, with which it coincides. On the second Sunday, we turn to John's Gospel for the reading. The Church leads us in a reflection on the first of Jesus' many signs, not all of which were recorded as John goes out of his way to remind us in 20:30–31. The reading is the story of the wedding feast of Cana (2:1–12). From the outset we

should note that the Gospel calls it a sign, not a miracle. The two refer to the same reality, but they approach that reality from very different points of view. The word "miracle" draws attention to the way the event evokes wonder. It is one of the great wonders of the New Testament. The word "sign" highlights the event's meaning. The event at Cana is presented as symbolic of many things. Indeed it is the chief of Jesus' signs, the one which includes all the others.

Cana is the story of a wedding banquet, one of the great symbols for the life of Israel in the company of God. It is the story of how this wedding banquet was marvelously transformed by the presence of Jesus and his disciples. Suddenly there was an entirely new banquet, in continuity with that of Israel, but as different as wine is from water. The old banquet had run out of wine, and all that remained was water. From that water of the old, there came a new and far superior wine for the banquet of the Lord's table. Of course, chronologically, it was not time for this. The hour had not yet come. But it could be celebrated by anticipation, just as today in the Church we celebrate the heavenly banquet of the fullness of history, so certain are we that Christ will fulfill his promises.

Jesus of Nazareth

Beginning with the third Sunday in Ordinary Time and until the end of the year (thirty-fourth Sunday), all the readings are taken from the Gospel according to Luke. On this third Sunday, the reading includes the Gospel's preface, a word from the author to the reader (1:1–4), and the first part of Jesus' inaugural presentation in the synagogue at Nazareth (4:14–21).

In the preface, Luke sets out his intention in writing the Gospel and Acts. He wants to go over the events which have been fulfilled in our midst and set them down in order. He would like Theophilus and all his readers to have a deeper insight into what they already know. It is clear that he means to lead us in a reflection on experience that will bring us to new understanding, one that is adapted to new circumstances.

Jesus reads the Scriptures in the Nazareth synagogue. The text he quotes from Isaiah summarizes his entire life and mission. He is the anointed one, endowed with the Spirit. His mission is to bear good news, the Gospel, to the poor, to liberate captives, bring sight to the blind, release prisoners and announce a year of jubilee, when all debts are forgiven. To appreciate the reading we must inquire into the identity of the poor, the captives and the blind. In varying ways, do they not include all human beings?

Jesus' Challenge

On the fourth Sunday in Ordinary Time, we continue with the story of Jesus in the synagogue at Nazareth. Last Sunday, Jesus was introduced and we heard him read a text from Isaiah. He also applied it to the present moment. Today we hear the reaction of the assembly (Lk 4:21–30). First it reacted favorably, but it also wondered who he might be. He certainly was not acting and speaking like Joseph's son. If he was the son of Joseph, he was one of them, and whatever he announced had implications for them and for their mission. On the other hand, if he was not Joseph's son, then whatever he said might be interesting, but it made no special demands on them.

The story now moves into a second stage, and Jesus challenges the assembly again. He wants to move their concerns beyond their own self-interest. To do this he calls on the example of Elijah and Elisha, both of whom reached out beyond Israel to the Gentile world. The assembly had not been able to deny that Jesus was one of them. Unwilling to accept his challenge, they had but one remaining option—that is, to destroy him—but Jesus made his way through their midst and walked away. The episode is a summary of Jesus' entire life, from the beginning of his ministry to his passion, resurrection and ascension.

The Call of Simon Peter

Most of us are familiar with the story of Peter as we find it in Mark's Gospel. On this fifth Sunday in Ordinary Time, we read Luke's version of the same story, and find that it is extremely different (Lk 5:1–11).

A large crowd has gathered by the sea. To teach them more effectively, Jesus sat in Simon's boat and had him pull away from shore. When he finished, Jesus asked Peter to head out into the lake for some fishing. At his word, which is the word of God (v. 1), Peter did so and soon found himself overwhelmed with an enormous catch. His reaction focuses entirely on the person of Jesus, whom he confesses as his Lord. In doing so, he also acknowledges his sinfulness. Amazement seizes the others as well, including his partners, James and John. In response, Jesus merely tells them not to fear, and he announces that henceforth they would be catching human beings. In all this, Luke's version of the event is much closer to life as we know it. That of Mark and Matthew is more stylized.

The Beatitudes

On the sixth, seventh, and eighth Sundays in Ordinary Time, the Gospel reading is taken from Luke's Sermon on the Plain, the Lukan equivalent of Matthew's Sermon on the Mount. The Lukan version (6:20–49) is much shorter than that of Matthew (chapters 5–7).

On the sixth Sunday the reading includes part of the introduction, in which Luke situates the discourse on a level stretch where many of Jesus' disciples have gathered together with a large crowd of people, including many who were sick or troubled with unclean spirits. It is in this context that Jesus raises his eyes to his disciples to speak the beatitudes and the woes. "Blessed are you poor . . . hungry . . . weeping." By reaching out and bringing good news to the poor, sick, and hungry around him, Jesus had just demonstrated why they were blessed. The woes are given by contrast. The reading also applies the blessings and woes to the persecutions experienced by the early Christians.

Loving One's Enemy

On the seventh Sunday, the reading takes up two important themes from Jesus' Sermon on the Plain— love of one's enemy and compassion (6:27–38).

Most would agree that the distinguishing characteristic of Jesus' ethic is his call to love one's enemies. It is also the most difficult. Certainly it is not easy to love anyone with the selflessness of Jesus even when the person is a friend. Even more difficult, however, is to love everyone, including those who are perceived as enemies. The Gospel spells out the implications of this demand very concretely. In the background we should retain the image of Jesus forgiving those who tortured him and put him to death. For Jesus, these people did not know what they were doing. Neither do those who strike out at the Church or at any of its members today.

Jesus himself did not judge and condemn. He forgave and he did so generously. That is what he asks of his disciples. They should be as compassionate as God himself is compassionate. Their forgiveness should be marked by generosity.

A Disciple's Life

For the third Sunday in a row, the reading is drawn from Jesus' Sermon on the Plain as presented by Luke. On this eighth Sunday, we hear three images concerning the life of a disciple (6:39–45).

First, we have the image of the seeing and blind. In the Christian community, as in all forms of discipleship, those who see guide the blind, and not the reverse. That is, the teachers, elders and prophets guide the disciples. One day, however, the disciples will have learned to see and then they may guide.

The second image also deals with sight. There are those who see but they have something blocking their vision. Isn't it interesting how those who have a huge beam or plank in their eye are so intent on removing a tiny speck from their brother's eye?

The third image is based on popular observation. The fruit you get depends on the kind and quality of the tree. So with human beings. From someone with a good heart, you will get only good things. "Each one speaks from the abundance of the heart."

A Centurion's Faith

In Luke's Gospel, Jesus does not formally undertake a mission to the Gentiles. This is left for the apostolic Church in the Acts of the Apostles. However, this does not mean that Jesus avoids all ministerial contact with Gentiles. Such was the case in Matthew, where Jesus expressly indicates that he was sent only to the lost sheep of the house of Israel (see Mt 15:24). In Luke, there are encounters with Gentiles. They announce the great Gentile mission which will be sparked by Pentecost.

On the ninth Sunday in Ordinary Time, we read about a centurion, an important military officer, whose servant was mortally ill. The centurion was a very humble man. Rather than go to Jesus himself, he sent some Jewish elders. Then rather than have Jesus come all the way to his house, he went to meet him on the way. He did not deem himself worthy of having Jesus in his home. His faith was as strong as his humility. It was not necessary for Jesus to come all the way. A word from Jesus would do. The centurion's extraordinary faith, surpassing any that Jesus had seen before, prepares the way for the future Gentile mission.

A Widow's Son

On the tenth Sunday, the scene returns to a Jewish context. A widow has lost her only son. As the large crowd carrying the body passed by, Jesus was moved with pity. After quieting the crowd, he addressed the young man directly: "I ask you to get up!" To everyone's astonishment, the young man did so (Lk 7:11–17).

The story has many implications. First, it is a source of divine praise. All present recognize the hand of God in the event. Surprisingly, the young man seems to be completely forgotten as all focus on the person of Jesus. The story's Christological emphasis is obvious. Second, the context in which the story appears, the story of the founding of the new Israel, also speaks to us of history and a new historical moment. The new Israel requires more than healing. It calls for a raising from the dead.

A Woman Who Loved Much

The new Israel was a world in which all could be reconciled, even those who had long felt excluded. On this eleventh Sunday in Ordinary Time, Jesus is in the home of a wealthy Pharisee, at table with a number of guests, when a woman enters, kneels behind Jesus and begins to weep over his feet (Lk 7:36–50). The Pharisee, who is at the center of this story, is astonished. He cannot imagine that a genuine prophet would allow the woman to do this. Jesus proceeds to show him that he welcomes the woman precisely because he is a true prophet. As a prophet, Jesus is a minister of reconciliation. He allows the woman to express her gratitude. Reconciled, she is filled with love, and she has come to express that love.

To bring the point home, Jesus dwells on the contrast between the way the Pharisee welcomed him and the way the woman has expressed her love. Like the Pharisee, we are left to ponder the event. Perhaps we take our relationship to Christ for granted!

The reading also includes the beginning of chapter 8 (vv. 1–3), where we see the circle of disciples expanded to include a group of women. The indication that these women were sinners should not be over-emphasized. The men also were sinners.

Profession of Faith

The first series of Sundays in Ordinary Time ends with the twelfth. Its theme is Peter's profession of faith (Lk 9:18–24). Important developments in the story of Jesus occur in the context of prayer. Once, while he was in seclusion with his disciples, Jesus turned from his prayer and asked his disciples about his identity. Who did the crowds say he was? Peter answered: "The Christ of God."

The passage then takes up the challenge which comes from such a profession. The Christ of God is the Son of Man, *the* human being, and as such he must suffer and die. Jesus also outlines the conditions of his death. In this we have a prophetic statement of the early Christian community. Every Christian had to face this reality. Moreover, it was a reality not only for Jesus but for all his followers. To those who heard Peter's confession, and his prophetic statement, Jesus added that all those who wanted to be his followers had to take up their own cross in his steps. His disciples received by giving to others. They would be saved by offering their lives with Jesus that others might live.

Introduction to Sundays 2–12 in Ordinary Time

Each catechetical session in this section contains the following movements:

  Focusing
  Looking at Life
  Sharing Our Life
  Knowing Our Faith
  Making the Faith Our Own
  Living Our Faith
  Closing Prayer

Additionally, the basic theme of the Sunday readings is suggested. A focusing activity provides the catechist with suggestions for shaping a conducive environment for prayer and sharing.

A variety of prayer experiences flow through these Sundays. The catechist may wish to expand upon these or to abbreviate them according to local needs. Most of the prayer experiences are more reflective than active. This type of structuring provides catechumens with some opportunity for a quiet that often is otherwise lacking in their busy lives. Music has been selected from *Glory and Praise* published by North American Liturgy Resources, Phoenix, AZ.

The process suggested in these sessions moves from reflection on personal stories to the tradition's story toward application in our on-going life stories. Invitations to sharing and to reflecting critically are integral to each session. In Knowing our Faith, the focal message of the Gospel is shared in relation to the theme. Two or three approaches appear in the development of this section. These approaches may be used singly or developed as one complete reflection. Making the Faith Our Own and Living Our Faith suggest directions and possibilities for engaging in an active faith response. Finally, the Doctrinal and Pastoral Issues most relevant to the readings are highlighted.

Second Sunday in Ordinary Time

Isaiah 62:1–5
1 Corinthians 12:4–11
John 2:1–12

Theme: Signs

FOCUSING

The room might be adorned with some familiar liturgical signs which carry us from Christmastide into Ordinary Time—water (baptism), light (Epiphany). The focusing event simply involves reflective music such as John Michael Talbot's "Come to the Quiet" and a reading on the sign of God's presence in our midst.

LOOKING AT LIFE

Which signs speak most powerfully to you in your everyday journey?

What are some of the signs of God's presence that you have experienced since we last gathered?

SHARING OUR LIFE

Share with someone in the group your experience of one sign of God's presence.

Why has that sign spoken to you?

What is its meaning in your life right now?

KNOWING OUR FAITH

Narrative reading of John 2:1–12
Narrator
Jesus
Mary

I. Today continues the themes of baptism and Epiphany. We see Jesus, the sign of God, manifest his power and concern at a wedding celebration in Cana of Galilee. John points out the importance of signs within the context of his entire Gospel. Signs are manifestations of Jesus' glory.

Let us be aware of the signs that surface for us as we probe the Gospel:

Mary's request as a sign of concern for the couple
Jesus' response to Mary
Jesus changing of water to wine
Waiter's surprise
Couple's belief
Disciples' belief
Jesus celebrating

We recognize the power of signs on many levels in this Cana experience and realize that it points toward the greater signs of Jesus' life and ministry. Cana represents the beginning of Jesus' signs. John relates Cana to the other miracles and to a concrete place in the ministry of Jesus.

II. Mary's role in this scene points toward her future role at the foot of the cross. Mary is the new Eve, the symbol of the Church. The Church has no role during Jesus' public ministry but only during the hour of his resurrection and ascension.

III. This first sign reveals the person of Jesus. Jesus is the one sent by God to bring salvation to the world. What shines through the Cana event is Jesus' glory, and the reaction on the part of the new disciples is belief.

MAKING THE FAITH OUR OWN

Which one of the signs within this story speaks to me?

Which one do I need to reflect upon more?

How do I experience Jesus within the Cana story?

LIVING OUR FAITH AND CLOSING PRAYER

Let us be aware of the signs of God's presence that come to us from within the many communities that we are part of as we listen to the second reading from Paul's First Letter to the Corinthians. Conclude with "Sing a New Song" by Dan Schutte S.J. (*Glory and Praise*, #47).

Doctrinal and Pastoral Issues: Signs, Sacraments, Covenant, Church as Sacrament, Miracles, Jesus, Mary

Nancy Sheridan

Third Sunday in Ordinary Time

Nehemiah 8:2–4, 5–6, 8–10
1 Corinthians 12:12–30
Luke 1:1–4; 4:14–21

Theme: Jesus' Mission

FOCUSING

A slide meditation highlighting poverty, bondage and blindnesses of various kinds, and imprisonment could provide an appropriate form of introduction to this week's reflections.

Narration: "Economic Justice for All," Nos. 31–55 "The Cry of the Poor" by John B. Foley, S.J. (*Glory and Praise, #93*).

LOOKING AT LIFE—SHARING OUR LIFE

What is your understanding of the word mission?

Do you have a mission in life?

Have you ever reflected on Jesus' mission?

What do you consider Jesus' mission to be?

KNOWING OUR FAITH

I. Luke's prologue sets forth Jesus' personal identity as a Gospel statement which clarifies the identity of the readers and challenges them to missionary discipleship. The Gospel presents Jesus as prophet. The Spirit of the Lord is upon Jesus at the very beginning of the public ministry. Jesus is the sole agent of the Holy Spirit throughout his ministry.

II. Luke's Gospel is often called the Gospel of prayer and the Gospel of the poor and outcasts. Luke impresses on the rich that it is their religious duty to share their good things with the poor. For all those in pursuit of a deeper and genuine spirituality, Luke shows us when and how to pray. All those who might be overwhelmed by the needs of people in our world and by the apparent inability of the Church and society in general to meet these needs are reminded that God guides history according to his plan and that we are at best instruments of the Holy Spirit.

III. Read Luke 4:14–21. Jesus' mission is proclaimed in the words of the prophet Isaiah. The particulars of the mission highlight concern for the outcasts—the poor, the captives, those in blindness, prisoners. The initial response of Jesus' hearers is one of awe. The mission indicates Jesus' universal outreach. Jesus' mission outreach must be the concern of all who claim relationship with him. The power of the Spirit endows Jesus' teaching with authority. Jesus' role as teacher is integral to his mission.

MAKING THE FAITH OUR OWN

Do we experience Jesus' invitation to mission as uncomfortable or challenging?

LIVING OUR FAITH

The U. S. bishops' pastoral letter on the economy, "Economic Justice for All," is a contemporary restatement of Jesus' mission as it touches our lives today. Let us reflect on the pastoral in light of Jesus' mission. A helpful aid would be the "Catholic Update" on the pastoral letter (St. Anthony Messenger Press).

CLOSING PRAYER

Once again sing "The Cry of the Poor"

Doctrinal and Pastoral Issues: Power of the Spirit, Jesus, Mission, Isaiah, Prophet, Law, Teacher, Economic Pastoral

Nancy Sheridan

Fourth Sunday in Ordinary Time

Jeremiah 1:4–5, 17–19
1 Corinthians 12:31—13:13
Luke 4:21–30

Theme: Prophet's Message

FOCUSING

"Be Not Afraid" by Bob Dufford, S.J. (Glory and Praise, #8). Reading: *The Prophetic Imagination*, pp. 110–11 (W. Bruggeman, Fortress Press, 1978)

LOOKING AT LIFE—SHARING OUR LIFE

Whom do you consider to be a prophet?

What is your understanding/experience of prophets?

Have you ever felt called to be a prophet?

Jeremiah received a call to be a prophet, and we might imagine that he experienced within himself some of the same questions we ask ourselves about what it means to be a prophet.

Reading: Jeremiah 1:4–5, 17–19

In the continuation of last Sunday's reading Jesus, too, moves from a moment of acceptance and adulation to a moment of hostility and rejection.

Reading: Luke 4:21–30

KNOWING OUR FAITH

I. The first reading and Gospel focus some basic reflections on the call of the prophet. Insight into Jesus' prophetic role among the Jews sets the tone for the Lucan readings that follow.

II. This portion of chapter 4 points out the challenge of Jesus' mission and signals unfavorable reactions to his teachings. Efforts to destroy Jesus led to a deepening sense of his mission and ultimately to his glorification.

III. Jesus' identity is a mystery for those who try to limit his mission to their own human and religious sphere. Jesus embodies the message that a prophet's message falls hard on the ears of those who are closest to him. Jesus' message extends beyond the Jews to all peoples.

IV. Rejection of Jesus in his own town becomes a symbol and an anticipation of the rejection he is to meet at the end of the Gospel.

MAKING THE FAITH OUR OWN

What do the experiences of Jeremiah and Jesus say to us about being prophets?

What can we expect? What can we look forward to?

LIVING OUR FAITH

Let us spend some time this week becoming more aware of the prophets in our midst.

CLOSING PRAYER

The motivation of the prophet comes to us from Paul's hymn on love (1 Cor 13).

Let us reflect on this reading as our closing prayer. Invite persons to read sections of the Corinthian letter reflectively.

Play some reflective instrumental music in the background such as "Winter" by George Winston.

Doctrinal and Pastoral Issues: Charity, Corinthians, Paul, Prophets, Prophecy, Rejection, Mission, Hebrew Scriptures, Elijah, Elisha, Naaman, Universal Mission

Nancy Sheridan

Fifth Sunday in Ordinary Time

Isaiah 6:1–2, 3–8
1 Corinthians 15:1–11
Luke 5:1–11

Theme: Call to Discipleship

FOCUSING—LOOKING AT LIFE—SHARING OUR LIFE

This guided imagery experience refocuses stories of personal call. It would be appropriate to introduce the process of guided imagery either before or after the exercise.

Background music: "Here I Am, Lord" by Dan Schutte, S.J. (*Glory and Praise*, #198).

Let us spend some moments realizing that we are surrounded by God's presence. As we reflect on the rhythm of our breathing let us be aware that our breath is a gift of life.

Realize that life is a gift, that life is a call to growth, to change, to struggle, to commitment.

Remember the moment when you first became aware of your call to life and who were the partners in that call.

What have been significant moments as the call has unfolded?

What have been the moments of fear, of struggle?

Recall my first awareness of Jesus' call to you.

What words of Jesus call you in a particular way?

What must you sacrifice to respond to the call?

Spend the next few moments remembering and being thankful.

Invite those who are willing to share their reflections. Be attentive to those who might have found the exercise painful or difficult. Read Isaiah 6:1–2, 3–8.

KNOWING OUR FAITH

The call of Isaiah parallels the experience of the call of the first disciples.

Proclaim Luke 5:1–11

I. The power of Jesus in word and deed is illustrated dramatically in the call of the first disciples. The miraculous catch of fish demonstrates the power of Jesus' word. The implications of the call to discipleship surface within this scene:

> they are not to be afraid;
> response to the call requires sacrifice;
> with Jesus' power they will bring God to others;
> they will share in a life-giving ministry.

II. Peter emerges as a central figure in relationship to Jesus. Peter's confessional statement points to his ongoing role in relationship to Jesus. Simon is overcome by the divine presence in Jesus. In the latter part of the passage we see him renamed Simon Peter. This passage points to other scenes wherein Peter will figure prominently.

MAKING THE FAITH OUR OWN—LIVING OUR FAITH

What similarities and/or differences do I see between the call stories of Isaiah and Jesus and my own?

CLOSING PRAYER

"The Journey," *Images: Women in Transition* (St. Mary's Press, 1977).

Doctrinal and Pastoral Issues: Call, Vocation, Discipleship, Ministry, Simon Peter, Apostles, Storytelling

Nancy Sheridan

Sixth Sunday in Ordinary Time

Jeremiah 17:5–8
1 Corinthians 15:12, 16–20
Luke 6:17, 20–26

Theme: Beatitudes, Synthesis of Christian Life

FOCUSING

A flowering bush or tree could provide a focal point for the prayer experience of the next three Sundays.

Pray Psalm 1:1–2, 3, 4, 6

Background: *The Quiet* by John Michael Talbot (Sparrow Corporation, 1985)

LOOKING AT LIFE

What are my basic values?

What factors have formed my values?

What are the basic values of our family?

What are the basic values of our society?

SHARING OUR LIFE

Do my basic values influence my present choices?

Have my basic values been instrumental in bringing me to this place in my life?

In what ways is Jesus a part of my value system?

These reflections may be journaled, shared in pairs, shared in a small group.

KNOWING OUR FAITH

Reading of Luke 6:17, 20–26 (individual readers for blessings and woes). Luke's Beatitudes show us Jesus in the throes of his Galilean ministry.

I. Luke's sermon occurs on the plain (an ordinary spot)

since Luke reserves mountaintops as places of special communication between Jesus and the Creator. Having defined the Church as the new Israel, Luke turns to its fundamental characteristics by presenting the Beatitudes as a synthesis of life. The general stance of the Beatitudes includes all Christian behavior.

II. Jesus addresses the sermon to the disciples. The blessings and woes are positive teachings on love and warnings against false teachers. Blessings declare certain groups of people to be privileged recipients of God's special gifts. God is on their side, not against them. When the coming of God's kingdom brings about a dramatic reversal of status, these people will be exalted. The woes parallel the blessings in form and content. Jesus' mission to the poor and lowly contrasts human justice and God's justice. The mission of the disciple appears in terms of a paradox. The mystery of Christian suffering and persecution undergirds the response to a Beatitude way of life.

III. The tradition of the Church's social teaching continues to articulate and clarify the spirit of the Beatitudes for our time. The recent pastoral letters of the American bishops touch upon concerns of peace, racism, Hispanic culture, and economic justice. The teachings of the Beatitudes amplify Jesus' mission as articulated in the Gospel of the third Sunday.

MAKING THE FAITH OUR OWN

Written Reflection

Which of the Beatitudes or woes do you find most consoling, most able to embrace in your own value system?

Which of the Beatitudes or woes offers the greatest challenge to your basic value system?

How do the Beatitudes fare in face of society's values?

How are the Beatitudes signs of hope?

LIVING OUR FAITH

Do the Beatitudes invite me to change anything in the way I live out my value system?

Is there any way in which I can positively contribute a Beatitude vision to my family, school, workplace, parish community?

CLOSING PRAYER

"What Is Hope" (Ruben Alves, *Tomorrow's Child*).

Doctrinal and Pastoral Issues: Beatitudes, Disciples, Justice, Witness, Conversion, Reign of God

Nancy Sheridan

Seventh Sunday in Ordinary Time

1 Samuel 26:2, 7–9, 12–13, 22–23
1 Corinthians 15:45–49
Luke 6:27–38

Theme: Living Out the Beatitudes

FOCUSING

Opening reflection provides an opportunity for a variety of persons to read short articles highlighting persons responding compassionately. Sources might be local newspapers and the *National Catholic Reporter*. The final reader shares Luke 6:27–38.

LOOKING AT LIFE—SHARING OUR LIFE

Who have been people of compassion in your life?

Who are historical or contemporary figures of compassion? (Mother Teresa, Dorothy Day, Pope John Paul II, AIDS ministers, Jesus)

What characterizes a compassionate response?

KNOWING OUR FAITH

I. In the continuation of the Sermon on the Plain Jesus speaks to the multitude in a series of traditional sayings. He includes a number of parables to explain attitudes and behaviors of those who accept a Beatitude lifestyle.

II. The positive teachings on love (6:27–38) include a basic principle, four extreme examples and four motives. The basic principle of loving one's enemies goes beyond the Hebrew Scriptures in their teaching about loving one's neighbor. The four cases in 6:29–30 give extreme examples of how the principle of loving one's enemies can shape our lives and change our behavior patterns. In each example our behaviors are challenged. The three motives (6:31–38) are an invitation to act toward other people in a way that we wish they would act toward us. Imitating the example of Jesus, we treat others in a way we hope to be treated.

III. We love our enemies in order to be like God. To be a disciple it is not sufficient to do justice. We must give example to others. A disciple mediates God's love to everyone by pardoning as God pardons through Jesus.

IV. The Gospel focuses love of enemies and generosity in giving. Love in action implies advocacy on behalf of others, sensitivity to the poor and a sharing of our goods. The rule and measure which we apply in dealing with others will in turn be applied to us.

MAKING THE FAITH OUR OWN—LIVING OUR FAITH

The catechist provides a brief introduction to intercessory prayer and its place in the tradition of the Church. Shape an intercessory prayer experience for those in need of our compassion. Is there one instance in which as a group we can witness our compassion during the coming weeks?

CLOSING PRAYER

"Peace Prayer" by John B. Foley, S.J. (*Glory and Praise*, #40).

Doctrinal and Pastoral Issues: Witness, Compassion, Lifestyle, Love of Enemies, Parables, Justice, Charity

Nancy Sheridan

Eighth Sunday in Ordinary Time

Sirach 27:4–7
1 Corinthians 15:54–58
Luke 6:39–45

Theme: By Our Fruits Will We Be Known

FOCUSING

The branch or bush that was used during the sixth Sunday may be adorned with words or phrases from the three readings.

Psalm 92 may be recited singing a simple response at the beginning and end.

LOOKING AT LIFE

Reflect upon a word or phrase that is particularly meaningful in your life.

If you were to describe your life in terms of a motto or saying, what might that saying be?

SHARING OUR LIFE

How do you integrate the motto or saying into your daily life?

Why has this motto or saying become so significant to you over the years?

KNOWING OUR FAITH

I. The final section from the Sermon on the Plain presents concluding warnings against false teachers. These sayings highlight Jesus' controversies with the Pharisees and scribes but also the controversies surrounding false teachers within the early Christian community. The continuing presence of false teachers continues to present a struggle in our own times and points toward the need for discernment in our experiences of hearing and acting upon the word of God.

II. Read Luke 6:39–40, 41–42. The parables emphasize the need for personal faith and conversion in order to be genuine in our response to our brothers and sisters and in our putting into practice Jesus' teachings. One who fails to recognize one's own blindness and whose eyes have not been opened in faith cannot lead, teach or heal. We need to be aware that conversion is on-going and that we experience the process of conversion at various levels in our life.

III. Read Luke 6:43–45. The saying on the fruit tree is a comment on the relation between actions and internal dispositions. Like other sayings in the sequence it illustrates the contrast between those who are genuine religious leaders or teachers and those who do not understand the message of Jesus. A person's words flow out of what fills his or her heart. Discipleship involves on-going discernment and conversion so that our actions may be rooted in genuine dispositions of heart.

MAKING THE FAITH OUR OWN

Does this Gospel clarify the meaning of discipleship for you?

What struggles do I experience with discipleship in my own life?

What has been my experience with false teachers?

LIVING OUR FAITH

Does the experience of this Gospel shed any light on the way we continue to live our personal mottos?

CLOSING PRAYER

Centering prayer experience uses as a beginning focus the adorned tree. People may begin by quietly adding their mottos or phrases to the tree.

Play some reflective music, e.g., "Sea of Tranquility" by Phil Coulter (K-Tel, Ireland, 1984).

Doctrinal and Pastoral Issues: Word, Motivation, Evil, Jesus as Teacher, Judging, Conversion, Discernment

Nancy Sheridan

Ninth Sunday in Ordinary Time

1 Kings 8:41–43
Galatians 1:1–2, 6–10
Luke 7:1–10

Theme: Faith

FOCUSING

"Go Up to the Mountain" by Gregory Norbert (*Glory and Praise, #259*).

LOOKING AT LIFE

Journaling Exercise on Tapestry of Faith: This exercise reflects on the faith journey by inviting people to identify key relationships, milestone events, key foci of involvement and key authority figures in terms of certain periods in their faith journeys. The facilitator determines the periods of time for use within the reflection.

SHARING OUR LIFE

Share your tapestry with your sponsor using the following questions as a guide:

Do you see any patterns that have been repeated throughout your life? What are they?

Are there some things that haven't changed—some continuities in your life?

Have any milestone events changed your sense of meaning or purpose in life?

What kind of spiritual resources have been important to you?

At what times have these been important?

KNOWING OUR FAITH

I. The Gospel for the ninth and tenth Sundays presents insights into Luke's understanding of the power of Jesus' healing word. Jesus re-enters Capernaum for the first time since his divinely ordained departure at the end of 4:31–44. This passage focuses a central Lucan theme, the mission to the Gentiles. The story opens up the mission of Jesus to the Gentile world.

II. The role of the elders within this scene indicates the importance of the Jewish leaders who were antecedents of the presbyters or elders within the community for which Luke is writing. These elders represent some of the leaders of the early Church communities.

III. The centurion recognizes God's presence among the people in the person of Jesus. He communicates with Jesus through the elders as a sign of respect for protocol in dealing with religious leaders. The centurion provides a model for all non-Jews who come to believe in the power of Jesus. His faith is not supported by national tradition. Yet it is a strong faith based on the witness of Jesus' miraculous deeds and preaching. Luke reinforces the historical foundations of Gentile Christianity with the centurion's extraordinary manifestation of faith which surpasses even that of Israel. Luke echoes Solomon's earlier prayer that foreigners may come to the temple, the symbol of God's presence.

IV. The Gospel calls us to reflection on faith. Faith is always a free gift of God. Faith is dynamic rather than static. Faith experience understands actional, rational and passional dimensions. Faith moves through a series of developmental sequences in our lives. (See *Christian Religious Education* by Thomas H. Groome, Harper & Row, 1980, pp. 56–73.)

MAKING THE FAITH OUR OWN—LIVING OUR FAITH

Spend some time during the coming week thinking about your Creed, your statement of faith belief. Share your creed with someone close to you. The catechist may model this experience by sharing his or her own creed.

CLOSING PRAYER

"Journeys Ended, Journeys Begun" by Gregory Norbert (*Glory and Praise, #263*).

Doctrinal and Pastoral Issues: Faith, Healing, Miracles, Jesus' Healing Ministry

Nancy Sheridan

Tenth Sunday in Ordinary Time

1 Kings 17:17–24
Galatians 1:11–19
Luke 7:11–17

Theme: Compassionate Healing

FOCUSING—LOOKING AT LIFE

The room may be darkened, using only a single candle for light.

Luke 7:11–17 lends itself to guided meditation.

Background music: "The Artistry of Jean-Pierre Rampal" (Pickwick International, 1980).

> Let us relax and realize that we are in God's
> presence . . .
> Picture yourself as part of the large crowd ac-
> companying
> Jesus to Naim . . .
> Stand beside Jesus as he sees the widow's only
> son being carried out . . .
> Feel the anguish of the widowed mother . . .
> Watch Jesus as he sees the mother and is
> moved with pity . . .
> Hear him say:
> Do not cry . . .
> Young man, get up . . .
> Hear the young man speak . . . What does he
> say? . . .
> Experience the emotion as Jesus gives him
> back to his mother
> and the awe-struck crowd frantically spreads
> the news of the miracle.

SHARING OUR LIFE

Spend some time in conversation with Jesus as you experience him in the scene. Be aware that his care and concern are gifts to you just as they were to the woman.

Speak to him of your needs; share your gratitude.

KNOWING OUR FAITH

I. Read 1 Kings 17:17–24

Jesus shows his compassion for the widow of Naim's son as did the prophet Elijah before him. Jesus reveals God's power and mercy by raising the son to life. This story's human environment is totally Jewish. For the Gentiles (centurion), participating in the new Israel required faith and radical healing. For the Jews it implied resurrection.

II. The widow's son comes to life by the power of Jesus' words. The same language is used later in Luke to speak of Jesus' own resurrection. The similarities become apparent in the description of the reaction of the crowd. Jesus is Lord of life; the young man comes back to life through Jesus' words. When Jesus commands life, it is communicated and the young man manifests his regained life by speaking. Jesus' act of power points toward his own resurrection as the ground for all hope for resurrected life.

III. God's compassion heals and restores grief. Luke is telling us what kind of God is revealed in Jesus. Jesus' decision to intervene is an example both of his compassion and of his fulfilling the mission of bringing good news to the poor and lowly.

MAKING THE FAITH OUR OWN—LIVING OUR FAITH—CLOSING PRAYER

This session calls for some simple ritual which might include some gesture of anointing as a sign of healing. A possible source that can be adapted is found in *Prayers for the Seasons* by Lois Kikkert O.P., pp. 38–39 (Paulist Press, 1983).

Doctrinal and Pastoral Issues: Compassion, Widows, Elisha, Miracle, Resurrection, Death

Nancy Sheridan

Eleventh Sunday in Ordinary Time

2 Samuel 12:7–10, 13
Galatians 2:16, 19–21
Luke 7:36—8:3

Theme: Forgiveness

FOCUSING

Present a dramatic reading of Luke 7:36–50

Jesus

Narrator

Simon

LOOKING AT LIFE

When have I experienced forgiveness?

Who have been persons of forgiveness, of reconciliation in my life?

How have I experienced Jesus' forgiveness?

SHARING OUR LIFE

Is my experience of relating to Jesus more like that of Simon or that of the forgiven woman?

KNOWING OUR FAITH

I. The criticism of Jesus for associating with tax collectors and sinners is taken up in the incident with the sinful woman at Simon's banquet. Jesus' role as prophet is questioned because he allows the sinful woman to touch him. Again, the story raises controversy about the question of Jesus' identity.

II. Jesus establishes an immediate contrast between the sinful woman and the Pharisee. Jesus explains the contrast to Simon by means of a parable that at first seems to have no immediate application. What criterion does

Simon use in judging the woman? What criterion does Jesus the prophet use? The final point of the parable emphasizes that love and forgiveness can never be separated.

III. Jesus' response to the woman confirms the view that Luke's basic point is found in 7:47. The woman already demonstrates her love and Jesus consequently forgives her sin. Her love springs from a faith response to Jesus whom she recognizes as Lord. Her salvation comes from loving faith which calls forth the Lord's peace. Jesus brings forgiveness of sins. His presence means forgiveness to Simon and to the woman. Yet each repents and receives Jesus differently. Simon does so grudgingly; the woman does so with great love.

IV. The summary shift in Luke 8 reintroduces earlier themes. Jesus travels through cities and villages preaching. His preaching is the good news of the kingdom of God. The mention of women provides a link with Jesus' forgiveness of the sinful woman.

The listing of women at the end of this passage assumes that we are aware that women accompanied Jesus and the twelve. Jesus opens the teaching of the kingdom and the invitation to discipleship to women. This introduction of the women prepares us for their role in the passion-resurrection narratives where they are identified as the women who had followed Jesus from Galilee. These women point us toward the prominent role of women leaders in the Church of the Acts of the Apostles.

MAKING THE FAITH OUR OWN—LIVING OUR FAITH

What vision of forgiveness does Jesus hold out to us?

What might I need to change in my own attitudes toward those who desire forgiveness in my own circle of family, friends, associates?

Where do I recognize the need for forgiveness in the world?

What insights do the end of the Gospel offer regarding Jesus' attitude toward women?

CLOSING PRAYER

A simple service of reconciliation could include:

Psalm 32, experience of personal and social forgiveness, exchange of peace. "Hosea" by Gregory Norbert (*Glory and Praise*, #262).

Doctrinal and Pastoral Issues: Parable, Pharisees, Forgiveness, Reconciliation, Sinners, Kingdom of God, Sexism, Women in Ministry

Nancy Sheridan

Twelfth Sunday in Ordinary Time

Zechariah 12:10–11
Galatians 3:26–29
Luke 9:18–24

Theme: The Cost of Discipleship

FOCUSING

Praying of Psalm 63 using simple gestures—this would provide a gentle introduction to body prayer.

LOOKING AT LIFE—SHARING OUR LIFE

Throughout a number of Sundays in this Ordinary Time we have gained insight into what it means to be a disciple.

Let us spend some time together creating a portrait of a Christian disciple. Are there people in our immediate surroundings who make this portrait come alive?

KNOWING OUR FAITH

I. The Gospel presents to us a portrait of Jesus at prayer. Prayer is the ordinary Lucan context for new disclosures of Jesus' identity and divine commissions. Peter's response to Jesus that he is the Messiah and the first prophecy of the passion are at once a climax and a turning point of his Gospel. This turning point turns us toward the mission of the Messiah.

II. Jesus accepts Peter's confession but explains that suffering, death and resurrection await him in Jerusa-lem. Just as the disciples share in Jesus' power as a teacher and healer and in his simple life-style, so they must be ready to share in his suffering and death. Jesus' charge to them not to speak is related to the first pre-diction of the passion.

III. Jesus presents a clear and unequivocal portrait of discipleship. The necessity of Jesus' suffering and death also defines the life of his followers. Luke calls for a daily taking up of one's cross. The Christian life then is lived in the struggle of everyday on-going history. We encounter another fundamental paradox: a life bent on personal survival is a life lost, but a life lost for Jesus' sake is a life saved. Death and resurrection mark the steps of the followers of Jesus.

MAKING THE FAITH OUR OWN

What is the meaning of the cross in my everyday journey?

How does the mystery of death and resurrection continue to exist in the world today?

LIVING OUR FAITH—CLOSING PRAYER

"We Are Claimed by Christ by the Sign of the Cross" (adapted) (*We Praise You, O Lord*, Patricia Fritz, O.S.F., Paulist Press, 1982).

Doctrinal and Pastoral Issues: Christology, Jesus' Iden-tity, Peter, Suffering, Cross, Prayer

Nancy Sheridan

Jesus and His Disciples

Part II: Destiny of the Church in the Journey of Jesus

By Eugene A. LaVerdiere, S.S.

In the first series of Sundays in Ordinary Time, we read from Luke's account of Jesus' Galilean ministry (4:14—9:50). In the second series which extends from the twelfth to the thirty-fourth Sundays, the readings are taken from Luke's account of Jesus' great journey to God (9:51—24:53). In the first series, we reflected on the Church's founding in stages. In this second series, we see how the Church was formed and purified by Jesus as it accompanied him toward its destiny in the presence of God. These readings include some of Luke's finest stories—the good Samaritan, Martha and Mary, the prodigal son, and Zacchaeus, all of which have left their mark on our Christian imagination.

Beginning of the Journey

The second series of Sundays in Ordinary Time presents the life of the Church as it moves on to its destiny in the life of God. It begins with the thirteenth Sunday. The first reading in the series tells of the beginning of Jesus' great journey to Jerusalem, a journey on which his disciples accompany him. From the beginning he is their prophetic teacher par excellence (9:51–62).

Jesus' journey to Jerusalem is a journey to the ascension, and that means it is a journey to God. The life of the Church, which participates in Jesus' journey, is in constant movement and development. As it precedes Jesus and prepares the way for his coming, the Church is like John the Baptist. It is the forerunner for Jesus' second coming or advent. As it goes about its mission, it must remember Jesus' way and his attitude toward people. It must not harshly condemn those who reject it or try to block its path (9:51–56). And once it has been invited to follow, it must set out on the journey with Jesus without hesitation and without looking back (9:57–62).

The Mission of the Seventy-Two

Among all the evangelists, Luke is the only one to tell of the mission of the seventy-two. Their number re-calls the seventy selected by Moses to assist in the leadership of Israel during the exodus. The seventy, who are called the elders or presbyters of Israel, were soon joined by two additional prophetic leaders to form seventy-two. In doing this, Luke provides the basis for the development of the ministry of the elders, prophetic teachers and leaders, in the life of the Christian community. Like those here in Luke 10:1–12, 17–20, later presbyters would also go in pairs. Among these we should include the two men in the tomb who greeted the women (24:1–11) and the two disciples of Emmaus (24:13–35).

The reading for the fourteenth Sunday in Ordinary Time thus shows us the seventy-two going forth as prophetic witnesses and teachers to prepare the way for the coming of the Lord. Jesus gives them instructions for their missionary journey: they go as lambs among wolves, but, even so, they should go simply, accepting the hospitality that is offered. Jesus also welcomes them on their return. It is not just that they have cast out demons. Satan himself is falling from the sky. The kingdom of God is at hand!

The Good Samaritan

The story of the good Samaritan (Lk 10:25–37) is one of the best known from Luke's Gospel. We read it on the fifteenth Sunday in Ordinary Time. A lawyer has two questions: what must I do to inherit everlasting life, and who is my neighbor? The second, of course, presupposes Jesus' answer to the first, as he asks what the law says and the lawyer gives his well-known response. Both questions have been with us throughout history, and they remain with us today.

The question concerning everlasting life is a personal question. Its answer, however, involves the neighbor and all the social questions which confront us today. The second question is an effort to blunt the sharp edges of social responsibility. Surely not all are my neighbor! As usual Jesus' approach is to tell a story. He seems to be answering the lawyer's second question: even the Samaritan is your neighbor. The condition for everlasting life includes loving the Samaritan. But Jesus is not satisfied with the question, and he brings the conversation around to answering another. The real question is not "Who is my neighbor?" but "How am I to be neighbor to others?" To this Jesus answers: "Go and be compassionate like the Samaritan was compassionate to the man who had been victimized by robbers."

Martha and Mary

On the sixteenth Sunday in Ordinary Time, we read the story of Martha and Mary (Lk 10:38–42), a story which captures the imagination but which also easily is misunderstood. Martha and Mary do not represent two different ways of life, one contemplative and one active, much less does it pass judgment on these ways of life. It is about every Christian, everyone who embarks with Jesus on the journey to God.

Martha exemplifies a problem on the journey, one which affects our ministerial responsibilities in the Christian community. She feels overwhelmed by all that needs to be done. She feels unassisted by her fellow Christian, her sister in the faith. And it seems to her that the Lord does not care. Jesus calls her attention to the one thing necessary: sensitivity to the person of the guest and communication, active listening to the word of the Lord. Mary exemplifies these. Without this one necessary attitude, everything else Martha is doing is meaningless.

The Lord's Prayer

All of us can recite the Lord's Prayer as it comes to us from Matthew's Gospel. This is the form we use in the liturgy and this is the form we learn from childhood. Few of us, however, are aware of the shorter form of the prayer provided by St. Luke in 11:2–4. So far as its actual length goes, most scholars agree that the Lukan version is closer to the prayer's earliest form.

The prayer is included in the reading for the seventeenth Sunday in Ordinary Time (Lk 11:1–13). Its context should be noted. A disciple asks Jesus, the Lord, to teach his disciples how to pray after experiencing and observing Jesus himself at prayer. When Jesus answers with the Lord's Prayer, he is thus responding to a felt need. In this we have a good pattern for prayer catechesis. After the prayer, Jesus continues with instruction on perseverance in prayer. At the end he sums up the whole prayer as a prayer for the Holy Spirit. The petitions of the Lord's Prayer are like the light of the Holy Spirit once it has passed through a prism.

Wealth and Greed

Someone has completely misunderstood what Je-

sus is all about. When Jesus is asked to intervene in a dispute over an inheritance, he reaffirms his true mission. He has not come to judge or arbitrate. Rather, he is to be a prophet, a teacher, a compassionate healer. His work is to unite, not divide. To these ends he tells a story about a rich man (Lk 12:13–21). This is our reading for the eighteenth Sunday in Ordinary Time.

Instead of arbitrating an inheritance, Jesus speaks about the foolishness of accumulating wealth. His story is about a man who provided abundantly for what he thought would be a long future. But that night he died. Who would inherit all he had labored for?

Here was someone before Jesus hoping to gather up wealth by acquiring an inheritance. Someday, perhaps that very night, the inheritance might be left to someone else! It is quite different with things which represent true wealth in the sight of God.

The Master's Return

On the nineteenth Sunday in Ordinary Time, the reading continues with the theme of possessions and their fleeting nature (12:32–48). Jesus says that our Father has given the disciples the true and enduring treasure. It is the kingdom, the same kingdom for which we pray in the Lord's Prayer. Nothing else deserves their single-minded attention. They must set their heart on the kingdom.

They will receive the kingdom at the return of the Son of Man, an event which could take place anytime. Luke's Gospel looks forward to a long history in which the Church must be deeply involved. Its journey is a missionary journey. However, as it makes its way among peoples and pursues its mission to the ends of the earth, it must live and act under the sign of the imminent return of Christ. This will guarantee a proper Christian attitude as it works in the world. What is true for all is true *a fortiori* for Jesus' close associates in the mission.

Unity and Division

Jesus does not come to judge, arbitrate and divide, but to unite (Lk 12:13–21), and yet his life and message is in fact a deep source of division. Jesus' whole life on earth is in view of the fire of Pentecost, a fire of rebirth, sprung from Jesus' own baptism of the passion. On this twentieth Sunday in Ordinary Time, the Gospel forces us to face the issue of birth and rebirth.

We are born into particular families, ethnic groups and races. Normally our life would unfold within the context of these social groupings, and even if we move about a larger world, our personal identity remains tied to our family, ethnic background and race. Reborn into the life of the Lord, we become brothers and sisters to all who welcome the same life of Christ, to all who are reborn in the fire of his Spirit. When some, but not all, are open to this, Jesus becomes a source of deep division. Those who are reborn experience the anguish of Jesus' own baptism in the passion.

The Narrow Door

From time to time, the Gospel makes special mention of the great journey to Jerusalem. In this way, we never lose sight of the forest for the trees. Such is the case on this twenty-first Sunday in Ordinary Time (Lk 13:22–30). As so often happens, Jesus is presented with a question but he answers another. This time, someone asks Jesus whether those who will be saved will be few. Earlier, in chapter 10:25–37 (see fifteenth Sunday), the question had been: "What must I do to inherit everlasting life?" This time, it has to do with the number. We do not know whether the questioner would like to see a large number or a small one, but either way it is plain that he would like to be among that number.

In his answer, Jesus says simply that the door is narrow and that at some point it will be bolted. So come in through the narrow door and do so before the Master comes to close it. Men and women will come from everywhere, from all four points of the compass to take their place at the banquet of salvation. Rather than be concerned about the number who will make it, consider that many who do were not expected to do so. On the other hand, those you expect to find may not be there.

The Humble Exalted

The setting is the home of a leading Pharisee, where Jesus and a number of people have gathered for a meal on the sabbath (Lk 14:1, 7–14). The event includes the healing of one suffering from dropsy (vv. 2–6), Jesus' message to the guests (vv. 7–11), his message to the host (vv. 12–14), and a general message in response to one of those present (vv. 15–24).

Today's reading presents Jesus' messages to the guests and to the host. Both messages addressed problems surrounding the Lord's Supper in the early Christian communities addressed by Luke. On this twenty-second Sunday in Ordinary Time, they speak to our own difficulties.

There are those who seek to be honored. They need to be in important positions, the places up front near the people that matter. Jesus notices some of the guests scrambling for such positions. Using the hypothetical case of a wedding banquet, Jesus warns against seeking the first places. If someone more important comes along, the one who has already occupied the first place will be shamed in public by having to step down to the lowest place. On the other hand, if the host sees him or her in the last place, he or she will be asked to come higher. It is a great thing to be exalted, but a very bad thing to exalt oneself.

The same applies to the host, but in another way. The host may seek to exalt himself or herself by inviting only people of rank and prestige. They take the last place, humble themselves, by welcoming the poor beggars, the crippled, the lame and the blind. At this, one in the party announces how such a one will be exalted. His statement is a beatitude: "Blessed is the one who eats bread in the kingdom of God!"

Taking Up the Cross

Today's reading is one of the most difficult. It actually sounds contrary to the basic commandment that we are to honor father and mother. As we read Luke 14:25–33, with its reference to turning one's back on father and mother, wife and children and brothers and sisters, we should recall what was said concerning Luke 12:13–21 on the twentieth Sunday. It provides an immediate context for understanding the Gospel for the twenty-third Sunday.

As in Luke 12:13–21, it is a matter of discerning what Christian life is all about and how the new life in Christ transcends the life received in the family of our earthly origins. Today's text goes further, however, when it adds that we must turn our back on our very self. In following Christ we must be as selfless as he was. That is what it means to take up one's cross. This selflessness requires that we be equally selfless in our relationships, and in particular in our family relationships. They must not be extensions of our person supporting us so much as extending our selfless mission to others. The Gospel helps us focus properly with two parables which exemplify single-mindedness in the following of Christ.

Providing for One's Future in the Kingdom

For the twenty-fourth Sunday in Ordinary Time, when we read Luke 15:1–32, see the fourth Sunday of Lent (Lk 15:1–3, 11–32) and the feast of the Sacred Heart of Jesus (Lk 15:3–7). On the twenty-fifth Sunday, we are confronted by a clever manager—often referred to as an unjust steward (Lk 16:1–13). To grasp Jesus' story, it is first necessary to know the cultural context to which it refers. A manager of a large estate was responsible for the estate and had discretionary powers over debts and obligations. In this case, the manager provided very generous conditions for repayment and thereby obtained the favor of the debtors on the eve of his own retirement. He thus provided for his personal future. Even the owner had to give his employee credit for being so enterprising.

The disciples, whose interest is with far greater things, indeed with lasting things, should be more clever and show more initiative than the wily manager. Besides, if in the ministry they have not managed their stewardship of others, why should they expect anything of their own Master?

Wealth and Poverty

As in so many places today, the world of the New Testament often saw extravagant wealth alongside of abject poverty, and as always the two challenged one another. The story for this twenty-sixth Sunday in Ordinary Time takes a familiar Lukan theme a step further. It is the story of a very rich man, conspicuous in his dress and sumptuous in his dining, and a miserably poor man, lying half-dead at his gate (16:19–31). Both eventually die, and of course their fortunes are reversed. The gulf between them now, however, is even wider than the passage which had run from the rich man's gate to his table. There is no crossing it.

As a last resort, the rich man, far from Abraham and in torment, pleads that at least someone be sent to warn his brothers living in the house he had once enjoyed with them. Would they not believe someone returning from the dead? Abraham's answer is addressed to the early Christians as well: "If they do not listen to Moses and the prophets, they will not be convinced even if one should rise from the dead" (16:31). Jesus did rise from the dead, and he is present to the Church, and still we are not convinced that wealth must be shared with the rest of God's family.

Sayings of Jesus

From the Gospels we can tell that Jesus loved parables and sayings which dealt with simple things. On this twenty-seventh Sunday in Ordinary Time, we reflect on two of Jesus' sayings (Lk 17:5–10). The first deals with faith. When the apostles ask for faith, Jesus responds with a hyperbole about a mustard seed of faith. Sayings such as this are to shake up the apostles. They are not meant to define expectations. Literal interpretations have one of two effects. Either we feel guilty, or we decide that the Gospel sayings of Jesus are not to be taken seriously. Both effects are bad.

The second saying also concerns expectations. Those who do what is expected of them, namely their role of service in the ministry, should be happy that they have done so. They should not expect a piece of the kingdom or any other special consideration. They are but servants, as Jesus was. As such they serve in the kingdom; they do not rule. See Luke's presentation of Jesus' discourse at the Last Supper (22:24–30).

The Grateful Foreigner

One of the great themes which threads its way through Luke's Gospel and Acts can be called the Samaritan theme. In Luke 9:51–56, Jesus' disciples want to call down fire from heaven on the Samaritans who refuse to welcome them. Jesus rebukes his disciples for this. A short time later he tells a story about a good Samaritan. Now on the twenty-eighth Sunday in Ordinary Time, Luke adds the story of ten lepers whom Jesus healed (Lk 17:11–19). Only one returned to thank him, a Samaritan, a foreigner. As Jesus says, his faith has healed him; it has been his salvation.

The theme of faith and salvation has been well-prepared in the Gospel. Even in the preaching of John the Baptizer, people had been warned that having Abraham as one's father was no guarantee of salvation. Children could be raised to Abraham from stones (3:8). The story of the Samaritan tells us something else as well. Those who appear to be bad because they oppose us often turn out to be the best associates. In Acts, Luke also shows how this was true of St. Paul. His whole two-volume work demonstrates how it was true of the Gentile world of the Roman Empire.

The Widow and the Judge

On the twenty-ninth Sunday in Ordinary Time, we read the first of two Lukan parables on prayer (18:1–8). The author begins by giving the reader the theme of the parable: the necessity of praying always and of not losing heart. For Luke, the reason that people ceased praying was because they lost heart. It was not a matter of losing one's faith in God, or, as sometimes happens today, of someone's discovering that he or she never did have faith in God. It was a matter of giving up hope that God would ever respond to someone's prayer.

The parable is about a widow who could not obtain her rights from a corrupt judge. Apart from her husband, now deceased, a widow easily was taken advantage of. Now if the widow finally can wear down such a judge, surely God will do justice for his chosen ones. The problem, however, is not there. Rather, when the Son of Man comes to meet that justice, will there be anyone left who still believes that his or her prayer will be answered?

The Pharisee and the Tax Collector

Last Sunday we heard a parable on the need to pray always. Its purpose was to counter any tendency we might have to lose heart. On this thirtieth Sunday, we hear a second parable on prayer. This one is addressed to those who are taken up with their own self-righteousness and who hold all others in contempt (Lk 18:9–14).

The parable contrasts two men, a Pharisee and a tax collector, at prayer in the temple. The description of the two is succinct but could not be drawn more sharply. The Pharisee prays with head unbowed; the tax collector does not even dare raise his eyes to heaven. The Pharisee's prayer focuses on everyone else. By lowering others, he thinks he is exalted. The tax collector refers only to himself, a sinner. He is in need of mercy. As Jesus indicates, the Pharisee failed to exalt himself. The tax collector, on the other hand, exalted himself by his humility.

Zacchaeus

The story of Zacchaeus is extremely well told. Its description of Zacchaeus and the crowd is simple and brief, but we have all we need to picture them clearly (Lk 19:1–10). The body of the story is enclosed between Jesus' initial statement to Zacchaeus: "I mean to stay at your home today" (v. 5), and his later statement: "Salvation has come to this home today" (v. 9). The meaning is obvious: for Jesus to be someone's guest is for salvation to be that person's guest. To be host to Jesus is to be host to one's own salvation. The thirty-first Sunday in Ordinary Time thus continues to focus our attention on the way Jesus sought out and welcomed those who were lost over the objections of those who thought they themselves were saved.

Jesus and the Sadducees

In the time of Jesus, the Pharisees and their scribes were among those who believed in the resurrection of the dead. In their view, the event was to take place at the end of time in conjunction with a general judgment. The Sadducees, on the other hand, denied the resurrection, and since this was the only way they had of envisioning personal life after death, their denial was an implicit denial of immortality. On this thirty-second Sunday in Ordinary Time, Jesus responds to a challenge of the Sadducees in this regard (Lk 20:27–38).

The Sadducees come to Jesus with a hypothetical story which they feel will pose an insoluble dilemma to one who believes in the resurrection. In his response, Jesus denies the story's presuppositions. Since there is no marriage in the resurrection, the question concerning the widow's husband in the resurrection is pointless. He then takes up the deeper question of life beyond death, however it may be imagined. The Sadducees place their faith in the God of Abraham, Isaac and Jacob. Is he not the God of the living?

Patient Endurance

All three of the Synoptic Gospels include a discourse of Jesus which, at least loosely, can be termed apocalyptic. Its language and imagery of strife, persecution, and cataclysm is easily recognized. However, this does not mean that these discourses are formally apocalyptic. Even Mark's, which comes the closest, is a reaction to apocalyptic thinking. All three Synoptics insist that, contrary to appearances, the end is not yet. First the Gospel must be preached to all the Gentiles. Mark, who presents the fall of Jerusalem as the beginning of the events which lead to the end, may envision a relatively short future, but he does insist on a future in which the Christian mission must be pursued in spite of persecution. Luke envisions a long future. He separates the fall of Jerusalem from the events which herald the end (21:5–24, 25–36).

The reading for the thirty-third Sunday in Ordinary Time (Lk 21:5–19) looks to the future in general and introduces the section on the fall of Jerusalem (21:20–24). The discourse faces the difficulties which lie ahead quite squarely. To be saved when these come, the disciples will need patient endurance. (For further development of this, see the first Sunday of Advent.

Christ the King

The liturgical year ends with the thirty-fourth Sunday in Ordinary Time, the feast of Christ the King. In this year of Luke, the reading is Luke 23:35–43, a passage from the passion narrative.

Jesus is hanging on the cross. He is taunted by those who stand about, especially by the leaders of the people. Their theme is simple: if he is the Messiah, the king of the Jews, why does he not save himself? Jesus is taunted even by a condemned criminal. Why does he not save those who have been crucified along with him?

Luke has an extraordinary sense of irony. Jesus, of course, is saving all humankind by dying on the cross. It is through the cross that he is coming into his kingdom, and those who are open to him will be with him in paradise.

Introduction to Sundays 13–23 in Ordinary Time

Each catechetical session for the thirteenth through the twenty-third Sunday in Ordinary Time contains the following steps:

> Gathering Prayer
> Catechist Instruction
> Thematic Reflection Processes
> –Reading of Scripture
> –Silence
> –Reflection Process
> Integration
> Closing Prayers

The gathering prayer consists of an opening song which can either be sung or meditatively played. The song is followed by an opening prayer led by the catechist which reflects the particular theme chosen for the breaking open of the word. Instead of a prayer or in addition to it, a psalm may be read, reflected upon or recited antiphonally by the group.

At the beginning of each session a brief instruction is given to assist the catechist. Generally, one thematic reflection process is chosen for each Sunday. When it is appropriate, though, a combination of two processes may be used. Sometimes at first hearing of a Gospel reading certain immediate images or reactions may occur because of the "hard news" of the good news. When this occurs it would be appropriate to let the participants explore their initial reactions to the Gospel. Some of the following catechetical sessions allow for this initial reflection process. The catechist chooses a specific reflection process based upon the needs, questions and concerns of the participants.

The session begins with the reading of the chosen Scripture passage, followed by silence (for a minimum of two to three minutes). After the silence an open-ended reflection process follows which may begin with a brief focus on the meaning of the Gospel. The main purpose of the reflection process is to lead the participants into the focus questions. The focus questions begin with the experience of the participants. It is recommended that the participants be invited to record their responses to the questions in a journal. Following this, participants break into small groups (no more than five) and share their responses to the questions. The reflection process continues as suggested in each of the catechetical sessions.

At the end of the reflection and discussion the participants are invited to integrate their responses into their daily life and to reflect upon the Catholic questions, concerns or issues that the process raised for them. During the integration time participants are challenged to make concrete decisions and commitments for living out the Gospel.

At the end of the session or the end of the following Sunday's session, the catechist or other presenter gives input in response to the Catholic questions, concerns or issues raised by the participants (for a maximum of thirty minutes).

Each of the following catechetical sessions lists suggested doctrinal and pastoral issues which arise in the readings, especially the Gospel.

Each session ends with prayer. Various forms are suggested, recommending that participants be invited to join their prayers to the concluding prayers.

Thirteenth Sunday in Ordinary Time

1 Kings 19:16, 19–21
Galatians 5:1, 13–18
Luke 9:51–62

GATHERING PRAYER

Song: "Seek the Lord," by Roc O'Connor, S.J. (*Glory and Praise, #46*).

Prayer: Lord, Jesus Christ, you are our light, guiding us on our life journey to you. Open our eyes and our hearts to see you and know you in all our lives. Guide us and lead us to live as your followers. We ask this in your name, Jesus our Lord. Amen.

CATECHIST INSTRUCTION

Choose one of the following thematic reflection processes to lead the participants, inviting them to record their responses in their journals.

I. Theme: Welcome and Hospitality

A. Reading of the Gospel (9:51–56)
   1. Silence

B. Reflection Process
   1. Focus: In the Gospel, Jesus and the disciples experience being unwelcome in a Samaritan town because they are journeying to Jerusalem, the center of worship for the Jews. In reaction to the rejection, the disciples would like to bring down the wrath of God on the Samaritan town but Jesus reprimands them for their attitude and they continue on their journey.
   2. Recall a specific time or event in your life when you felt unwelcome or when you experienced rejection.
   3. Recall the feelings you had before, during and after the experience of feeling unwelcome or rejected.
   4. How did you respond and what decisions did you make as a result of your experience of feeling unwelcomed or rejected?
   5. Small group sharing.

C. Rereading of the Gospel
   1. Silence

D. Reflection Process (continued)
   1. In your Christian community, in your family, at work or in your neighborhood, how do you welcome or extend hospitality in your family?
   2. How does the Gospel challenge, affirm or enlighten your experience of welcoming or hospitality?
   3. Large group sharing.

II. Theme: Welcoming the Gospel into Our Lives

A. Reading of the Gospel
   1. Silence

B. Reflection Process
   1. Focus: Presented in the Gospel are three anonymous persons who desire to follow Jesus. Before they can, though, they tell Jesus that they must fulfill a prior obligation. To the first person, Jesus says that to be his follower one needs to be detached from the security of a home or from the comfort of things. To the second person Jesus says that in order to be his follower one needs to be detached from former responsibilities. And, finally, Jesus responds to the third person by saying that to be his follower one is called to detachment from past relationships. Nothing is to stand in the way of a radical commitment to Jesus and the proclamation of the kingdom of God by one's life.
   2. What attitudes, fears or past experiences in your life keep you from hearing or responding to the Lord's invitation to live the Gospel? Be specific and concrete.
   3. Where in your life do you hear the Lord inviting you to a greater response to the Gospel?
   4. Small group sharing.
   5. How do you hear the Lord inviting "Church" to a greater response to the Gospel? Be specific and concrete.
   6. Small group sharing followed by large group response.

III. Theme: Following Jesus

A. Reading of the Gospel (9:57–62)
   1. Silence (2–3 minutes)

B. Reflection Process
   1. Focus (refer to Focus in II)

2. Recall a person in your life who best exemplifies for you what it means to be a Christian. Name the person's attributes, characteristic values, way of life that made you choose that person.
3. Small group sharing.
4. What does it mean for you in your life to be a follower of Jesus Christ, a Christian?
5. What attributes, character values, way of life or qualities do you have that exemplify for you that you are a Christian? Give one specific concrete example.
6. Small group sharing.
7. As in the Gospel, what do you need to be detached from, to let go of, in order to follow Jesus?
8. Small group sharing followed by large group reflection.

INTEGRATION

1. As a result of hearing the word of God proclaimed in the homily and in the breaking open of the word, what questions does the Gospel raise for you about Catholic teaching, faith or way of life?

2. (Optional:) Input in response to questions raised about Catholicism.

3. How do you hear yourself called to life by the Gospel this coming week?

4. What needs to happen in your life in order for you to live the Gospel this coming week? How are you asked to change and are you willing to?

5. What do you need from yourself, your family, this community, your sponsor to help you live the Gospel this coming week?

CLOSING PRAYER

As a group pray Psalm 16, followed by petitionary prayer.

Doctrinal and Pastoral Issues: Church, Christian Life, Hospitality

Kathy Brown

Fourteenth Sunday in Ordinary Time

Isaiah 66:10–14
Galatians 6:14–18
Luke 10:1–12, 17–20

GATHERING PRAYER

Song: "Anthem," by Tom Conroy (*Glory and Praise*, #83).

Prayer: All-powerful God, through your Son you call us to be missionaries, announcing the reign of God. Empower us and guide us as your witnesses to be the good news of your love for all people. We thank you for calling us to journey with your Son, our Lord Jesus Christ. Amen.

CATECHIST INSTRUCTION

In the following reflection processes use "I" with all the themes. Invite the participants to record their responses in their journals.

I. Theme: First Hearing of the Gospel

A. Reading of the Gospel
   1. (Before reading the Gospel the catechist asks the participants the following:) Listen for the word or phrase that speaks to you or touches you in your life today.
   2. Reading of the Gospel
   3. Silence

B. Reflection Process
   1. Without discussion in small groups speak only the word or phrase that touches you from the Gospel.

II. Theme: Preparing for the Journey

A. Reading of the Gospel
   1. Silence

B. Reflection Process
   1. When Jesus sent out the seventy-two disciples he gave them instructions on what they were to take and not to take for the journey, and what attitude they were to have.
   2. As you reflect honestly on your life, what gifts, talents or abilities do you bring with you on the Christian journey of life? Be specific and concrete.
   3. As you listen to the Lord in your life, what do you believe you need to leave behind or let go of in your life as you continue the Christian journey?
   4. Small group sharing.

III. Theme: Peacemakers

A. Reading of the Gospel
   1. Silence (3 minutes)

B. Reflection Process
   1. Focus: Jesus instructed his disciples to go forth in peace, offering peace to those they met along the journey. Jesus was aware that some would welcome and others would reject the disciples' offer of peace. Peace has come to mean many things in our world today.
   2. Reflect on your own understanding of peace in the following areas: family, work place, city, country, world, personal life. What are the similarities and differences in your understanding of peace?
   3. Small group sharing.
   4. In a specific and concrete way, how do you hear yourself called to be a person of peace in your family, in your work place, in the Church, in your neighborhood or in the world?
   5. Small group sharing followed by large group response.

IV. Theme: Empowerment

A. Reading of the Gospel
   1. Silence

B. Reflection Process
   1. Focus: In sending the seventy-two disciples, Jesus empowered them for their ministry as his followers. Upon their return, the seventy-two reported the power they had experienced in the name of Jesus.
   2. Name a time or experience in your life of being empowered or empowering another person. What were the feelings you had before, during or after the event? As a result of being empowered or empowering another person, what

changes did you experience in your own life in your values, behaviors, attitudes?

3. Each of us is empowered by God for our Christian journeys. Recall a time in your life when you experienced the power of God acting in your life? Recall the feelings you had before, during and after the event.

4. As a result of that event in your life, did you experience any change or conversion in your life?

5. Small group sharing.

INTEGRATION

1. From the homily and the word shared today, what are the questions that it raises for you about Catholic teaching, life or faith?

2. (Optional:) Input in response to the questions raised.

3. As a result of the breaking open of the word, how do you hear yourself called to live the Gospel this coming week?

4. What are the obstacles you face in living the Gospel, and are you willing to overcome them?

5. What do you need from your family, your friend(s)/sponsor, yourself, in order to live the Gospel?

CLOSING PRAYER

As a group read/pray Psalm 66 together, followed by prayers of thanksgiving and the kiss of peace.

Doctrinal and Pastoral Issues: Ecclesiastical Documents on Peace, Baptism, Mission, Theological Virtues, Charisms, Authority and Power in the Institutional Church, Discipleship

Kathy Brown

Fifteenth Sunday in Ordinary Time

Deuteronomy 30:10–14
Colossians 1:15–20
Luke 10:25–37

GATHERING PRAYER

Song: "Blest Are They" by David Haas (G.I.A. Publications).

Prayer: Loving God, you teach us through your Son the way to live our lives authentically. Lead us to your truth; strengthen us as we reach out to all our neighbors so that we may come to be authentic witnesses of your truth and love for all. We ask this through Christ our Lord. Amen.

CATECHIST INSTRUCTION

Choose one of the following reflection processes to guide the participants, inviting them to record their responses in their journals.

I. Theme: Reaching Out

A. Reading of the Gospel
   1. Silence

B. Reflection Process
   1. Recall an event in your life when you experienced pain (physical or emotional), depression or loneliness. Remember the issues and the feelings that led up to the event, and the feelings during and after that time in your life.
   2. What were the questions that this event or time in your life raised for you about relationships, about God and about your life?
   3. Who was there to be with you or help you during this time in your life?
   4. Invite the participants to go off in twos, sharing their reflections on the above questions.
   5. (After the participants return, continue the reflection process:) Rereading of the Gospel
      a. Silence
   6. How does the Gospel affirm or challenge your experience? Is there another Gospel that speaks more to your experience?
   7. Small group sharing followed by large group discussion.

II. Theme: Neighbor

A. Reading of the Gospel
   1. Silence (3 minutes)

B. Reflection Process
   1. Focus: As children each of us was taught that there are people we ought to avoid. Most of the time, these lessons, whether implicit or explicit, were to protect us as children.
   2. As a child, who were the people you were told to avoid?
   3. What were the assumptions being made about these particular people?
   4. Small group sharing.
   5. In the following examples, report your immediate response to the following people:
      a. a drunk man sitting on the sidewalk
      b. "the homeless"
      c. a friend just admitted to a psychiatric hospital
      d. a dying friend or relative
      e. a friend who is depressed
      f. an American Indian who just lost his job
      g. a black man on drugs
   6. What are the assumptions you have about the people in the above examples?
   7. What persons or groups would you avoid today as an adult?
   8. Small group sharing.
   9. Reread the Gospel.
      a. Silence (1 min)
   10. How does the Gospel affirm or challenge your understanding of who is your neighbor?
   11. Large group sharing and discussion.

III. Theme: Engagement in Life

A. Reading of the Gospel
   1. Silence

B. Reflection Process
   1. Input: At its root the Gospel story is less about who the individuals were that passed by the beaten man and more about the attitude of the one man who chose to help him. Not just a lesson on helping others or doing works of charity, the story invites us to reflect on how deeply we become engaged in life.
   The story does not tell us why this particular

man was beaten and left half-dead by the robbers. The beating was apparently senseless and meaningless, raising the question for the reader as to whether evil has the final word. On the one hand, the man assisting the beaten man did so for no apparent reason, personal gain or ulterior motive for himself. In fact he put himself in a certain amount of danger by responding to the man, for the robbers may still have been nearby. On the other hand, the other two men passed by the beaten man, avoiding suffering and death, because there was a certain risk in "getting involved." The man who helped restored the beaten man to life so that he could continue his story, thus stating clearly that evil does not have to have the final word. To engage in life, to not pass by, to not avoid life, suffering or death is to be empowered by God.

C. Action
1. Catechist Instruction: One week prior to this Sunday, arrange with the parish social action group or local neighborhood/city organization for the participants to volunteer for a day or an evening in one of the possible following areas:
   a. the homeless
   b. a soup kitchen
   c. migrant workers
   d. a convalescent center

D. Praxis
1. After the activity is completed have the participants reflect as a large group on the following questions:
   a. Describe your experience.
   b. What were the feelings, the hesitations, the fears you had before, during and after this experience?
   c. As result of this experience, have you changed your thinking or your understanding about this particular group? Be specific and concrete.
2. Reread the Gospel.
   a. Silence
3. Is there another Gospel story that your experience reminds you of? Why?
4. As a result of hearing the word of God and reflecting on your experience, how have you been challenged or affirmed in your thinking, your values, your beliefs?

INTEGRATION

1. As a result of hearing the word of God in your group and in the homily, what are the questions that it raises for you about Catholic teaching, faith, or way of life?
2. (Optional:) Input in response to questions raised about Catholicism.
3. After breaking open the word, how do you hear yourself called to live the Gospel this coming week? Be specific and concrete.
4. What will it cost you to live the Gospel, and are you willing to pay the price?
5. What do you need from this group, from the Church, from your family, from your friend(s)/sponsor in order to live the Gospel this coming week?

CLOSING PRAYER

Song: "Blest Are They"

Doctrinal and Pastoral Issues: Sacraments of Anointing and Reconciliation, Church Law, Hope, Paschal Mystery, Charity, Social Justice, Church and Politics

Kathy Brown

Sixteenth Sunday in Ordinary Time

Genesis 18:1–10
Colossians 1:24–28
Luke 10:38–42

GATHERING PRAYER

Song: "Lord, You Have the Words" by David Haas (*We Have Been Told*, GIA Publications).

Prayer: Lord God, you have shown us the way to peace and hope in our world which is busy about so many things. Gently guide us back to recognize you as our center, the one whom we need to focus our lives on. We give you thanks for your care and guidance. We pray this through Christ our Lord. Amen.

CATECHIST INSTRUCTION

Choose one of the following thematic reflection processes to guide the participants, inviting them to record their responses in their journals.

I. Theme: Letting Go

A. Reading of the Gospel
   1. Silence

B. Reflection Process
   1. Focus: In the Gospel Martha was upset and worried. This anxiety kept her from being present to the Lord. In our own lives we are confronted by many things that can upset or worry us, keep us uncentered or unfocused on what is truly important in life, Jesus Christ. We need to find ways to let go of those things in our life that keep us worried, upset or unfocused.
   2. Recall a recent time in your life when you were worried or upset and describe it briefly. What were the events that led up to it? What were the feelings you had during and after the event?
   3. How did the event resolve itself?
   4. If the event is not resolved, what is the hope you have? What would resolve the event for you?
   5. Small group sharing.

C. Imagination Exercise
   1. Take the participants through a relaxation exercise, following it by the imagination journey.
   2. Imagine yourself on a path. It is a beautiful day, the sun is shining and a gentle breeze is blowing. See the path lead you to your favorite place where you sit or lie down and relax.
   3. See a friend who loves you very much coming to you. Invite your friend to sit with you.
   4. Share with your friend the time when you experienced being worried or upset.
   5. After a while your friend takes your hand and leads you down a path. Coming toward you is Jesus who calls you by name.
   6. As you come face to face with Jesus, tell him about the time when you were worried or upset. Hear him respond to you by saying a word or a phrase. Hear him speak.
   7. After a while you say goodbye to Jesus and return with your friend to your favorite place. Your friend says goodbye to you, and you sit and ponder all that has happened to you.
   8. Rereading of the Gospel
      a. Silence
   9. After hearing the Gospel, you reflect on what it means for you.
   10. Rising, you walk down the path that leads you back into this room.
   11. Share your story and experience with one other person. (30 minutes)
   12. When the participants gather again invite them to journal to the following questions:
      a. As a result of this experience what have you learned, relearned or what new insights do you have about how you deal with worry or upset or feelings of being uncentered in your life?
      b. What do you hear the Lord calling you to do, to change, to let go of?

D. Large Group Response
   1. Invite the participants to share their experiences of the meditation and of their dialogue, respecting the confidentiality of the conversation.

II. Theme: Centering Prayer

A. Reading of the Gospel

1. Silence

B. Process
    1. Focus: One of the great traditions of the Church comes to us from the early Church and the "desert Fathers," men who chose to spend their time, their energy, their lives, in remote places, contemplating on the mystery of God. Coming from that tradition is the prayer of centering. The Gospel reminds us that we are to keep our hearts and minds on Jesus and the coming of God's kingdom. The prayer of centering may be one way for us in our prayer life to focus and enter into silence with the Lord.
    2. Catechist Instruction: Lead the participants through a centering prayer experience, keeping them focused through use of the "Jesus Prayer." (20–30 minutes)
    3. Reflection
      a. Describe your experience of the centering prayer, being sure to include any feelings before, during or after the experience.
    4. Small group sharing
    5. What prayer forms are you comfortable or uncomfortable with, and why?
    6. Large group response.

III. Theme: Hearing the Lord

A. Reading of the Gospel
    1. Silence

B. Reflection Process
    1. Focus: In a world of many distractions, with its different values and high-powered media, it is sometimes difficult to hear the Lord speak to us in our daily life.
    2. Recall and describe a recent event or experience when you knew the Lord was speaking to you.
    3. In what ways or through whom does the Lord speak to you? Where do you hear the Lord speak to you in your life?
    4. What keeps you from hearing the Lord in your life?
    5. Small group sharing
    6. What do you need to happen in your life so that you can hear the Lord speak to you?

IV. Theme: Prayer

A. Reading of the Gospel
    1. Silence

B. Reflection Process
    1. Focus: In the Gospel Martha comes to Jesus with her problem about the burden of hospitality and fulfilling her many tasks while Mary, her sister, does not help her. At the end, Jesus tells Martha that Mary has chosen the better way, the message being that what is primary is to keep one's life centered on Jesus. A very specific way to keep one's life centered on Jesus is through prayer.
    2. Describe your daily prayer life. Does it include silence, private time, reflection on the Scriptures, etc.?
    3. How does your prayer reflect that Christ is more and more the center of your life? Do you bring your daily life to Christ?
    4. Small group sharing
    5. How does the Gospel and the sharing in your group challenge or affirm you in your daily prayer life?
    6. What keeps you from a daily prayer life?
    7. What do you do in order to develop a daily prayer life?
    8. Large group discussion

V. Theme: Gospel Values

A. Reading of the Gospel
    1. Silence

B. Reflection Process
    1. Catechist instruction: Invite the participants to be involved in the following action activity:
      a. During the coming week listen to commercials, read advertising, be alert during casual conversations, become aware of the values being promoted in our society. Make a collection or a list of your findings.
    2. Focus: Recognizing the difference between the values of the Gospel and the values of the world is not always easy. Often the values are similar.
    3. Compare and contrast the values you heard expressed during the week with your own personal values and the values expressed in the Gospel.
    4. Small group sharing.
    5. In order to keep our lives centered on Christ, sometimes our values need to be challenged by Gospel values. How and where in your life do you experience your values being challenged or affirmed by the Gospel?
    6. Small group sharing followed by large group discussion.

INTEGRATION

1. As you listen to the Gospel, the homily and the breaking open of the word today in your group, what

questions are raised for you about Catholic teaching, practices, way of life or faith?

2. (Optional:) Input in response to questions raised.

3. How do you hear yourself called to live the Gospel this coming week?

4. In order to live the Gospel, what commitment or action is being asked of you?

5. What will you need to change, give up or let go of in your life in order to live the Gospel this coming week? Are you willing to change?

6. What do you need from this group, from your friend(s)/sponsor, from your family, from yourself, in order to live the Gospel?

CLOSING PRAYER

Psalm 134 followed by spontaneous prayer and petitions.

Doctrinal and Pastoral Issues: Catholic Prayer Forms, Christology, Contemporary Understanding of Prayer and Action

Kathy Brown

Seventeenth Sunday in Ordinary Time

Genesis 18:20–32
Colossians 2:12–14
Luke 11:1–13

GATHERING PRAYER

Song: "As a Deer," by Huijbers and Oosterhuis (Team Publications—Oregon Catholic Press).

Prayer: Lord God, you are a just God, never closing your ears to our voices. Look upon our lives with kindness and gentleness. Know the deepest desires of our hearts and answer them. May we by our lives come to be one with you, announcing your kingdom. We ask this through your Son, our Lord, Jesus Christ. Amen.

CATECHIST INSTRUCTION

In the following thematic reflection processes use "I" followed by one of the other processes. Invite the participants to record their responses in their journals.

I. Reading of the Gospel

A. As you hear the Gospel, listen for the word or phrase that most touches you in your life today.
  1. Reading
  2. Silence

B. Reflection Process
  1. In your journal, write the word or phrase from the Gospel that touches you in your life today.
  2. Briefly describe why that word or phrase touches you at this time in your life.
  3. Small group sharing.

II. Theme: Expectations and Hope

A. Reading of the Gospel
  1. Silence

B. Reflection Process
  1. Focus: We very often recite the Lord's Prayer, often not reflecting on the meaning of the words we say. The Lord's Prayer is a prayer for the Christian journey, as well as a challenge to the Christian community.

2. If this is your prayer for the Christian journey, then what do you understand is expected from you?
3. The prayer also tells us what is our hope. Hearing the prayer addressed to you in your daily life, what can you hope for from God?
4. Small group sharing.
5. How does the Lord's Prayer affirm, challenge or console you in your life?
6. Large group response.

III. Theme: Prayer Development

A. Reading of the Gospel
  1. Silence

B. Reflection Process
  1. Focus: What is prayer? Why pray? Does God hear my prayer? What is required of me in prayer? These are questions that are often asked about prayer, especially when we begin to speak about petitionary prayer. Both the Genesis reading and the Gospel speak about our prayer lives with God.
  2. Recall the various ways you have prayed through your life starting as a child and coming to the present.
  3. In what ways has your prayer life changed or remained the same throughout your life?
  4. Small group sharing.
  5. Recall a time in your life when you have asked God for something. Was your prayer answered? How?
  6. Small group sharing.
  7. Where do you feel God is calling you in your prayer life today? What is being asked of you and are you willing to respond?
  8. Small group sharing followed by large group sharing.

IV. Theme: Forgiveness

A. Reading of the Gospel
  1. Silence

B. Reflection Process
  1. Focus: Forgiving someone who has hurt us, deceived us or caused problems for us can be very difficult. Yet the Gospel speaks strongly

about the need to forgive as we have been forgiven by God.

2. Recall a time in your life when you were forgiven for something you said or did. Recall the events and the feelings you had during and after the experience of forgiveness.

3. Small group sharing.

4. Recall a time or experience in your life when you were hurt, deceived or burdened with the difficulties another person had brought into your life. Remembering the event, recall the feelings you had before, during and after the experience.

5. How was the person(s) involved in your experience of being hurt, deceived or burdened forgiven by you?

6. If you have not forgiven the person(s) involved, describe what keeps you from forgiveness.

C. Reading of the Gospel (first half)
   1. Silence

D. Reflection Process
   1. As "Church" we are called to be reconciled. In your experience of "Church," where do you see a need for forgiveness and reconciliation?
   2. What do you think is required of "Church" in order to live out the Lord's Prayer in its daily life? Do you believe "Church" is willing to do what is necessary to live the Lord's Prayer?
   3. Small group sharing.
   4. As you listen to the Gospel and as you reflect on the Lord's Prayer, how do you hear the Lord calling you to change or calling you to deeper reconciliation in your life?
   5. What do you need in your life in order to be a more forgiving person?
   6. Large group response.

INTEGRATION

1. As a result of hearing the word of God, what questions are raised for you about Catholic teaching, way of life, or faith?

2. (Optional:) Input in response to the questions raised about Catholicism.

3. How do you hear yourself called to live the Gospel this coming week? What will be required of you to live the Gospel and are you willing to do what is necessary?

4. What do you need from this group, from your family, your friend(s)/sponsors or yourself, in order to live the Gospel this coming week?

CLOSING PRAYER

Read Ephesians 3:14–21 (prayer for the Christian community)

Doctrinal and Pastoral Issues: Kingdom of God, Reconciliation, Prayer, Eucharist, Petitionary Prayer, Perseverance, Old Testament Prayers, New Testament Prayers, Various Catholic Prayer Forms, Faith, Hope and Love, Divine Revelation.

Kathy Brown

Eighteenth Sunday in Ordinary Time

Ecclesiastes 1:2, 2:21–23
Colossians 3:1–5, 9–11
Luke 12:13–21

GATHERING PRAYER

Song: "Take, Lord, Receive," by John B. Foley, S. J. (*Glory and Praise, #53*).

Prayer: Psalm 95 (read as a group).

CATECHIST INSTRUCTION

Choose one of the following thematic processes to lead the participants, inviting them to record their responses in their journals.

I. Theme: Vanity of Vanities

A. Reading of Ecclesiastes 1:2; 2:21
   1. Silence

B. Reflection Process
   1. In your journal dialogue with Qoheleth about his words. Do you agree or disagree? How do you respond to Qoheleth?
   2. Does the reading challenge or affirm your own understanding of life?
   3. Small group sharing.
   4. How does your faith in God challenge or affirm the words of Qoheleth? How does Qoheleth challenge your faith?
   5. Where in your life do you hear God calling you to change, to deeper faith, to hope?
   6. Small group sharing followed by large group sharing.

II. Theme: Focusing on the Kingdom

A. Reading of the Gospel
   1. Silence

B. Reflection Process
   1. Focus: In the Gospel, Jesus is asked to solve a problem for a man requesting that his brother give him his inheritance. Jesus does not solve the problem but instead goes to the root of the real issue, the attitude of the brother demand-

ing his share of the inheritance. Jesus' challenge to the disciples is that they keep their focus on God's kingdom and all else in life will be taken care of.
   2. As you reflect on your own life, what attitudes or desires keep your focus off God? Be specific and concrete.
   3. What in your life helps to keep you focused or attentive to God?
   4. Small group sharing.
   5. How do you hear yourself called to change your life or your attitude(s) so as to keep your focus and attention on God?
   6. Large group reflection.

III. Theme: Possessions

A. Reading of the Gospel
   1. As you hear the Gospel, listen for the words, phrases, ideas or images that touch you in your life.
   2. Silence

B. Reflection Process
   1. As you listened to the Gospel, why did those words, phrases, ideas or images touch you?
   2. Small group sharing.
   3. Rereading of the Gospel
      a. Silence
   4. Being specific and concrete, what do you consider as your possessions?
   5. Make a list of everything that you consider to be of value to you. Then put the items on the list in order of priority, placing at the top of the list the most important item of value in your life. As you prioritize them, what could you live without and not live without?
   6. Small group sharing.
   7. How does the Gospel challenge or affirm your attitude toward your possessions?
   8. What have you learned, relearned or had a new insight about your attitude, feelings about "possessions" or items of value?
   9. Large group sharing.

IV. Theme: Material Goods

A. Reading of the Gospel
   1. Silence

B. Reflection Process
  1. In the United States what are the assumptions and the values we live out of regarding the goods of the earth (environment, food, clothing, shelter, etc.)?
  2. How do these assumptions and values affect third world countries?
  3. Small group sharing.
  4. Rereading of the Gospel
     a. Silence
  5. As you reflect on the Gospel, compare and contrast the values of the Gospel with the values of first world countries in relationship to third world countries.
  6. How are your own beliefs about the use of the goods of the earth challenged or affirmed by the Gospel?
  7. Small group sharing.
  8. How can you approach the goods of the earth more authentically and honestly as a result of reflecting on Gospel values?

INTEGRATION

1. As a result of the homily and of hearing the Gospel broken open for you today, what questions does it raise for you about Catholic teaching, way of life, faith, etc.?

2. (Optional:) Input in response to the questions raised about Catholicism.

3. How do you hear yourself called to live the Gospel this coming week?

4. What is it going to cost you to live the Gospel? Are you willing to pay the price?

5. What do you need from your family, your friend(s)/ sponsors, this group, the Church, yourself, in order to live the Gospel?

CLOSING PRAYER

Almighty and powerful God, through the life of your Son you have shown us the way to care for all people throughout the world. We are a selfish people, constantly in need of your help and guidance. Hear our petitions that we pray for all your creation . . .

Prayers of Petition

Closing Song: Final verse of opening song, "Take, Lord, Receive."

Doctrinal and Pastoral Issues: Pastoral Letters on the Economy, Sharing the Goods of the Earth, Lives of Saints (e.g., St. Francis of Assisi), Stewardship, Old Testament Understanding of Giftedness of Creation

Kathy Brown

Nineteenth Sunday in Ordinary Time

Wisdom 18:6–9
Hebrews 11:1–2, 8–19
Luke 12:32–48

GATHERING PRAYER

Song: "The Cry of the Poor," by John B. Foley, S.J. (*Glory and Praise*, #93).

Prayer: Psalm 33 (read together)

Silence

Prayer: Lord God, through your Son you announced the coming of the kingdom into our world. You call us to live in the hope of your kingdom, to be a sign to all of the inbreaking of your kingdom. Open our hearts and minds to recognize your kingdom in our lives and in our world. Guide us toward that kingdom. We ask this through Christ your Son. Amen.

CATECHIST INSTRUCTION

Choose one of the following thematic reflection processes to lead the participants, inviting them to record their responses in their journals.

I. Theme: Recognizing the Kingdom

A. Reading of the Gospel
   1. Silence

B. Reflection Process
   1. Focus: The Gospel speaks of a fundamental Christian attitude in life: the expectation and belief in the coming of God's kingdom into our lives and our world. Sometimes it is recognizing the breaking in of God's kingdom that is difficult because it is here but not completely.
   2. Where do you experience God's kingdom breaking into your life? Be specific and concrete.
   3. Where in your life do you hear the Lord asking to open your life for the breaking in of the kingdom?
   4. What keeps you from letting the Lord into your life?
   5. Small group sharing.

6. In what ways do you hear the Lord asking to be invited into all your life?
7. What keeps you from letting Christ into your life?
8. Large group discussion.

II. Theme: Preparing for the Lord

A. Reading of the Gospel
   1. Silence

B. Reflection Process
   1. Focus: The Gospel speaks about what we need to do and the attitudes we need to have as we wait for the Lord's coming.
   2. Reflect on what it means for you to prepare for someone to come and visit you. List all the things you do to prepare for the visit.
   3. Listen to the Gospel and write all the things the disciples are asked to do in preparation for the coming of the Lord. What stands out for you in the reading?
   4. Rereading of the Gospel
      a. Silence
   5. Reflecting upon your life, how are you open and ready for the coming of the Lord?
   6. What do you need in your life to change, to let go of, to forgive, etc., in order to be more open and ready for the coming of the Lord? Be specific and concrete.
   7. Small group sharing.

III. Theme: Reading the "Signs of the Times"

A. Reading of the Gospel
   1. Silence

B. Reflection Process
   1. Focus: We are invited to listen to the Lord calling out to be recognized, to be heard in the world. The Second Vatican Council referred to this as listening to the "signs of the times," those places and times in our world that call out to have the light of the Gospel shed upon them.
   2. As you reflect on the world, our nation, your neighborhood, where do you see and hear God's people crying out to be heard, to be set free, to be healed?

3. Where are the signs of hope and where are the signs of despair in our world?
4. In your understanding of Church today, what do you see as the role of "Church" in response to the signs of the times?
5. How do you understand you are to personally respond to the signs of the times?
6. Small group sharing.
7. As you hear the Gospel proclaimed, how are you affirmed or challenged in your understanding of the Church's responsibility and your responsibility to listen to the signs of the times?
8. Large group discussion.

IV. Theme: Faith and Truth

A. Reading of Hebrews 11:1–2, 8–19
   1. Silence

B. Reflection Process
   1. As you listen to the word of God, what do you hear in your heart God saying to you about trust, faith or hope? Record your response in your journal.
   2. Where in your life do you hear God calling you to deeper truth, faith or hope? Be specific.
   3. Participants share in twos (20 minutes)

C. Reflection Process Continued
   1. What do you need to let go of or to change in order to respond to God's call?
   2. What do you need from friend(s), sponsor, family, this community, yourself, in order to respond to God's call to a deeper faith, trust and hope?
   3. Small group sharing followed by large group reflection.

INTEGRATION

1. From the word shared today, what are the issues or the questions that have been raised for you regarding Catholic teaching, way of life, faith?

2. (Optional:) Input in response to the questions that were raised.

3. As a response to the homily and to the word broken open in your group, how do you hear yourself called to live the Gospel this coming week?

4. In order to live the Gospel, what will be required of you?

5. Are you willing to do what is necessary to live the Gospel this coming week?

6. What do you need from those gathered here, from your family, from your friend(s)/sponsor, from yourself in order to live the Gospel this coming week?

CLOSING PRAYER

O God of our past, God of our present, God of our future, listen to our hearts. We desire to come to know you, to let you into our lives, to be your instruments and witnesses of your kingdom breaking into our world. Send us your gifts, your faith that we may be strong and truthful to you and all your people. Listen now to the prayers of our heart. (Petitions and spontaneous prayer)

Doctrinal and Pastoral Issues: Kingdom, Heaven, Eucharist, Eschatology, Salvation, Social Justice, Theological Virtues, Vatican II Document "Church in the Modern World."

Kathy Brown

Twentieth Sunday in Ordinary Time

Jeremiah 38:4–6, 8–10
Hebrews 12:1–4
Luke 12:49–53

GATHERING PRAYER

Opening Song: "Sing Out, Earth and Skies" by David Livingston (GIA Publications).

Prayer: O Lord of peace, you challenge us to follow you in all that we do. We know that your way leads us to the cross and to baptism by fire. Lord, guide us and protect us on our journey with you. Give us your strength and courage to continue. We thank you for hearing our prayers and for your mercy. We praise you, O Lord Jesus Christ. Amen.

CATECHIST INSTRUCTION

To begin the process use "I" followed by one of the other thematic reflection processes. Invite the participants to record their responses in their journal.

I. First Reading of the Gospel

A. (Before reading the Gospel:) Listen for the word, phrase, idea or image that most speaks to you or touches you.
  1. Reading of the Gospel
  2. Silence

B. Reflection Process
  1. Record in your journal the word, phrase, idea or image that spoke to you in the reading. Why did it speak to you?
  2. What question(s) does the Gospel raise for you in your life, in your family, in your work, in your neighborhood, in the Church?
  3. Small group sharing.

II. Theme: Prophetic Community

A. Reading of the Gospel
  1. Silence

B. Reflection Process

1. Focus: Both Jeremiah and Jesus were considered prophets in their times. As a result of their prophetic mission, both stood over against established and accepted power structures, behaviors and values in their respective times in history. One of the themes of Luke's Gospel is the birth of the prophetic community of the Church.
2. Reflecting on people you have known or known about, whom would you consider modern day prophets?
3. What are the qualities, attitudes, values that these people represent for you?
4. Small group sharing.
5. In your own life, recall a specific or concrete experience of being a prophet in your work place, in your family, among your friends or in the community.
6. What were the feelings you had before, during and after your experience of being a prophet?
7. If you have never had an experience of being a prophet, what are the feelings you have about the possibility of becoming a prophet?
8. Small group sharing.
9. In your experience of "Church," how do you see "Church" being prophetic in the world, in the neighborhood, in the community, in the parish, in the homilies?
10. How do you hear "Church" being called to be prophetic? Be specific.
11. Small group sharing.
12. How has the Gospel and the sharing of the word challenged or affirmed your understanding of your role as a Christian in your family, in your work place, in your community?
13. How do you hear "Church" being challenged or affirmed in its prophetic calling?
14. Large group response.

III. Theme: Faithfulness

A. Reading of the Gospel
  1. Silence

B. Reflection Process
  1. Focus: By being faithful to himself and thus to his Father, Jesus knew that his life and message would bring division and his ultimate

death. The early Christian community also understood that to be a faithful follower of Jesus was a radical life and death decision for the kingdom. As followers of Jesus, we often have painful decisions to make, decisions that may cause division or make us unpopular.

2. Reflect on what it means for you to be faithful to yourself. What is asked of you in order to be faithful and who asks it of you?

3. Recall an event, a time in your life when you were faithful to yourself or when you knew you were unfaithful to yourself: a time when you compromised your beliefs, your values, your integrity, your faith in God, etc.

4. What were the feelings you had before, during and after the event?

5. What questions did the event or time in your life raise for you about the meaning of your life, about relationships, about God, about being a follower of Christ, about your self-worth?

6. Small group sharing.

7. As a result of this experience, what changes have taken place in your life, in your values, in your understanding of what it means to be faithful to yourself?

8. As you reflect upon the event, what changes would you make in the future regarding the process of decision making?

9. Small group sharing followed by large group reflection.

INTEGRATION

1. Write three questions that today's reading raises for you about Catholic teaching, way of life or belief.

2. (Optional:) Input in response to the Catholic questions raised.

3. After hearing the Gospel proclaimed to you in the homily and through the breaking open of the word, how do you hear yourself called to live the Gospel this coming week?

4. What will be the obstacles to keep you from living the Gospel this coming week? What will be necessary for you to change in your life, to give up or to let go of in order to live the Gospel?

5. Are you willing to make the changes?

6. What do you need from this gathered community, from the Church, from your family, from your friend(s)/sponsor, from yourself in order to live the Gospel this coming week?

CLOSING PRAYER

Read Jeremiah 20:8–10, 11, 13, followed by spontaneous, petitionary prayer.

Doctrinal and Pastoral Issues: Social Justice, Prophecy, Prophets, Kingdom, Paschal Mystery, Early Christian Community, Martyrs, Redemption

Kathy Brown

Twenty-First Sunday in Ordinary Time

Isaiah 66:18–21
Hebrews 12:5–7, 11–13
Luke 13:22–30

GATHERING PRAYER

Song: "People of Peace," by Lowenthal and Oosterhuis (Team Publications—Oregon Catholic Press).

Prayer: Lord our God, all truth is from you, and you alone bring oneness of heart. Give your people the joy of hearing your word in every sound and of longing for your presence more than for life itself. May all the attractions of a changing world serve only to bring us the peace of your kingdom which this world does not give. Grant this through Christ our Lord. Amen.

CATECHIST INSTRUCTION

Choose one of the following thematic reflection processes to guide the participants, inviting them to record their responses in their journals.

I. Theme: One People

A. Reading of Isaiah 66:18–21
  1. Silence

B. Reflection Process
  1. Focus: In the reading from Isaiah we are presented with a picture of the hope and promise of the future. It is a picture of all the nations gathered in unity, giving glory to God.
  2. In what ways do you experience personally in your life a feeling of unity, of being one with others, in your family, in your work place, in your neighborhoods, in the Church?
  3. In what ways do you experience disunity in your life, in your family, in your work place, in your neighborhoods?
  4. What contributes to the disunity that you experience?
  5. In what ways do you contribute to unity or disunity?
  6. Small group sharing.
  7. In your experience how do you see "Church" contributing to unity or disunity in your neigh-

borhood, in your city, in the world, in people's lives?
  8. Large group discussion.
  9. How do you hear Isaiah inviting you to contribute to unity in your life? What is the hope and promise offered to you?
  10. How do you hear Isaiah inviting "Church" to contribute to unity? What is the hope and the promise offered to "Church"?
  11. Large group discussion.

II. Theme: First Hearing of the Gospel

A. Reading of the Gospel
  1. Before reading the Gospel: Listen for the word, the phrase, the idea that most speaks to your life.
  2. Reading of the Gospel
  3. Silence

B. Reflection Process
  1. Reflect and write on why that word, phrase or idea spoke to you at this time in your life.
  2. Small group sharing.

III. Theme: The Good News

A. Reading of the Gospel
  1. Silence

B. Reflection Process
  1. Focus: Sometimes the reading of the "good news" does not sound like "good news." The Gospel is very often the hard news, the radical invitation to live the Christian life without compromise.
  2. As you listened to the Gospel, was it good news or hard news for you? Why?
  3. Reflecting on all the Scriptures can you think of other "hard news" readings, stories, etc.?
  4. What makes a reading "hard news" vs. "good news"?
  5. Small group sharing.
  6. How is the Gospel also a reading of hope and not just hard news for your life?
  7. How does the Gospel challenge and affirm you in your life, in your job, in your family, in your beliefs?
  8. Small group sharing followed by large group discussion.

IV. Theme: Salvation

A. Reading of the Gospel
   1. Silence

B. Reflection Process
   1. Focus: The Gospel speaks about how those who were first invited to feast in the kingdom will in fact be passed by while others, those least expected, will gain entry to the kingdom's feast. That which was thought to be necessary to enter into the kingdom of God is in reality not sufficient. The Gospel challenges the reader to a personal response.
   2. As we grew up we were introduced to the religious concept of "to be saved." For you what does it mean to be saved?
   Has your understanding of "to be saved" changed for you during your life, and, if so, how?
   3. If you did not grow up being introduced to the religious concept of "to be saved" at this time in your life and reflecting on the Scriptures, what do you believe "to be saved" means for you personally?
   4. Small group sharing.
   5. As you listen to the word of God and reflect upon its meaning for your life, how does the Gospel challenge or affirm you in your understanding of who will be saved or who will enter the kingdom of God?
   6. What other Scripture passages raise questions for you about who will be saved?
   7. Small group sharing followed by large group reflection.

INTEGRATION

1. As you reflect upon the homily and the word broken open today, what are the questions it raises for you about Catholic teaching, way of life, faith?

2. (Optional:) Input in response to the Catholic questions raised.

3. Name one concrete and specific way you hear yourself called to live the Gospel this coming week.

4. What do you see as the obstacles to living the Gospel this week? Are you willing to overcome the obstacles?

5. What do you need from this gathered community, from your family, from the Church, from your friend(s)/sponsor to help you live the Gospel this coming week?

CLOSING PRAYER

Read Psalm 117 together, followed by spontaneous petitionary prayers.

Doctrinal and Pastoral Issues: Conversion, Ecumenism, Salvation, Kingdom of God, Hope, Faith, Heaven and Hell

Kathy Brown

Twenty-Second Sunday of Ordinary Time

Sirach 3:17–18, 20, 28–29
Hebrews 12:18–19, 22–24
Luke 14:1, 7–14

GATHERING PRAYER

Song: "One Bread, One Body," by John B. Foley, S.J. (*Glory and Praise*, #127).

Prayer: Loving God of creation, who has made us in your image and likeness, you call us to become one with you, to be a people enlightened by your Word made flesh. Create in us a new spirit, opening our minds and hearts to receive you in and through all your people. May we become a humble and caring people for all your creation. We ask this through Christ our Lord. Amen.

CATECHIST INSTRUCTION

Choose one of the following thematic reflection processes to guide the participants, inviting them to record their responses in their journals.

I. Theme: Christian Humility

A. Reading of Sirach 3:14–17, 20, 28–29
   1. Silence

B. Reflection Process
   1. Reflecting upon your childhood, how did you grow up understanding the meaning of humility? What did this mean for your daily life?
   2. As an adult has your understanding of what it means for you to be humble changed? What are the similarities and differences?
   3. Small group sharing
   4. Rereading of Sirach
      a. Silence
   5. How does the reading from Sirach add to or detract from your understanding of humility?
   6. How does the reading challenge or affirm your understanding of what it means to be humble?
   7. Small group sharing followed by large group response.

II. Theme: Invitation to the Table

A. Reading of the Gospel
   1. Silence

B. Reflection Process
   1. Focus: The Gospel speaks about those who are invited and those who ought to be invited to the table of the Lord. Instead of inviting those familiar to us, Jesus tells us that we are to invite beggars, the crippled, the lame and the blind.
   2. As you reflect upon your life, your neighborhood, your work place, our country, identify who the beggars, the crippled, the lame and the blind are for you in your life. Be specific and concrete.
   3. In your experience of "Church" who are the beggars, the crippled, the lame and the blind?
   4. As you look around the members of your parish community, who would you say is invited into the community and who is not?
   5. Small group sharing.
   6. Compare and contrast those whom you consider to be the "beggars, crippled, lame and blind" with those you experience being welcomed in "Church" and in your parish community.
   7. Small group sharing.
   8. Reading of the Gospel
      a. Silence
   9. How does the Gospel challenge or enlighten your experience of who is welcome in your life, in your family, in your work place or in your parish community?
   10. Where in your life do you hear the Gospel calling you to change?
   11. Large group response.

INTEGRATION

1. What questions, concerns or issues, does the Gospel raise for you regarding Catholic teaching, Catholic practice, Catholic law, Catholic belief?

2. (Optional:) Input in response to questions raised.

3. As you listen to the word opened up for you today,

how do you hear yourself called to live the Gospel this coming week?

4. In order to live the Gospel this coming week, what do you need to do, to let go of or to change?

5. Are you willing to do what is necessary to live the Gospel?

6. What help do you need from this community, from the Church, from your friend(s)/sponsor, from your family, from yourself, in order to live the Gospel this coming week?

CLOSING PRAYER

Loving and compassionate God, we know that you are there for us, guiding us along the path to you. Help us to be faithful to ourselves and to you; help us to hear and see all those you call to the table. May we by our lives invite others to come to know you and to experience acceptance in your family. Strengthen and empower us to be your body of hope for all people. In Christ's name we pray. Amen.

Doctrinal and Pastoral Issues: Fruits of the Spirit, Eucharist, Church Law, Authority, Ecclesiology, Social Justice, Ministry and Mission of the Church, Divorce and Remarriage, Healing, Sacrament of Reconciliation

Kathy Brown

Twenty-Third Sunday of Ordinary Time

Wisdom 9:13–18
Philemon 9–10, 12–17
Luke 14:25–33

GATHERING PRAYER

Song: "My God and My All," by David Haas (GIA Publications).

Opening Prayer: Psalm 90 (read together)

CATECHIST INSTRUCTION

Choose one of the following thematic reflection processes to guide the participants, inviting them to record their responses in their journals.

I. Theme: Wisdom

A. Reading of Wisdom 9:13–18
   1. Silence

B. Reflection Process
   1. Reflecting on your childhood, what was the image of God you grew up with? Was God absent, present or "out there"?
   2. What is your image of God as an adult? Is God absent, present or "out there" or some other image?
   3. In what ways has your image changed or remained the same, similar or different?
   4. Small group sharing.
   5. How does your understanding of God respect the distance and difference between God and yourself? How does your prayer respect those differences? What are the differences and distances between God and you? In other words, how is God intimate to you?
   6. Small group sharing.
   7. How do you hear the reading and the sharing challenging your understanding of who God is and is not for you?
   8. How does the reading speak to you of hope and promise in your life? How do the differences and distance between yourself and God extend to you both hope and promise in your life?

10. Small group sharing followed by large group reflection.

II. Theme: Proclaiming Our Faith

A. Reading of the Gospel
   1. Silence

B. Reflection Process
   1. Recall an experience of being uncomfortable speaking or living your faith or your Christian convictions or your religious practices. What were the feelings you had before, during and after the experience?
   2. What were the issues involved and how did you resolve them?
   3. Small group sharing.
   4. What were the assumptions you had about the people involved and about the consequences of proclaiming your faith?
   5. Reading of the Gospel
      a. Silence
   6. How does the Gospel speak to your experience? What does it affirm or challenge in your experience?
   7. Small group sharing.

III. Theme: Cost of Discipleship

A. Reading of the Gospel
   1. Silence

B. Reflection Process
   1. Focus: The Gospel speaks about the single-mindedness required of those who desire to follow Jesus. Discipleship requires that we follow the way of Jesus which leads to the cross. To follow Jesus calls for total renunciation, for self-giving, to place God's kingdom before all else and to persevere in the journey. Discipleship calls for us to renounce all our possessions and our relationships that keep us from focusing upon Christ.
   2. Recall an experience in your life when you set a goal to be achieved. Remember all the feelings, reasons and motivations you had for achieving the goal.
   3. What were the qualities and attitudes you needed to achieve the goal?

4. What were the obstacles you faced to achieve your goal?
5. Small group sharing.
6. As you look at your life as a follower of Jesus, what do you see as your goal?
7. What do you need in order to persevere in your discipleship and in your singlemindedness in following Jesus?
8. What keeps you from totally committing your life to being a disciple of Jesus?
9. Small group sharing.
10. As you hear the Gospel addressed to you, how are you being invited and called to a different or deeper life of discipleship?
11. What fears, anxieties, concerns does the call to discipleship raise for you?
12. Large group reflection.

INTEGRATION

1. As you listen to the Gospel and the homily, what questions does it raise for you regarding Catholic teaching, way of life, beliefs, etc.?

2. (Optional:) Input in response to the questions raised.

3. As you hear the Gospel proclaimed to you in the homily, and in the group sharing, how do you hear yourself called to live the Gospel this coming week?

4. What is it going to cost you to live the Gospel and are you willing to pay the price?

5. What do you need from your family, from God, from your friend(s)/sponsor, from the Church in order to live the Gospel this coming week?

CLOSING PRAYER

Read Ephesians 1:15–22, followed by spontaneous petitionary prayer.

Doctrinal and Pastoral Issues: Discipleship, Mission of the Church, Ministry, Evangelization, Judgment, Sin, Conversion, Trinity, God, Mystery, Revelation

Kathy Brown

Introduction to Sundays 24–33 in Ordinary Time

In the following each catechetical session follows these steps:

> Gathering Prayer
> Reflection Questions
> Key Points for Reflection (Input)
> Integration Questions
> Closing Prayer

Each session is written with a 2 to 2½ hour time frame in mind. It is hoped that the sessions could take place immediately following dismissal from the Sunday liturgy. If however this is not possible, then it is recommended that a reading of the word be incorporated into the Gathering Prayer. This will serve as a "refresher" since several days may have elapsed since the Sunday liturgy. Using some variations in the method of presenting the readings may be helpful. For example, the Gospel may be presented in a dialogue reading.

The third step in the process involves using the key points for reflection. In most sessions it will be necessary to choose only a few of these points to incorporate into the "input" time. The needs of catechumenate groups vary and the catechist should determine which points are of particular relevance to his or her group. In most cases, the length of the input step should be limited to 10–15 minutes. The response of the catechumens within their small groups is of primary importance in the session. Always allow plenty of time for this integration step, even if that means a shorter input period.

Assumed, but not always stated, is that each session allows time for questions. This can be done following the input step or following the integration sharing. One method of drawing forth their questions is to ask them what they have seen or heard that raised a question or a concern for them regarding God, Christ, Church, etc. Another suggestion is to ask them to respond to these two questions:

• What has been clarified for you during this session?
• What has caused you confusion or doubt during this session?

These responses can be done either in writing or verbally. In either case, it is important for the catechist to listen or read carefully. These responses will provide valuable guidance as to the needs of the group and the effectiveness of the catechetical sessions.

Twenty-Fourth Sunday in Ordinary Time

Exodus 32:7–11, 13–14
1 Timothy 1:12–17
Luke 15:1–32

GATHERING PRAYER

"Hosea" by Gregory Norbert (*Glory and Praise #262*), or "Redeemer Lord" by John B. Foley, S.J. (*Glory and Praise, #233*)

REFLECTION QUESTIONS

(These questions should be answered individually and then shared in small groups of three or four persons.)

1. What does the word "mercy" mean to you? How have you experienced God's mercy?

2. When was the last time you met up against a block in your life that forced you to re-evaluate your pattern of living? Describe this situation and how you responded to it.

KEY POINTS FOR REFLECTION (INPUT)

1. All of these readings are stories of God's mercy—mercy toward Moses' people, toward Paul, and toward all who stray. "God's mercy endures forever." Share what that statement means in your life. How have you experienced God's mercy? How has the enduring quality of God's mercy affected your life?

2. The son who returned had to come to grips with himself before he was willing to amend his ways, to return home. We must evaluate ourselves periodically, too. We have to face the areas in our lives that are pulling us away from the Father. Then we must make the decision to change. This is the on-going conversion process to which we are all called. Share how this has happened in your life recently.

3. In the Gospel story the faithful son resents the way in which the father celebrates his brother's return. While the father celebrates in joy, the faithful son is sulking and engages in self-pity. As Christians we are told to rejoice in one another's joys, to share in one another's sorrows. Relate a situation in your own life where this was/is difficult. How did you respond? What are some ways that you have worked through this difficulty?

4. The story of the lost sheep urges us to see ourselves one-to-one with the Lord. We find it quite easy to accept that God loves *us*, in the flock. But when we reduce the *us* to *me*, it's often more difficult to fully accept. Reflect on the statement that God rejoices over our return.

5. The Church offers us many opportunities for conversion through the sacraments of Eucharist and reconciliation. Talk about how these sacraments call us to change continually. Explain how God's mercy is an important factor in each of these.

INTEGRATION QUESTIONS

(These questions should be answered, and even "journaled" if possible. Then allow time for sharing.)

1. Reread the Gospel story. With whom do you identify in the story—the father, the son who returns, or the faithful son? What has happened in your own life that puts you in that character so easily?

2. Summarize, in one or two sentences, the message of this Gospel for your life. How are you called to grow in the coming week?

3. Recall how you responded to the question of how you have experienced God's mercy. Perhaps other occasions have come to mind during this session. Offer a prayer of thanksgiving for his gift of mercy.

CLOSING PRAYER

Psalm 136 (as a responsorial)

Response: His mercy endures forever.

> Give thanks to the Lord for he is good.
> Give thanks to the God of gods.
> Give thanks to the Lord of lords. ℟.
>
> Who alone does great wonders,
> Who made the heavens in wisdom,
> Who spread out the earth upon the waters. ℟.

Who made the great lights,
the sun to rule over the day,
the moon and the stars to rule over the night.
℞.

Who leads his people through the wilderness,
Who remembers us in our abjection,
And frees us from our foes. ℞.

*Doctrinal and Pastoral Issues: Mercy, Faithfulness,
Forgiveness, Celebration, Reconciliation*

Khris Ford

Twenty-Fifth Sunday in Ordinary Time

Amos 8:4–7
1 Timothy 2:1–8
Luke 16:1–13

GATHERING PRAYER

Sing: "Gather Us In," words and music by Marty Haugen (GIA Publications, 1982), especially verses 1, 2, and 4. Verse 3 would not be appropriate.

Leader prays: (Begin with sign of the cross) O Lord, you gather us in, to be your people, to be one in you. Open our ears this day that we may hear your words of truth and justice. Open our eyes to see the injustice in the world about us. Strengthen us that we may respond as your loving people. In Christ we pray. Amen.

REFLECTION QUESTIONS

(These questions should be answered individually and then shared in groups of three or four.)

1. Reread Amos 8:4–8. What phrase/word struck you? Describe your reaction and why you think you reacted in that way.

2. What is your overall reaction to the story of the clever manager in today's Gospel? What does this reading say to us about discipleship and the "business world" of today?

KEY POINTS FOR REFLECTION (INPUT)

1. Amos' reading mandates that we must be concerned for the poor and makes a strong statement regarding those who "trample upon the needy." This is not merely an Old Testament story but one fitting for the situation in our world today. Share some stories of injustice from your own experience. Find articles in today's newspaper regarding this. Share also some ways that you and/or the Church are working to build up the poor, to fight against some injustice.

2. Often we fail to pray for those with whom we disagree, especially those in positions of authority over us. Timothy's letter bids us to pray always for those who are in authority. Perhaps we should pray at least as often as we donate and/or write letters to our leaders. In Mass we include specific prayers for Church leaders and for government leaders, regardless of their political stance.

3. Discipleship involves being well informed on world affairs as well as "Church" affairs. Christ invites us to use wisely all the gifts he has given us. Through wise and prudent use of material goods we can lessen the hurt of the poor and come closer to living out the kingdom values.

4. Introduce at least part of the pastoral letter on the economy. The Church mandates that we uphold the Gospel values as we plan and work through the economic issues in our personal life as well as those of our country. Talk about some of the implications of this in your personal life.

5. Money—you can't live with it, you can't live without it! How we live with it can be an important test of who we are as Catholic Christians. Give some examples of Christian money management in your own life. How can money become an "evil" in our life?

6. If we are dishonest in our business dealings, worship on Sunday becomes a lie, according to Amos. Share what this statement means to you. How does sharing in the celebration of the Eucharist call us to a different way of living?

INTEGRATION QUESTIONS

1. How will you live out the challenge of this Gospel in the coming week, especially in your "work environment"? Is there some particular situation that needs to be looked at in light of this Gospel?

2. Injustice is all about us, if we but open our eyes to it. How will you respond to this in the coming week?

CLOSING PRAYER

Say a prayer for those in authority in this country and throughout the world. Insert the names of specific local leaders as well. Respond to these petitions with: The Lord hears the cry of the poor. Blessed be the Lord.

Conclude this prayer of petitions with the Lord's Prayer and a song of peace.

and/or

Listen to or sing: "The Cry of the Poor" by John B. Foley, S.J. (*Glory and Praise #93*).

Doctrinal and Pastoral Issues: Justice, Economic Pastoral, Stewardship, Authority and Power, Social Sin, Social Consciousness

Khris Ford

Twenty-Sixth Sunday in Ordinary Time

Amos 6:1, 4–7
1 Timothy 6:11–16
Luke 16:19–31

GATHERING PRAYER

Lord, our God,
in you justice and mercy meet.
With incredible love you have saved us from
  death
and have drawn us into your life.

Open our eyes to the wonders this life sets before us,
that we may serve you free from fear,
offering to others your life and your love.

Help us in your mercy to see those things we
  would rather avoid,
and give us strength to do the deeds of love
  that you would have us do.

We ask this through Christ our Lord and Savior. Amen.

REFLECTION QUESTIONS

1. Luke paints a picture of vivid contrast between the lifestyle of Lazarus and that of the rich man. Have you ever experienced these "extremes" in society? How does it make you feel?

2. "But if someone would only go to them from the dead, then they would repent." Could this statement be made about us today? How do you react to this statement?

KEY POINTS FOR REFLECTION (INPUT)

1. The contrast between Lazarus and the "rich man" is stark and unmistakable. The contrast between the "haves" and the "have nots" of our society is equally as clear. Yet, too often we sit by as uninvolved by-standers. In doing so, we become "involved part-ners" in the injustice. The ten commandments mandate that we not murder or steal. Often we dis-miss these when we look at ourselves. Of course we haven't killed anyone or stolen anything. But have we been partners in "killing" the dignity of others or in taking from them what is their God-given right to life?

2. Through our identification with the body of Christ, we are in union with the poor and the helpless. They too are a part of Christ's body. If one part of the body suffers, we all suffer.

3. Material things are good because they are created by God. But we are obliged to use them to meet the needs of all. Share what this means in your life. How is this a challenge to what the world tells us?

4. Christ united us in relationship to God and to one another. The two relationships are intimately bound to one another. Thus, our response to God is shown in our love and service to our neighbors. To love our neighbors implies that we recognize and reverence their dignity and rights.

5. The mission of the Gospel is to liberate humans for the sake of justice. Justice happens when persons are free to become all that God intended them to be.

6. In the reading from Amos, the upper class of the Is-raelite society believed they were deserving of the benefits handed down to them from their ancestors. They were, after all, God's chosen people. Quite often we get caught up in our many blessings and begin to believe that we deserve them because of our hard work, cleverness, talent, etc. Let us not forget that all that we have is gift. We deserve noth-ing.

7. To be God's chosen people is a special calling. Like all special "callings," it comes with responsibility and demands accountability. What does this mean in your life as a Catholic Christian? How would your life be different if you were not a "chosen" person?

INTEGRATION

Invite men and women who are involved in social jus-tice activities to join you for this session (Catholic Worker House, Catholic Charities, men's and women's shelters, prison ministry groups, etc.). Divide into small groups with one "guest" in each. Ask them to

share their experience and its impact on their lives.
Also, they may wish to share any pressing needs of
their "group." Allow those in the group to interact with
each "guest."

Bring the whole group back together for any comments
that they may have regarding what they have heard.
Then pose the following questions:

What is the Lord asking of me through today's readings?

How will I respond to him during the coming week?

CLOSING PRAYER

Sing together "The Harvest of Justice" by David Haas
(GIA Publications, 1985).

Leader: Go in peace to love and serve the Lord and
              one another.

All: Thanks be to God.

Doctrinal and Pastoral Issues: Christian Lifestyle, Justice, Body of Christ, Stewardship, Humility

Khris Ford

Twenty-Seventh Sunday in Ordinary Time

Habakkuk 1:2–3; 2:2–4
2 Timothy 1:6–8, 13–14
Luke 17:5–10

GATHERING PRAYER

Give us, O Lord, a greater faith. We often get mixed up—we confuse faith with believing, with creeds, and with lists of teachings.

Help us to understand that creeds and teachings are only our human way of putting words on that which takes place within our hearts when we turn to you.

Help us to respond in faith to the world about us, to nourish our faith with your word and presence.

In Jesus' name, we pray. Amen.

REFLECTION QUESTIONS

1. 2 Timothy calls our faith a "rich deposit" and exhorts us to guard this faith. What is your reaction to this statement? How do you "guard" your faith?

2. What does this title of "useless servant" mean to you?

KEY POINTS FOR REFLECTION (INPUT)

1. Faith is gift. We do not earn it or deserve it. Faith transforms us and allows us to see with "new vision." How often we take this great gift for granted!

2. The good works we perform in response to the gift of faith, are expected of us. "Faith without works is dead." But these works do not earn us salvation. They are simply the work of being disciples of Christ.

3. All things are possible with God, even the transplanting of a sycamore tree into the sea. Do we really believe that? Our faith gives us the power of the Spirit. Do we exercise that power to glorify God in our lives?

4. Quite often we think of faith as that quiet, strong foundation for us. Today's readings remind us that our faith must be alive, afire, compelling, and dynamic. Share how someone's dynamic and alive faith witnessed to you recently.

5. God does not need our good works to accomplish his purpose. Yet he does allow us to live out his purpose and to respond to this gift of faith by doing good works.

6. The term "useless servant" may make us bristle. But it is a statement of understanding what we are expected to be and do as disciples of Christ. The word "useless" reminds us that there is no room for boasting of these deeds. The grace already given impells us to serve, enduring many hardships. The term "useless" also reminds us that it is especially in our weakness that God is able to use us most effectively.

7. Paul's letter to Timothy tells him to guard the faith. We too must guard our faith as we would a love relationship. Our faith must be nurtured and tended, watered and pruned. We do this through reading and studying God's word, personal and shared prayer, and in fellowship with other Christians. We guard our faith through frequenting the sacraments of the Church, especially the Eucharist and reconciliation. Share some special ways you have guarded your faith.

8. An "unguarded faith" may fall prey to the many evils of the world—to doubting, to pride, etc. Share an experience or a time when your faith faltered because you did not guard it.

9. As in the situation of Habakkuk, violence and disaster often cause us to "take stock" of our faith and our entire life. In such times we may also say, as was said in the Scriptures, "Increase our faith."

INTEGRATION

1. Have you ever prayed for an increase in faith? What was the situation? What was the "fruit" of your prayer?

2. Often we are tempted to try to impress others with our many "good works." Is this happening in any area of your life? What would Christ say to you concerning your tasks? Is yours the attitude of a "useless servant"?

3. How has your faith been a "gift" during the past week? How will you "guard your rich deposit of faith" during the coming week?

CLOSING PRAYER

Leader: Lord, you have given us the gift of faith, whereby we affirm that Jesus is the Son of God. We hold fast to this faith we have received. We guard this rich deposit within us.

Response: Lord, increase our faith.

Leader: We believe that God loves us unconditionally and desires for us the fullness of life.

Response: Lord, increase our faith.

Leader: We believe that God calls us to constantly turn toward him and grow in his likeness.

Response: Lord, increase our faith.

Leader: We believe that God forgives our sins if we but ask in faith.

Response: Lord, increase our faith.

Leader: We believe that in Jesus Christ's death he won victory over sin for us.

Response: Lord, increase our faith.

Leader: We believe that one day we shall meet Christ face to face and we shall reign with him.

Response: I believe, Lord. Help my unbelief.

Sing: "We Thank You, Father" by Gregory Norbert (*Glory and Praise #272*).

Doctrinal and Pastoral Issues: Faith, Doubt, Creed, Salvation, Thanksgiving, Eucharist, God's Healing

Khris Ford

Twenty-Eighth Sunday in Ordinary Time

2 Kings 5:14–17
2 Timothy 2:8–13
Luke 17:11–19

GATHERING PRAYER

Sing: "All the Ends of the Earth" by Robert Dufford, S.J. (*Glory and Praise, #174*), or "Save Us, O Lord" by Robert Dufford, S.J. (*Glory and Praise #234*).

REFLECTION QUESTIONS

1. Recall a time in the recent past when God revealed his saving power to you. What was your response? Describe the situation. How do you feel now as you "relive" this event?

2. To the one who returned, Jesus said: "Get up and go. Your faith has made you well." What is your reaction to this statement? What about the faith of the other nine who were cured?

KEY POINTS FOR REFLECTION (INPUT)

1. Jesus came for the salvation of all people—Jews and Gentiles, Samaritans and Galileans, blacks and whites, etc. Is this the message of salvation that our daily lives proclaim?

2. The lepers in the Gospel were not only suffering from a terrible disease that diminished their ability to live fully, but they were also isolated from society. They suffered from discrimination as well. Their lives were broken both physically and psychologically/spiritually. Today we see the disease of AIDS doing much the same thing to people. How will we respond?

3. The Samaritan leper is the only one who returns and expresses his gratitude to Christ. He has experienced, first-hand the power of God. This brings him to faith and his response is one of thanksgiving. Share an experience of God's healing power. Share how you responded to this experience. When we respond in thanksgiving the graces received are multiplied.

4. Quite often we take God's power and healing for granted, especially when life goes smoothly. We do not respond in thanksgiving. In fact, often we don't even consider the source of the "smoothness." Like the other nine lepers, our experience of God does not lead us to a deepening in faith.

5. It is important to remember and to retell the stories of God's saving power in our life, and to give thanks. We do this when we gather for Eucharist each week. Each time we remember and give thanks we are deepened in our faith. When difficult times confront us we need only recall how God has always been there for us. Our faith has been and will be our salvation.

INTEGRATION

1. Recall the events of this past week (both personal and community/world events). How was God most present to you? What is/was he doing in your life? Share this with someone.

2. Tell the Lord, either in writing or in thoughts, how thankful you are for his work within you.

3. Anticipate the next few days. How will your memory of God working within you help you to live the next few days more fully for the Lord?

CLOSING PRAYER

Leader begins with a spontaneous prayer of thanksgiving, focusing on Christ's action in our lives. All are invited to participate in the prayer by adding their own special intention.

In between each intention, respond by singing the refrain to: "Remember your mercy (or your kindness), O Lord" (David Haas, GIA, 1985).

Close the prayer by praying for the outcasts of society; like the lepers, Christ offers them salvation. Specific groups and/or individuals who are oppressed or living on the fringes of society should be mentioned by the leader.

Exchange the sign of peace as a sign of wholeness and of our thanksgiving for Christ present in one another.

Doctrinal and Pastoral Issues: Salvation, Healing, Faith
"Outcasts," Power of God, Prejudice

Khris Ford

Twenty-Ninth Sunday in Ordinary Time

Exodus 17:8–13
2 Timothy 3:14–4:2
Luke 18:1–8

GATHERING PRAYER

Prayerfully read Psalm 115.

and/or

Sing: "If God Is for Us" by John B. Foley, S.J. (*Glory and Praise*, #25).

or

Listen to: "Our Help Is From the Lord" (Wood Hath Hope, NALR, 1978).

REFLECTION QUESTIONS

1. Name one or two ideas or concepts that you feel strongly enough about to "plead for" and to argue persistently as did the widow. Recall a time when you did this.

2. What part does your community of faith play in your prayer life? How was this a part of our Exodus reading?

KEY POINTS FOR REFLECTION (INPUT)

1. The widow was rewarded for her persistence in coming before the judge to beg for justice. How often have we been willing to be this persistent and vulnerable for the sake of just treatment (especially someone else's)? Share some occasions when this persistence has been rewarded.

2. Persistence in prayer is a message of this Gospel reading, as well as the reading from Exodus. Often we find it difficult to pray—times of distress, times when we don't "feel" God's presence. These are the times when we most need to pray. Share some personal experience of "dryness" or "difficulty" in prayer.

3. Our parish community can help us to sustain our prayer and to keep from getting too discouraged during difficult times. Share examples of parish support. Perhaps several people could give personal examples of this. Bring in some special "guest" to share on this.

4. We often doubt our ability to be faithful, persistent in our faith, in times of difficulty. These stories reassure us of this power within us. Remember that we are created in God's image.

5. We are reminded in Paul's letter to Timothy that the Scriptures should be our source of strength. This should be true at all times, but, most especially, when we are in times of trial and testing of our faith. Share a time when the word has been a source of strength.

6. All Scripture is inspired by God and is useful for teaching the truth, rebuking error, correcting faults, and giving instructions for right living. Share the teachings of the Church concerning the "divine origin" of the Bible. (See Vatican II's Dogmatic Constitution on Divine Revelation.)

INTEGRATION

1. Reflect on the past few days. In what area of my life have I not been persistent enough in my pursuit of the Lord and his ways? When/where have I settled for less than the Gospel asks of me?

    What will I do this week to be stronger (more faith-filled) in this area? How will Scripture and prayer help me in this?

2. Reflect on the past few days. Remember especially those times when Christ was faithful to his promise, when he was there for you. Take time to "bask" in this recognition of God's caring and loving you. Offer him your thanks.

CLOSING PRAYER

Ask each person to identify a favorite verse or phrase from Scripture that has been personally helpful in times of need. After a period of silence ask that each person read his or her Scripture passage aloud. Each person concludes by saying: "Our help is from the Lord."

All respond, "Thanks be to God."

The leader might close the time of prayer by saying: "Glory be to the Father . . ."

Doctrinal and Pastoral Issues: Justice, Christian Action, Prayer, Revelation

Khris Ford

Thirtieth Sunday in Ordinary Time

Sirach 35:12–14, 16–18
2 Timothy 4:6–8, 16–18
Luke 18:9–14

GATHERING PRAYER

Sing: "Come, My Children" by the Dameans (*Glory and Praise*, #189), or Read Psalm 34 prayerfully.

REFLECTION QUESTIONS

1. There is a popular saying often seen on plaques. It reads: Be patient. God isn't finished with me yet! How does this relate to the two prayers heard in the Gospel? How does this statement relate to you?

2. Describe someone whose life is an example of humility. How has this person been a witness to you?

KEY POINTS FOR REFLECTION (INPUT)

1. To "keep the faith" is not only to preserve and keep intact the gift of faith. It is also to live the faith. Paul writes about his lived faith, his life sacrificed for Christ.

2. The sacrifices we offer the Lord must be sincere and honest. We must offer the gift of ourselves, above all. In doing this, our rituals of sacrifice are not hollow and mere "motions." Rather the ritual becomes a celebration of our giving of our very selves. Talk about how the Mass is this kind of celebration.

3. How easy it is to fall into the trap of the "Pharisee," performing good works for the glorification of self. Doing the right thing for the wrong reason brings condemnation on us. Often times it also diminishes the way others see Christ.

4. The humility of the tax collector makes his prayer a true offering to the Lord. In his humility he is raised to greatness in the Lord's sight. Share a story of someone who exhibits this quality of humility. Tell how this person strengthens your faith and knowledge of Christ.

5. Salvation and justification are gifts from God, not something we accomplish through any deeds. To believe and live otherwise is to set ourself up as a kind of God.

6. Like the tax collector, we are seen as "upright" when we recognize and confess our sinfulness before the Lord. The Lord comes to the needy, those who recognize their incompleteness and brokenness.

7. On our faith journey, the "race" Paul speaks about, we can only compare ourselves to Christ. No other measure is of consequence in a life lived for Christ. What does this say about the "race" for status in today's world?

8. Only God can be the judge of life's "victories and failings." To judge others is to put ourselves in place of God. We can only be concerned with our own journey in response to God's love for us.

INTEGRATION

1. What is the Lord's personal message for you in today's readings?

   How do the readings speak to you about your prayer life? about the abundance/lack of humility in your life? about your motives in the good deeds that you do? about judging others and comparing yourself with others?

2. Like the tax collector we must recognize our sinfulness, our "incompleteness." Where do you need the Lord to fill the void? Where/what is the "missing piece" right now? Share your thoughts about this with the Lord in prayer.

3. Paul speaks of his life as a "race" with the victory prize to be awarded to those who wait with love for Christ. In the coming week how will you "wait with love for him to appear"?

CLOSING PRAYER

Leader: Let us pray for the grace of humility. (allow time for silent prayer)

Leader: "For when we were still helpless Christ died for the wicked at the time that God chose" (Rom 5:6).

All:	To him be all honor and glory forever.
Leader:	"Though he was in the form of God, he did not deem equality with God something to be grasped at. Rather he emptied himself and took the form of a slave, being born in the likeness of men." (Phil 2:6–8).
All:	To him be all honor and glory forever.
Leader:	"Because you are God's chosen ones, clothe yourselves with heartfelt mercy, kindness, humility, meekness, and patience."
All:	To him be all honor and glory forever.
Sing:	"There Is one Lord" by the Dameans (*Glory and Praise*, #242) or album *Path of Life*, Dameans, 1981 or "Eye Has Not Seen" by Marty Haugen (GIA Publications, 1982).

Doctrinal and Pastoral Issues: Patience, Prayer, Humility, Faith, Sacrifice, Self-Gift, Pharisees, Salvation, Eucharist

Khris Ford

Thirty-First Sunday in Ordinary Time

Wisdom 11:22—12:1
2 Thessalonians 1:11—2:2
Luke 19:1–10

GATHERING PRAYER

Sing: "The Lord Has Seen Me" (from *Justice Like a River*, B. Huijbers, Oregon Catholic Press, 1984), or "I Long for You" by the Dameans (*Glory and Praise*, #204) or album *Path of Life*, Dameans, 1981)

Pray: Late have I loved you,
             O Beauty ever ancient, ever new,
             Late have I loved you!

             You were within me,
             but I was outside,
             and it was there that I searched for you.
             In my unloveliness
             I plunged into the lovely things which you
                 created.
             You were with me, but I was not from you;
             Created things kept me from you;
             yet if they had not been in you
             they would not have been at all.
             You called, you shouted
             and you broke through my deafness.
             You flashed, you shone,
             and you dispelled my blindness.
             You breathed your fragrance on me;
             I drew in breath and now I pant for you.
             I have tasted you,
             now I hunger and thirst for more.
             You touched me,
             and I burned for your peace.

             In the name of the Father . . . Amen.

             (Prayer of St. Augustine)

REFLECTION QUESTIONS

1. Zacchaeus longed to just get a glimpse of Jesus. Recall a time when you longed to experience the presence of Jesus. Describe this situation, what you felt and what you did.

2. Insert your own name in the "blank" and visualize Jesus saying these words to you:
   "_____, hurry! I mean to stay at your house today!" What is your response to those words directed to you?

KEY POINTS FOR REFLECTION (INPUT)

1. Our reading from Wisdom reminds us that God can do all things, and that our very existence is in God's hands. That we are here is a sign that God loves and us and has called us to some purpose here on earth.

2. Zacchaeus was physically short and could not see above the crowd to view Jesus. Often we see ourselves as small, and we are unable to view Jesus because of our blindness, our sins. Failure to live out our calling diminishes us and distorts our vision.

3. In order to bring Christ into focus in our lives we have to climb up, too. We must see our failures and repent. We must commit to a new way of living, with Christ as our focal point.

4. Jesus sought out Zacchaeus—not the other way around. It was Jesus who spotted Zacchaeus along the mobbed roadway. It was Jesus who approached Zacchaeus and spoke to him. The name Zacchaeus means "God remembered." Just as God remembered Zacchaeus, he remembers each of us too. He seeks us out and comes to our house to stay. How often we get that twisted and convince ourselves that it is we who have chosen God when in actuality it is God who has chosen us.

5. Jesus comes to us right where we are, in the simplest of surroundings. Quite often he comes when we least expect him. God wants us to be transparent before him. He wants us to welcome him into our heart and to tell him our deepest secrets and yearnings. Like Zacchaeus, when we trust in God's love enough to admit our failings, then we can receive his gift of salvation.

6. The crowds on the road to Jericho were blinded by their own judgmental attitude toward others. They were shocked when Jesus chose the house of a sinner for a visit. Share a time when attitudes like this blinded you. How was your "vision" restored?

7. Zacchaeus went beyond the requirements of the law

to repay for his sins. The Beatitudes remind us that to just follow the laws (the ten commandments) is not enough. Jesus asks more of us. He asks us to strive for perfection in loving as he did.

8. In order to see Jesus, Zacchaeus was willing to go to considerable effort, to climb a tree and go out on a limb. Are we willing to go to efforts, to go out on a limb to come to know God better? Share some ways we might do this, individually and in community.

9. Like Jesus we are called to love the sinners and to look beyond their sin to their goodness. When we do this we enable them to "walk taller" and perhaps to see a glimpse of Jesus. Sometimes this may mean that we will have to risk and be willing to trust in the Lord.

INTEGRATION

1. Jesus speaks his words to us concerning how we accuse and judge one another. Instead we are told to be like sons and daughters of Abraham and respond beyond the law. How can I reach out to someone on the "fringes of life" during the coming week? What individual or group have I accused unjustly or made judgments about? How can I make reparation for this?

2. What special efforts will I make in the coming week to put Jesus into clearer focus in my life?

3. Recall a time when you got an "unexpected visit" from Jesus. That is, recall a time of special awareness of his indwelling presence. Describe this time, remembering the place, the events, the people, and your feelings. How did you respond to his presence? How do you respond now, as you bring it to mind?

CLOSING PRAYER

Lead the group in a meditation using the Gospel story of Zacchaeus. Ask them to picture in their mind a favorite place anywhere—real or imagined. Visualize Jesus somewhere in this scene, and you nearby, just watching Jesus. Be in this place for a few moments. Savor the colors, the sounds, the smells, the feelings of seeing Jesus and wanting to be nearer to him.

(Use quiet, instrumental music here and allow plenty of time for people to "experience" the scene.)

Now Jesus is aware of your presence and your longing to be near him. He turns to you and says:

"Come, I mean to stay with you this day."

(Allow for silence here—time to respond to Jesus' words.)

How do you respond? Speak to him in prayer.

(Once again allow time for everyone to respond in silent prayer.)

Let us close our prayer in song.

Sing: "Alleluia, People of God" by Lucien Deiss (*Glory and Praise* #176) or "Beginning Today" by The Dameans (*Glory and Praise* #183) or "You Are the Voice" by David Haas (GIA Publications, 1983).

Doctrinal and Pastoral Issues: Real Presence, Sin, Repentance, Call, "Fringe People," Justice, Beatitudes

Khris Ford

Thirty-Second Sunday in Ordinary Time

2 Maccabees 7:1–2, 9–14
2 Thessalonians 2:16—3:5
Luke 20:27–38

GATHERING PRAYER

A Reading: Romans 6:2–11

Prayer (adapted from Psalm 73:23–28)

Lord, I want to always stay close to you
with my hand held in yours.
You will guide me with your instruction
and in the end you will receive me with
    honor.
What else will I have in heaven but you?
And since I have you, what else could I want
    on earth?
My mind and body may weaken,
but God is my strength.
He is all I ever need.
Those who abandon you will surely perish;
the unfaithful ones will be destroyed.
But for me Lord, how wonderful to be near
    you,
to be sheltered by you!
How wonderful it is to proclaim your won-
    drous deeds!
AMEN

REFLECTION QUESTIONS

1. Write down three things that you believe about your life after death. Also write down the strongest feeling you have as you ponder this subject.

2. What does the quote "God has no use for dead people; he is God of the living" mean to you?

KEY POINTS FOR REFLECTION (INPUT)

1. Christ won victory over the power of death by his own death. Christians experience his power over death when we share in his death, through baptism and the Eucharist (Rom 6:2–11; Jn 6:50–51).

2. Through Christ, suffering and death may come to

have meaning for us. Apart from Christ these have no meaning and can be a cause for despair (Pastoral Constitution on the Church in the Modern World).

3. The reality of death brings all of life before us. We see those ideas/persons/events which really matter stand apart from all else. Priorities align themselves very quickly in the face of death. Share an experience in dealing with the death of a friend or loved one. How have you seen this to be true?

4. Despite the certainty of death, life does make sense in the context of Christ's intended purpose for us.

5. Every person will stand before God to be judged on his or her individual actions. Even now we are judged by God as we accept or reject Christ and his Gospel within our lives.

6. Like the Sadducees we may wonder about what life after death will be like. But, unlike them, we are rooted in hope. In Scripture we are promised that we shall see God (Mt 5:8). Paul says we shall see God face to face (2 Cor 3:12–18). Seeing God's face will transform us in his likeness (1 Jn 3:2). (See Credo of the People of God, Pope Paul VI, 1978.)

7. As Christians, the hope of resurrection gives us cause to live our lives in a meaningful way. We strive to live in full union with God and in our striving are pulled beyond ourselves. We reach beyond ourselves to others, unselfishly.

8. The model for human death is Jesus. He freely accepted death. We too must approach our death in freedom.

9. In the Apostles' Creed we proclaim our belief in the resurrection of the body. (See "Letter of Certain Questions Concerning Eschatology," 1979, Congregation for the Doctrine of the Faith.) This is the foundation for our belief in the communion of saints. Life after death is communal just as is our earthly life.

INTEGRATION

1. What does it mean to share in Christ's death and resurrection, daily? How have I done this today?

2. How is my life a reflection of my belief that I will be

resurrected? How would it be different if I did not believe this?

3. What are my feelings about death? How are these changing as I grow in relationship to the Lord?

CLOSING PRAYER

Psalm 16, read antiphonally

and/or

Sing: "We Walk by Faith" by Marty Haugen (GIA Publications, 1984)

or

"I Am the Bread of Life" by Suzanne Toolan (GIA Publications, 1970).

Doctrinal and Pastoral Issues: Death, Heaven, Hell, Resurrection, Afterlife, Hope, Communion of Saints

Khris Ford

Thirty-Third Sunday in Ordinary Time

Malachi 3:19–20
2 Thessalonians 3:7–12
Luke 21:5–19

GATHERING PRAYER

Psalm 98—using the refrain of either of the two songs below as a "response."

"Sing a New Song" by Dan Schutte, S.J. (*Glory and Praise* #47), or "Sing Out, Earth and Skies" by Marty Haugen (GIA Publications, 1985).

REFLECTION QUESTIONS

1. Describe your reaction to the Gospel reading. Re-read it again if necessary. Name your strongest feelings and any questions raised in your mind. Share these in small groups.

2. What one phrase or sentence stands out to you as you read this passage? Why?

KEY POINTS FOR REFLECTION (INPUT)

1. Both the Malachi and the Thessalonians readings speak to us of our attitude toward the "end times." Both exhort us to live today in service to one another. If we do this, we need not worry about tomorrow.

2. Quite often we hear the preaching of those who seem to be saying that the end is very near. The whole of their message seems to warn us of the horrors of tomorrow, and the signs of evil that are all about us. Paul's letter and Jesus' teaching remind us to center ourselves on the saving power of Christ and the strength of God in difficult times. The focus is totally different, and thus our outlook on living today is quite different also.

3. To be a follower of Christ is to be a person of hope. Though we recognize that this world will pass away, we live in the hope of the world to come. This quality of hopefulness permeates our living day-to-day.

Today we live willing to sacrifice and be persecuted for the sake of the kingdom. Today we seek to serve those less fortunate and those who hate us. We do this so that when "end times" comes no one can use our actions as a witness against Christ.

4. As Christians our hope for the kingdom to come gives our living today greater meaning and a sense of urgency. Our responsibilities in this life include sharing this hope with others (Pastoral Constitution on the Church in the Modern World).

5. Jesus Christ's resurrection is the first fruits of the kingdom. It is the beginning of the fulfillment of his promise.

6. The sacrament of the Eucharist reveals the Church's anticipation and hope for the kingdom, where we will all join at the Lord's table to eat and to drink.

7. We must not be like Jerusalem and fail to recognize God's presence among us now. He has come to us in Christ, and he remains with us. His words and presence are our strength to live today. Aware of these, we need not be afraid. But those who concentrate on the signs of the "end times" will be too consumed to see Christ present in our time. They will fail to share his message of love and hope.

8. Persecution may be seen as our opportunity to witness for Christ, to share his love. To endure persecution for Christ's sake is to do more than survive. Rather it is to be victorious over evil, to show God's glory to all.

INTEGRATION

1. In what way have I shared Christ's message of hope during this past week?

2. How do I feel when I anticipate the "end times"? Have these always been my feelings? If not, how have they changed?

3. Describe a time when you were persecuted for something and you held firm to your position. How have you been called to stand firm in your faith? How has persecution been a part of your faith story?

4. What particular message did today's Gospel hold for you?

CLOSING PRAYER

A Reading: Read pp. 288–289 from *That Man Is You,*
Louis Evely, Paulist Press, 1967.

Prayer: Father of our Lord Jesus Christ,
       ever faithful to your promises
       and ever close to your people:
       the earth rejoiced at the coming
       of our Savior
       and looks forward with longing
       to his return at the end of time.

       Prepare our hearts and remove any obsta-
         cles
       that hinder us from feeling the joy and
         hope
       which his presence will bestow.
       Strengthen us to endure the tests of our
         faith,
       Keep our hearts and minds always on
         watch
       for Christ's presence among us,
       for he is Lord for ever and ever.
       Amen.

*Doctrinal and Pastoral Issues: Service, Eschatology,
Hope, Kingdom of God, Persecution, Cost of Discipleship*

Khris Ford

Christ the King

2 Samuel 5:1–3
Colossians 1:12–20
Luke 23:35–43

GATHERING PRAYER

Read Psalm 93, vv. 1–3, 5 together (pause for silence)

Leader begins a prayer of petitions for justice in our world.

All are invited to respond with:
     Jesus, our King, hear our prayer.

The petitions should be current places/situations of injustice worldwide and/or community.

Leader: Father, Lord and King, you created the earth and all its inhabitants to glorify your name. You loved us beyond measure, even unto death. You made of us a royal nation. Today we come before you a wounded world, struggling to hold your banner of love above all else. We bring to you this day a world besieged by your enemies: hatred, famine, discrimination, and war. In prayer we bring you (those children and adults who have been victims of abuse.)

Response: Jesus, our King, hear our prayer.

In prayer we bring you the people of (Ethiopia)

Response: Jesus, our King, hear our prayer.

In prayer we bring you all those (whose lives have been touched by AIDS).

Response: (same as above)

ALLOW OTHERS TO OFFER THEIR PARTICULAR NEEDS.

REFLECTION QUESTIONS

1. We relate to Jesus in many ways, in many roles. He is often consoler, teacher, lover and healer. Today we celebrate "Christ the King." What does that mean to you?

2. With kings come kingdoms. What role do you see the Church playing in God's kingdom?

KEY POINTS FOR REFLECTION (INPUT)

1. In today's world the concept of "kingship" is often difficult to relate to, and Jesus is the exception to those things we believe to be "norms" for kings.

   – he wore no crown or royal vestments.
   – he did not rise to power like most monarchs.
   – he had no army, no servants, and no palace.
   – most of his followers were not the powerful or the rich.
   – he didn't even have a geographic area that "belonged" to him, a kingdom.

2. Jesus the King and King David did have much in common. Both were anointed for their kingship and possessed the power of the Spirit. Both are associated with shepherding. David became king by the consent of those he ruled. Jesus rules over those who invite him into their hearts. He waits for us to consent and commit.

3. When we think of a king, we often think of his "subjects." Jesus the King offers us a new understanding of this, and we would more likely speak of his "followers." This distinction is indicative of the kind of "kingship" introduced by Jesus. Jesus was/is a servant king.

4. Jesus' life is the example of the "servant" that we are to be no matter how much power and responsibility may be given to us. His is a "kingship" of offering ourselves to our "people."

5. The scene in our Gospel is full of irony on the one hand, and serves to affirm the uniqueness of the kingship of Christ. He hangs on a cross between two common thieves and over his head is the sign that reads: This is the King of the Jews. Those about him affirm this title by calling out for him to save them, to save himself, to save all. Even as he hangs upon the cross, seemingly helpless, he promises the one thief that he will join him in paradise. He reigns even in this scene at Calvary.

6. The word Christ comes from the word "Christos," which is a Greek translation for the word Messiah

(meaning "anointed one"). It is related to the word "chrism," the oil used to anoint kings. Kings of Israel were anointed and then enthroned. When we say Christ the King, we are really being redundant. A better way to proclaim him King is to say Jesus the King, or Jesus the Christ. The word "Christ" is really a title which we have reduced to almost a "last name" in addressing Jesus. Perhaps we would do well to consciously call him Jesus *the* Christ, as we consider this special feast day.

7. Jesus redefined the word "authority." In Matthew 20:26–27 we are told that those who aspire to greatness must serve the rest. Those who wish to rank first must serve everyone's needs. Authentic leadership is characterized by selflessness, by the total gift of self to others.

8. Jesus was a revolutionary, a rebel in his time. He was non-violent, but not passive. Jesus was a king with a new message. His message was of a kingdom not of this world. Yet he did not just speak of a strange new kingdom to come, unrelated to the living in this world. His rule had many implications for our world and our living—ideas such as loving your enemy, turning the other cheek, blessed are the poor, and forgiving your brother seventy-times seven. Jesus' kingship disturbed others who were in authority. Today is not so different. Many are disturbed by the witness of Christians who seek to live out Jesus' definition of authority.

9. Present with Jesus in the Gospel scene are two others. One asks Jesus for forgiveness and proclaims that he is the Savior. The other is unwilling to ask. One is promised salvation and the other is not. We make it so difficult to accept the gift that Jesus offers us. He offers it so freely and we complicate it and often refuse. Share how these opportunities come to us day by day.

INTEGRATION

1. Let us imagine ourselves in a fairy-tale-like situation. I imagine a leader, a human who has been raised up by God himself. All of us are drawn to this leader, to listen to his message, and to follow his call. We hear this leader say to us:

> I have come to rid the world of disease, poverty, oppression, ignorance—anything that is an enemy of people. All are invited to join me in this task. However, if you join me you must follow my example in all areas of my living. You must eat what I eat, drink what I drink, etc. When I am at work, you must also be at

work, day or night. Those who share in the work with me will also share in the victory. (Adapted from *The Spiritual Exercises of St. Ignatius: A Contemporary Reading*, David L. Fleming, Institute of Jesuit Sources, 1978)

It would seem that no one could refuse such an invitation. Yet some will refuse this call to follow. Why?

2. Jesus is just such a leader as is described above, and much more. He calls us to follow. How will you respond during the coming week?

Write a brief prayer that you can use throughout the coming week. Ask that you may have the grace to hear God's call and to respond to him fully. Pray for the strength to follow in his example of selflessness, offering yourself for God's service. Give thanks to the Father for the gift of his Son, our King.

CLOSING PRAYER

Sing: "Praise Canticle" by David Haas (GIA Publications, 1982)

or

"Glorious in Majesty" arranged by Jeff Cothran (GIA Publications, 1982)

or

"Witnesses" by Gregory Norbert (*Glory and Praise* #274)

and/or

A Guided Meditation: "The King" (from *Wellsprings*, by Anthony de Mello, Doubleday and Co., 1985)

Doctrinal and Pastoral Issues: Christ the King, Kingdom of God, Power, Authority, Leadership, Justice

Khris Ford

HOLY DAYS

Mary and the Saints

By Eugene A. LaVerdiere, S.S.

Besides all the feasts and solemnities which we have already seen, the liturgical year includes two great feasts of Our Lady and the feast of All Saints. The feasts of Mary are that of the Immaculate Conception, which comes on December 8, during Advent, and that of the Assumption, which we celebrate on August 15, during Ordinary Time. The readings for these feasts are from Luke's prologue. The feast of All Saints is celebrated on November 2. Its Gospel reading is from the prologue to Matthew's account of Jesus' Sermon on the Mount.

The Promise

With the feast of the Immaculate Conception we celebrate the story of God's promise of salvation, from the first covenant to the fulfillment of the covenant in Christ. The story is epitomized by the person of Mary through whom God's life and word became flesh. Mary also embodies the vocation of the Church and of every Christian.

The reading for the feast is Luke 1:26–38, the story of Gabriel's annunciation that Mary would be the mother of the Son of God. Touched by grace, she was open to the Holy Spirit and accepted to be the servant of the Lord. In such a life and commitment, there is no sin. The Church is called to the same selfless service and to bring forth the life of God into the world. Unlike Mary, we are not sinless, but we do have her as an ideal expression of what humanity ought to be. Mary is the vision of humanity's fulfillment in the reign of God. As such she stretches our hopes beyond the horizon of our personal lives and beyond history itself.

The Fulfillment

With the feast of the Assumption we celebrate the story of how God's promise is fulfilled over and over again throughout history. It is because we have seen the promise fulfilled so often that the promise is a source of hope for us. The story of fulfillment, like the story of the promise, is epitomized in the person of Mary, whom Elizabeth greeted in the name of the entire Old Testament as well as in our own name as the mother of the Lord.

The reading for the feast is Luke 1:39–56 which includes the Magnificat, Mary's song of praise, in which her rejoicing sings of how God is glorified in what has been done through her person. Her song is also the prayer of the Christian fulfillment. All that we pray for in the Lord's Prayer is now celebrated in anticipation as already fulfilled. No longer need we pray that God's name be hallowed. His name is hallowed. His reign is established in the reversal of worldly values. The lowly have been raised up and the mighty toppled from their thrones, and the hungry have been filled with good things. Thus it is that in the person of Mary we celebrate both the promise and the fulfillment of life and history.

Life in the Kingdom

On the feast of All Saints, we celebrate all those who enjoy the fullness of life but most especially the unsung Christian heroes, many of whom we have known personally. In celebrating them, the Church asks us to reflect on Jesus' vision of the kingdom of God as expressed in the Beatitudes (Mt 5:1–12).

The Beatitudes introduce Jesus' discourse on the mountainside, in which Matthew gathered many sayings of Jesus into a great synthesis of Christian living. The Sermon on the Mount is the law of Christian discipleship. The mountain which Jesus ascends to interpret the old law and present the Christian way of life is not so much geographical as theological, the place where revelation is given, as had been the case at Sinai.

The Beatitudes present Jesus' challenging vision in a form characteristic of wisdom literature: "Blessed are . . . for they shall. . . ." Note, however, that for the poor in spirit (5:3) and those who are persecuted for righteousness' sake (5:10), we read: "Blessed are . . . for theirs is. . . ." since the reign of God already has broken into the world in the life and teaching of Jesus. The reason that the poor in spirit, those who mourn, etc., are blessed is not that they are poor in spirit or that they mourn, but because they have been granted the kingdom of God and they shall be comforted. The good news is proclaimed to the poor. The form of the last Beatitude is very different. In it, Jesus speaks directly to the persecuted community of Matthew. The other Beatitudes must have formed a rhetorical whole framed by "theirs is the kingdom of God" (Mt 5:3, 10) before the addition of this last Beatitude at the time of Matthew's writing of his Gospel.

Introduction to the Feasts of the Assumption, Immaculate Conception and All Saints

The sessions in this section contain the following parts:

Opening Prayer
Focus Questions
Reflections
Integrating Questions
Closing Prayer

The opening and closing prayers suggest a variety of prayer forms. The focus questions aim at helping catechumens reflect on their experience and the readings; responses to the focus questions could be shared in small groups or noted in a personal journal. The reflections center on themes in readings; the catechist can develop one or more of these themes and lead into a discussion with catechumens.

The integrating questions aim at helping catechumens integrate a response to God's word in their lives. Again, responses could be shared in small groups or noted in journals. Both focus and integrating questions demand time for reflection. Finally, doctrinal and pastoral issues relevant to each feast are enumerated.

Assumption of the Blessed Virgin

Revelation 11:19a; 12:1–6a, 10ab
1 Corinthians 15:20–26
Luke 1:39–56

OPENING PRAYER

Leader: My being proclaims the greatness of the Lord.

All: My being proclaims the greatness of the Lord.

Leader: All creation proclaims the greatness of the Lord.

All: My being proclaims the greatness of the Lord.

Leader: God has redeemed us from darkness.

All: My being proclaims the greatness of the Lord.

Leader: God has blessed and called each of us.

All: My being proclaims the greatness of the Lord.

Leader: God offers us the promise of everlasting life.

All: My being proclaims the greatness of the Lord. (Invite individuals to offer spontaneous prayers of praise.) Response to each prayer: My being proclaims the greatness of the Lord.

All: Gracious God, we give praise for your constant care. Give us the wisdom and trust of Mary, your servant, to proclaim your goodness. We ask in the name of Jesus through the power of your spirit. Amen.

FOCUSING QUESTIONS

(Reflect and discuss your reactions in small groups.) Identify an experience of hope in your life. What happened? Who was present? What meaning did it have for you? How did you respond to the experience?

REFLECTIONS

1. The assumption of Mary is a sign of hope. She trusted, hoped in God, and she is with God. The message of the Gospel is that God can work wonders through us. Hope involves trust. To develop trust we need to spend time getting to know God and God's message. Develop the meaning of Christian hope.

2. The canticle of Mary in the Gospel reading bears witness to proclaiming the kingdom. The kingdom of God is not for selfish possession. It is meant for everyone. The canticle highlights the need to care for the poor, the concern for justice and use of power. What are the injustices that surround us? How can we respond as Catholics to the injustice and to the poor? Discuss the meaning of the U.S. bishops' pastoral on the economy, *Economic Justice for All*.

3. Each of us is called to hope in God's promises. God promises forgiveness, mercy and abundant love to each person. God's love can empower us to be messengers of these promises. In the Gospel, Elizabeth serves as messenger of God's love and promise. Mary accepts the challenge of God's promise to proclaim to others mercy and forgiveness, to offer hope to others, especially those who are powerless and helpless. How do we accept and proclaim the promises of God?

INTEGRATING QUESTIONS

How do you show God's mercy to the helpless, poor and powerless in your life?

How do you experience God's promises in your life?

CLOSING PRAYER

Slowly pray together the canticle of Mary (Lk 1:46–55).

Doctrinal and Pastoral Issues: Assumption of Mary, Christian Hope, Mary as Servant of God, Mercy and Justice, U.S. Bishops' Pastoral on the Economy.

Joseph P. Sinwell

Feast of All Saints

Revelation 7:2–4, 9–14
1 John 3:1–3
Matthew 5:1–12a

OPENING PRAYER

Pray together Psalm 113 by alternating verses or pray this response to each verse: "Saints of the Lord, bless the Lord."

FOCUSING QUESTIONS

Have you ever known or met someone who was described as a blessing or saint? Describe the person. What unique qualities did he or she have?

REFLECTIONS

1. We honor the saints because they serve as models. They are individuals who chose to live their lives in accord with the Gospel. They were ordinary people who struggled just as we do. They believed in the death and resurrection of Jesus and allowed God to change their lives. They were diligently committed to proclaiming God's reign. Tell the story of the patron saint of the parish or diocese or of a catechumen to highlight the saints as models of Christian living.

2. Each of us is called to holiness. What is holiness? Today's Gospel highlights a way of following Jesus: becoming holy. The Beatitudes describe attitudes for living the Gospel. Explore the meaning and implications of the Beatitudes. Identify people who exhibited one or more of the Beatitudes in their lives. The Beatitudes challenge each of us to examine our lives.

3. The Beatitudes in the Gospel reading present a vision of the reign of God. The Beatitudes demand that we care for those who hunger and thirst, who suffer from injustice and other sorrows. This vision demands a response or risk. The saints were willing to risk responding to the poor and unfortunate. Who are the poor, the persecuted, the suffering in our society? What is our Christian response to their cries?

INTEGRATING QUESTIONS

Review the Beatitudes in the Gospel. Which Beatitude most needs improvement in your life? What steps to change will you undertake to live this Beatitude?

CLOSING PRAYER

God, today we rejoice in remembering the holy men and women of every time and place. We are gratified for the witness of their lives.

(Pray the Litany of the Saints. Response to each name: Pray for us.)

> Mary, Mother of God . . .
> St. Elizabeth . . .
> Sts. Peter and Paul . . .
> St. Stephen . . .
> St. Frances Xavier Cabrini . . .
> St. John Neumann . . .
> St. Elizabeth Ann Seton . . .

Continue with the names of catechumens and other saints you prefer to mention.

> All holy men and women of God . . .

All: We pray in the name of Jesus who is both Redeemer and Brother through the power of your Spirit. Amen.

Doctrinal and Pastoral Issues: Communion of Saints, Beatitudes, Holiness, Justice, Care of the Poor

Joseph P. Sinwell

Feast of the Immaculate Conception

December 8

Genesis 3:9–15
Ephesians 1:3–6, 11–12
Luke 1:26–38

OPENING PRAYER

Sing together "Be Not Afraid" by Bob Dufford, S.J. (*Glory and Praise*, #8) or pray together Psalm 98 with the response "Sing a new song to the Lord; God has done wondrous things."

FOCUSING QUESTIONS

In the Gospel, Mary experiences the call of God. What events or persons have helped you experience the call of God? How did they help you? What was your response to this experience?

REFLECTIONS

1. The first reading focuses on the consequences of sin. Sin is a refusal to respond to the word of God. Sin weakens and harms our relationship. The curses of God described in the second reading highlight the alienation caused by sin.

   Sin does have social consequences and dimensions. Racism and sexism in our society are examples. Examine how sin affects relationships and society.

   As Christians we are called to heal the divisions caused by sin. What are the divisions in our lives? How do we heal these divisions?

2. Today's Gospel states that Mary is highly favored by God. The feast of the Immaculate Conception celebrates that Mary was conceived without sin. Mary is blessed, gifted. Each of us is gifted. Ask those present to list their God-given gifts.

   Mary recognized her giftedness and freely chose to bring forth life. The Gospel challenges us to follow the example of Mary. How do we appreciate the gifts of others? How did we use our gifts to bring life to others?

3. Reflect on these words of the Gospel: "I am the servant of the Lord. Let it be done to me as you say." The concept of service demands an openness to God's word and willingness to embrace the unknown. Mary is a model of Christian service. Service will challenge us to put aside our petty concerns and look at the needs of others and the community. It is willingness to say yes to God's word. What are the needs of the suffering, the hungry, the homeless, the poor, the alienated? How do we say yes to them? How do we respond to injustice? How do we let God's word become more alive in our daily actions?

INTEGRATING QUESTIONS

What attitudes or habits in my lifestyle hinder me from saying yes to God's word? How can I begin to change these attitudes or habits?

CLOSING PRAYER

Slowly pray together the Hail Mary or the prayer from today's second reading (Eph 1:3–6).

Doctrinal and Pastoral Issues: Immaculate Conception, Social Sin, Reconciliation, Christian Service, Giftedness

Joseph P. Sinwell

Additional Catechetical Resources

Listed on this bibliography are additional resources for a catechumenate director. Books listed in the various sections of this text are not necessarily reiterated here. This is a list of additional resources. This list is also in no way meant to be the last word. There are other exceptional materials available. Hopefully, there will be many more developed in the future.

Bausch, William J. *Storytelling: Imagination and Faith.* Twenty-Third Publications, Mystic, CT., 1984.

Bergan, Jacqueline and Schwan, S. Marie. *Forgiveness: A Guide for Prayer.* St. Mary's Press, Winona, 1985.

Coughlin, Kevin. *Finding God in Everyday Life.* Paulist Press, New York, 1980.

DeBoy, James. *Getting Started in Adult Religious Education.* Paulist Press, New York, 1979.

DeMello, Anthony. *Sadhana: A Way to God.* Institute of Jesuit Sources, St. Louis, 1979.

———, *The Song of the Bird.* Image Books, New York, 1984.

Duggan, Robert, Editor. *Conversation and the Catechumenate.* Paulist Press, New York, 1984.

Farrell, Edward. *Celtic Meditations.* Dimension Books, New Jersey, 1976.

Fischer, Kathleen. *The Inner Rainbow: The Imagination in Christian Life.* Paulist Press, New York, 1983.

Forum. Newsletter of the North American Forum on the Catechumenate. Washington, D.C.

Groome, Thomas. *Christian Religious Education.* Harper & Row, New York, 1980.

Halpin, Marlene. *Imagine That.* Wm C. Brown, Dubuque, Iowa, 1982.

Hays, Edward. *Prayers for the Domestic Church.* Forest of Peace, Easton, Kansas, 1979.

Hefling, Charles C. *Why Doctrines?* Cowley Publications.

Hestenes, Roberta. *Using the Bible in Groups.* Westminster Press, Philadelphia, 1983.

Huck, Gabe. *Teach Me to Pray.* Sadlier, New York.

Ivory, Tom. *Looking at Our Faith.* Sadlier, New York.

Link, Mark. *Breakaway.* Argus Communications, Allen, Texas, 1980.

Maloney, George. *Centering on the Lord Jesus: The Whole Person at Prayer.* Michael Glazier, Inc., Delaware, 1982.

McCauley, George. *The Unfinished Image.* Sadlier, New York, 1983.

McMakin, Jacqueline. *Doorways to Christian Growth.* Winston Seabury, 1984.

Palmer, Parker. *To Know as We Are Known: A Spirituality of Education.* Harper & Row, San Francisco, 1983.

Rite of Christian Initiation of Adults. USCC, Washington, D.C.

Share the Word. Paulist Evangelization Center, Washington, D.C.

Simons, George F. *Keeping Your Personal Journal.* Paulist Press, New York, 1978.

Smith, Gregory Michael. *The Fire in Their Eyes.* Paulist Press, New York, 1976.

Wallis, Jim. *A Call to Conversion.* Harper & Row, New York, 1981.

Warren, Michael, Editor. *Sourcebook for Modern Catechetics.* St. Mary's Press, Winona, 1983.

CALENDAR: ADVENT TO PENTECOST: 1987–1999

Year	Sunday Cycle	1st Sunday of Advent	1st Sunday of Lent	Easter Sunday	Pentecost
1987–88	B	Nov. 29	Feb. 21	Apr. 3	May 22
1988–89	C	Nov. 27	Feb. 12	Mar. 26	May 14
1989–90	A	Dec. 3	Mar. 4	Apr. 15	June 3
1990–91	B	Dec. 2	Feb. 17	Mar. 31	May 19
1991–92	C	Dec. 1	Mar. 8	Apr. 19	June 7
1992–93	A	Nov. 29	Feb. 28	Apr. 11	May 30
1993–94	B	Nov. 28	Feb. 20	Apr. 3	May 22
1994–95	C	Nov. 27	Mar. 5	Apr. 16	June 4
1995–96	A	Dec. 3	Feb. 25	Apr. 7	May 26
1996–97	B	Dec. 1	Feb. 16	Mar. 30	May 18
1997–98	C	Nov. 27	Mar. 1	Apr. 12	May 31
1998–99	A	Nov. 29	Feb. 21	Apr. 4	May 23

Contributors

Kathy Brown is currently a member of the staff at the North American Forum on the Catechumenate. She received her Master's in Theology from St. Paul University in Ottawa, Canada. Ms. Brown was formerly the Adult Education Coordinator and Catechumenate Director for a parish in Tempe, Arizona.

Clare M. Colella is Director of Electronic Communications for the Diocese of San Bernardino. She formerly was Director of the Office of Sacramental Formation there and continues to serve them as resource person, as well as being on her parish catechumenate team. For several years she served on the Board of the North American Forum on the Catechumenate. Mrs. Colella holds a Master's in Religious Education from Seattle University.

Khris S. Ford is the Director of Evangelization and the Catechumenate for St. Elizabeth Seton Parish in Plano, Texas. She holds a Master's in Education. Mrs. Ford, a teacher for many years, is active in the RCIA Council for the Diocese of Dallas and has conducted workshops for their catechumenal teams. She is a member of the National Conference on Evangelization.

Richard N. Fragomeni is a doctoral candidate in liturgical studies at the Catholic University of America. He was director of worship for the Diocese of Albany, New York and lectures regularly throughout the U.S. on liturgical formation.

Maureen A. Kelly is pastoral associate and director of religious education at St. Rose of Lima Parish, Gaithersburg, Maryland and chairperson of the Board of the North American Forum for the Catechumenate. She holds an M.A. in Theology from the Catholic University of Louvain, Belgium, and is the author of various articles and tapes. Ms. Kelly has given workshops throughout the United States and Canada.

Rev. Michael J. Koch is pastor of St. Philip Neri Church in Saskatoon, Canada. He received his education at the University of Saskatchewan and St. Joseph Seminary, Edmonton. He also studied at the University of San Francisco and in Jerusalem. Father Koch is a member of the steering committee of the North American Forum on the Catechumenate.

Rev. Eugene A. LaVerdiere, S.S. is the editor of *Emmanuel* magazine and an associate editor of *The Bible Today*. He holds a doctorate in New Testament and Early Christian Literature from the University of Chicago. Father LaVerdiere is the author of many books as well as audio and video cassettes. His most recent books include *The New Testament in the Life of the Church* and *When We Pray* (both Ave Maria Press).

Elizabeth S. Lilly is the Liturgy Coordinator and Director of the Catechumenate in St. William Parish, Los Altos, California. She holds a Master's in the History of Art from the University of California, Berkeley. She is a member of the Diocesan Committee on the RCIA, Diocese of Monterey.

Ron Oakham, O.Carm. is Director of Institutes for the North American Forum on the Catechumenate. He holds an M.A. in theological studies from the Washington Theological Union and was director of the R.C.I.A. in the Archdiocese of Newark.

Karen Hinman Powell served for five years as Executive Director of the North American Forum on the Catechumenate. She is presently director of the Professional Development Program at Georgetown University. Past experience includes work with three parish catechumenates in Mississippi, Maryland, and Virginia. She is the author of *How To Form A Catechumenate Team* (Liturgy Training Publications) and co-editor of *Breaking Open the Word of God* for Cycle A. and B. She holds a M.Div. degree from the Jesuit School of Theology in Chicago.

Nancy Y. Sheridan, S.A.S.V. is associate director of adult enrichment for the Diocese of Manchester, New Hampshire. She holds an M.A. in Religious Education from Boston College. Sister Sheridan is a member of the teams for the North American Forum on the Catechumenate and a contributor to the third volume of *Breaking Open the Word of God* (Paulist Press). She is a lecturer in the areas of adult formation, spirituality, and the Christian Initiation of Adults.

Joseph P. Sinwell is Diocesan Director of Religious Education, Diocese of Providence, and Co-Director of the Rhode Island Catechumenate. He is a founding member of the North American Forum on the Catechumenate and currently serves on its executive committee as treasurer. He holds Master's degrees in Religious Education and Agency Counseling and is a candidate for a Doctor of Ministry degree at St. Mary's University, Baltimore. Mr. Sinwell is co-editor of *Breaking Open the Word of God*, Cycle A. and B.